America's Best Newspaper Writing

A Collection of
ASNE Prizewinners

Second Edition

America's Best Newspaper Writing

A Collection of ASNE Prizewinners

Roy Peter Clark
Christopher Scanlan
The Poynter Institute

BEDFORD/ST. MARTIN'S

Boston ◆ *New York*

For Bedford/St. Martin's

Executive Editor: Erika Gutierrez
Senior Editor: Simon Glick
Developmental Editor: Michaela Garibaldi
Senior Production Supervisor: Joe Ford
Production Associate: Matthew Hayes
Project Management: Books By Design, Inc.
Cover Design: Lucy Krikorian
Cover Art: Jasper Johns (b. 1930). *FLAG*. Dated on reverse 1954. Encaustic, oil and collage on fabric mounted on plywood, 42¼ × 60⅝". Gift of Philip Johnson in honor of Alfred H. Barr Jr. (106. 1973). The Museum of Modern Art, New York, N.Y. Digital image © The Museum of Modern Art/Licensed by SCALA/Art Resource, N.Y. Cover art © Jasper Johns/Licensed by VAGA, New York, N.Y.
Composition: Macmillan India, Ltd.
Printing and Binding: RR Donnelley & Sons Company

President: Joan E. Feinberg
Editorial Director: Denise B. Wydra
Director of Marketing: Karen Melton Soeltz
Director of Editing, Design, and Production: Marcia Cohen
Manager, Publishing Services: Emily Berleth

For information, write: Bedford/St. Martin's, 75 Arlington Street, Boston, MA 02116   (617-399-4000)

ISBN: 0-312-44367-6
EAN: 978-0-312-44367-2

To our mothers,
Shirley Clark and Alice S. Harreys,
and in memory of our fathers,
Theodore R. Clark and James W. Scanlan

Preface

In 1978 the American Society of Newspaper Editors, under the leadership of Gene Patterson, created the Distinguished Writing Awards. The Poynter Institute, a school for journalists in St. Petersburg, Florida, administered the contest, interviewed the writers, and published an annual collection of the winners entitled *Best Newspaper Writing*. To date, 27 volumes have been published, but only the most recent are still in print. The chance to read some of the best of this work is now yours in *America's Best Newspaper Writing*—whether you are a student, teacher, or working journalist.

Our goal in collecting these pieces—the best of the best—from the first 25 years of award winners was to provide students of journalism, from first-semester news writing and reporting students to experienced working journalists, with exemplary and practical examples of the craft. While many collections purport to include "the best" articles available for reading and study, only ours focuses on providing a wide range of recent stories—including many brief local stories—the type journalism students are most often assigned to write. We selected the pieces that we felt would both be the most engaging and the best models for writers. After much reading and discussion, we used these standards for inclusion:

- The story had to continue to speak over time, with themes that transcended the events and issues of the day.

- The story had to exemplify an important story form and contribute to the whole collection as representative of a useful range of forms for students of the craft and their teachers, from deadline pieces, to profiles and features, to columns and editorials, to business and explanatory work, to sports and obits.

- The story had to help the reader learn something important about the process of reporting and writing.

- The story must serve as a strong model for students as well as for working professionals.

To enhance the collection as a learning tool, we have included a section on the craft of writing, revised extensively for the second edition. This covers issues of language, process, audience and purpose. In addition, throughout the volume, we have written brief introductory headnotes for each writer, offering biographical information, tips on what to look for in the writer's stories and commentary from the writer, drawn from our archives.

To our mix of contemporary writers, we have added a selection of "classic" stories, ones we think no serious student of journalism should fail to read. We think of them as stories that might have won an ASNE award if the contest had existed back then.

NEW TO THIS EDITION

We have strived to make the second edition of *America's Best Newspaper Writing* the most useful and up-to-date journalism anthology available by adding more stories—both new and classic—and powerful learning tools designed to keep students on the cutting edge of journalism trends and give them a deeper understanding of the writerly techniques that contribute to effective storytelling.

- **More stories; a broader collection of journalists.** We have updated this edition to provide students with more stories on which to model their writing (40 ASNE winners in all) and to showcase the broad range of voices that make up the community of journalists in America today, from Mirta Ojito writing on growing up in Cuba to Anthony Shadid writing on the war in Iraq.

- **Two new classic stories.** To our selection of classic pieces—ones we believe no serious student of journalism should miss—we have added two more: "Mary White" by William Allen White and Lorena Hickok's "Iowa Village Waits All Night for Glimpse at Fleeting Train."

- **New chapter, "Terrorism, War and Disasters."** As crisis coverage has become an increasingly important part of every paper's mission, the work of journalists who reported on recent disasters—from 9/11 to the war in Iraq—is featured in this edition to provide examples of great stories written under the most devastating of circumstances.

- New chapter, "Ethical Journalism and the Craft of Honest Writing." With journalistic scandals in mind—from Janet Cooke to Stephen Glass to Jayson Blair—this chapter has been designed to help students recognize the dangers of fabrication and plagiarism and to provide them with concrete techniques to ensure that their writing remains original.

- **Expanded writing instruction.** Chapter 10, "The Craft of Writing Great Stories," now provides more tips and advice covering issues of language, process, audience and purpose.

- New, annotated "X-Ray Reading" examples. Annotations on seven ASNE prizewinning stories show students how writerly devices such as repetition, quotations and specific details contribute to effective storytelling.

IN HONOR OF

We would like to honor three authors, whose work appears in this anthology, who have passed away. The very first ASNE winner was a columnist and editorial writer from the New Bedford *Standard-Times* named Everett S. Allen. With shocking white hair and weathered skin, he had the look of a Transcendentalist poet or a sailor on Herman Melville's *Pequot*. His remarks upon receiving the award are reprinted on pages xxiii–xxiv.

Saul Pett was among the AP's best writers, the apotheosis of a generation of reporters who never met a saloon, or a story told in a saloon, that they didn't like. You'll find his profile of former New York Mayor Ed Koch whimsically creative (p. 174).

Murray Kempton died in 1997, but not before leaving us a legacy of sharp commentary and adventurous sentences. He told us that he always wanted his writing to be good because he knew, somehow, its influence would last. He could not stand the thought of a young man—the next Theodore Dreiser, perhaps—picking up his column on a bus and finding it deficient. Kempton's opinion piece on police misconduct in New York City starts on page 140.

The work of Allen, Pett and Kempton—with nearly 40 of their brothers and sisters—endures herein and, we hope, for many years to come. To inspire the next generation, it must make its way into the right hands. If you're reading this, that part is now up to you.

ACKNOWLEDGMENTS

To create this book required the hard work and cooperation of many people and organizations. Since this anthology goes back to 1978, some of the labor to produce it was exerted more than two decades ago. Our special thanks go to Gene Patterson, whose leadership helped create the ASNE Distinguished Writing Awards. Each year, a committee of the nation's top editors comes to St. Petersburg, Florida, to judge the contest. We thank them for their careful attention and dedication to good writing.

The support we've received from the faculty and staff of The Poynter Institute continues to astonish and humble us. Don Fry, Karen Brown Dunlap, Keith Woods and Aly Colón have served as editors of the annual edition of *Best Newspaper Writing*. We're standing on their shoulders.

Billie Keirstead has been a partner in this project since its inception. Priscilla Ely, Martin Gregor, Nancy Emineth and Joyce Barrett have been strong allies. None of this support would have been possible without the vision of Poynter's top leaders over time, from Donald Baldwin to Bob Haiman to Andy Barnes to Jim Naughton to Paul Tash.

We would like to thank the following reviewers, whose comments and suggestions helped shape the second edition: G. Stuart Adam, The Poynter Institute and Carleton University; Jacqui Banaszynski, University of Missouri–Columbia; Gregory Borchard, University of Nevada, Las Vegas; Christopher Daly, Boston University; Sylvia Fox, California State University, Sacramento; Steve Giegerich, Columbia University; Barbara F. Luebke, University of Rhode Island; Shannon E. Martin, University of Maine; Tommy Mumert, Arkansas Tech University; Randy Pruitt, Midwestern State University; Lila Sarick, College of Charleston; William Ward, The Poynter Institute; and Kristal Brent Zook, Columbia University.

Reviewers who helped us on the first edition include James L. Baughman, University of Wisconsin–Madison; Bill Berry, University of Wisconsin–Stevens Point; Maria Brann, Purdue University; Marion Lewenstein, Stanford University; Richard J. Roth, Northwestern University; Carl Sessions Stepp, University of Maryland; George Sylvie, University of Texas at Austin; and Howard Ziff, University of Massachusetts–Amherst. We also thank Kevin Kerrane and Ben Yagoda of the University of Delaware for their help and support.

We are honored to have this work published by Bedford/St. Martin's and its highly professional team, including Joan Feinberg, president; Denise Wydra, editorial director; and Erika Gutierrez, executive editor, who all pursued the project with passion and persistence. Michaela Garibaldi, editorial assistant, helped make the second edition a much more valuable book and the process of producing it an enjoyable professional experience; we're also glad that Simon Glick, our editor for the first edition, once again came along for the ride. Emily Berleth, manager of publishing services, worked elegantly and diligently to turn the manuscript into a book.

Both of us owe much to our friend and writing coach Donald Murray, whose efforts to improve the crafts of writing and teaching now span a half century.

Special thanks go to the award-winning writers and their newspapers. We are merely preserving and celebrating their efforts to create stories that are instructive and inspirational.

Between us we have two spouses, six daughters, two dogs and three cats. Without their support and forbearance, our best efforts would be insufficient to any task.

Roy Peter Clark
Christopher Scanlan

Contents

2   LOCAL REPORTING AND BEATS   28

---

7 THE PROFILE AND FEATURE STORY 164

| 9 | THE CLASSICS | 243 |

10	**THE CRAFT OF WRITING GREAT STORIES**	287

---

11   **ETHICAL JOURNALISM AND THE CRAFT OF HONEST WRITING**   314

The Remarks of Everett S. Allen Upon Becoming the First Winner of the ASNE Distinguished Writing Award in 1978

I am profoundly grateful for all the obvious reasons, yet grateful beyond these for one reason which may not be at all obvious.

When I was about to graduate from college, one of my English professors, who apparently thought well of me, called me to his office. He said, "I believe that you have some ability to write and I am therefore most depressed to learn that you have decided to go into journalism."

At the moment, I was in no position to reply, but I resented the remark. In part, that may have been why I made such an effort, from the very beginning, to inject the best writing of which I was capable into such news stories as were assigned to me.

I believe that I am the only newspaper reporter who deliberately and successfully inserted in a general-alarm fire story a perfect iambic line. I was so titillated at being able to do it—and at getting it past the copy desk, and you know how copy desks are about perfect iambic lines—that even though it was something like 38 years ago, I remember it perfectly.

The line was, "Ten pumpers roared throughout the night in Sawyer Street." Now, if 13 pumpers had shown up at the fire, or if the fire had been, let us say, in Brock Avenue, I would have had to either (a) change the meter of the line, or (b) respectfully decline to cover the fire.

Happily, I did not have to make either choice. And since that time, I have persisted in attempting to introduce creative writing into the news columns whenever possible and, in these latter years, that has meant encouraging the young to do likewise.

I am most pleased that my peers, the prestigious leadership of ASNE, have, through the creation of these awards, moved to provide a fresh and important incentive to those on American newspaper staffs who can and wish to write creatively.

About the Authors

Roy Peter Clark is Senior Scholar at The Poynter Institute, a school for journalists in St. Petersburg, Fla. He has worked full time at Poynter since 1979 as director of the writing center, dean of the faculty and vice president.

Clark graduated from Providence College in Rhode Island and earned a Ph.D. from the State University of New York at Stony Brook, specializing in medieval literature. He taught writing, language and literature at Auburn University at Montgomery in Alabama. In 1977 he was hired by the *St. Petersburg Times* to become one of America's first writing coaches and worked with the American Society of Newspaper Editors to improve newspaper writing nationwide. Because of his work with ASNE, he was elected as a distinguished service member.

Clark has worked with journalists and taught writing in more than 40 states and on five continents and is widely considered one of America's most influential writing coaches. He is the founding director of the National Writers' Workshops, regional conferences that attract more than 5,000 writers annually. Clark edited seven volumes of *Best Newspaper Writing*, the annual collection of ASNE writing award winners. He is the author of *Free to Write: A Journalist Teaches Young Writers* (Heinemann, 1995). With Don Fry, he wrote *Coaching Writers: Editors and Reporters Working Together* (Bedford/St. Martin's, 2003). He is the co-editor of *The Values and Craft of American Journalism* and *The Changing South of Gene Patterson: Journalism and Civil Rights*, both published by the University Press of Florida. He and G. Stuart Adam edited *Journalism: The Democratic Craft* (Oxford University Press, 2005).

Clark has written more than 500 essays for The Poynter Institute Web site, www.poynter.org, including the popular series *The Writer's Toolbox*. He has written serial narratives for newspapers, including *Ain't Done Yet*, a serial novel syndicated by *The New York Times*.

Christopher "Chip" Scanlan is a senior faculty member in the reporting, writing and editing program at The Poynter Institute and is director of the National Writers' Workshops. He joined the Poynter faculty in 1994 from the Knight Ridder Newspapers' Washington bureau, where he was a national correspondent. During his five years in Washington, he created the bureau's first family beat and won awards for coverage of veterans' health care, consumer issues and America's garbage crisis. He also won a Robert F. Kennedy award for international journalism for a series on hazardous exports to the developing world. In two decades of reporting, his stories earned 16 regional and national awards.

Scanlan is a graduate of Fairfield University (B.A., English, 1971) and Columbia University Graduate School of Journalism (M.S., 1974). He served as a Peace Corps volunteer in West Africa, where he taught English as a second language in 1971–72. He spent the first years of his career at *The Milford* (Conn.) *Citizen*, the *Journal Inquirer* in Manchester, Conn., and the *Delaware State News*. From 1977 to 1985, he was a reporter at the *Providence* (R.I.) *Journal-Bulletin*, where he helped create and run the paper's writing program and edited *How I Wrote the Story*, a collection of news writing accounts.

From 1985 to 1989, Scanlan was a feature writer for the *St. Petersburg Times*. His articles, essays and short fiction have appeared in numerous magazines and anthologies, including *The New York Times*, *The American Scholar*, *The Washington Post Magazine*, *Redbook*, *Telling Stories/Taking Risks: Journalism Writing at the Century's Edge*, *The Chronicle of Higher Education* and the online magazine Salon.com. His work was also selected to appear in the 2003 and 2004 editions of *Best American Essays*. He is the author of *Reporting and Writing: Basics for the 21st Century* (Oxford University Press, 2000) and editor of the *Best Newspaper Writing* series from 1994 to 2000. Scanlan and his wife, Katharine Fair, are the authors of a novel, *The Holly Wreath Man* (Andrews McMeel, 2005), which originally appeared in serial form in 45 newspapers.

Introduction

We know of only three ways to grow as a writer. First you must read good writing. Then you must write. Then you must spend the rest of your life thinking and talking about good reading and good writing.

This anthology is meant to get you started. Just as you once read stories to learn the grammar of language, you can read the authors in this collection to learn the grammar of stories. It will help if you read the stories in certain ways:

- Read to understand the structure of stories—how they begin, how they move from one scene to another, how they end.
- Read to discover how the process of writing works for each writer, from the conception of story ideas, to the collection of raw material, to finding a focus, to the creation of order, to clarification and revision.
- Read closely to learn how language, rhetoric, syntax and sentence structure create the meaning the writer tries to convey.
- Read to hear the voice of the author through the story—the sum of the strategies the writer uses to create the illusion of speaking directly to you, the reader.
- Read to learn the difference between writing to convey information and writing to create an experience for the reader.
- Read to learn the variety of roles the journalist plays, from watchdog, to explainer, to investigator, to storyteller.

In this collection you will find a rich variety of story forms, many coming from those organized areas of coverage that journalists call "beats." Whatever the beat, the good reporter must learn to tell stories on deadline. In Chapter 1 you will meet expert practitioners at the top of their form, writing dramatic stories, under difficult circumstances, from all over the world.

Many reporters begin and spend their entire careers covering local news, so Chapter 2 reveals the way beat coverage—from politics, to sports, to medicine—can be made interesting and relevant to all

1

readers. Chapter 3 is a showcase of stories that remember those who have died, a common task for all journalists and one that can be practiced with empathy and literary care.

Many stories in our culture concern crime and the courts, topics that have attracted some of our greatest writers. Chapter 4 demonstrates the ways dramatic narrative and civic purpose can be joined together on behalf of the reader.

As news becomes increasingly complex and technical, society needs writers who can clarify and explain. Chapter 5 offers three such writers, who specialize in making the often confusing worlds of business, government and technology understandable to the reader.

Language can be used to persuade, develop arguments and support opinions with evidence. These skills employed by columnists and editorial writers are on display in Chapter 6. From there the focus shifts, in Chapter 7, to profiles and feature stories, the source of some of the most innovative writing in American journalism.

Since September 11, 2001, much of the most important news around the world has been about terrorism, war and disasters. Such events inspire courageous reporting and brilliant writing, a wonderful sample of which you will find in Chapter 8, which is new to this collection.

The forms of writing in journalism have evolved over the decades, as our collection of "classic" stories in Chapter 9 reveals. We have dusted off these precious gems to remind readers that, however styles change, the search for the great story has been enduring.

Since 1978, we have learned much about the craft of writing from interviewing the writers in this collection. We have gathered from them tools we have used in our own writing. We have come to understand the processes many writers have in common. We have admired writers who see the world with a special creative vision, who take risks when most are cautious, who base their work on thorough reporting and critical thinking, and who seek originality in the land of the trite and conventional. The strategies we've collected over the years on the craft of writing great stories are described in Chapter 10.

Where good writing is concerned, we believe that ethics and excellence go hand in hand. To help writers avoid plagiarism and fabrication, we have added a new section, Chapter 11, on these twin perils that continue to trouble journalists, damaging their careers and eroding reader trust in newspapers.

To enhance student learning, we have added a new feature called X-Ray Reading. To reveal the strategies of writers, we have chosen seven stories for close reading and careful analysis. X-Ray Reading allows you to see through the surface of the story to the invisible machinery of grammar, language, syntax and rhetoric, the tools of making meaning.

Many of the writing tools described in this anthology have been borrowed from others. We'd like to recognize some of them, not only to express our gratitude but also so their names can become familiar to you and so their work can become your resources.

Donald M. Murray has devoted his life to the craft of writing, as a teacher, researcher, columnist and Pulitzer Prize-winning editorial writer. He has taught us that though writing can seem magical, it is not magic. It is the product of reason and intuition, a process that can be learned, practiced and perfected.

No one takes the craft of journalism more seriously than Melvin Mencher. As a journalism professor and textbook author, he has described how reporters learn, how they conceive stories, how they define what is important. We embrace his maxim of responsible journalism, that it is immoral not to be excellent in your craft.

Our colleagues at The Poynter Institute, Don Fry, Karen Brown Dunlap, Keith Woods and Aly Colón, have interviewed many of the authors in this anthology. They have shared their insights with us, and their work as teachers and authors continues to inspire a new generation of excellent writers.

You can join that generation, and this collection can be your guidebook. Read it carefully. Talk it over with your teacher and other students. Argue about what works in these stories and what still needs attention. Discover your favorite passages. Mark them up. Copy them down. Use them as models.

Then go out and report and write with all parts of your body: your feet, your heart, your hands and your soul. Write with the belief that one day you will write a story that will inspire other readers and writers the way some of these stories inspire you.

Roy Peter Clark and Christopher Scanlan
The Poynter Institute, St. Petersburg, Florida
May 2005

Chapter 1

DEADLINE
WRITING

Not too many years ago, when newspaper journalists talked about their craft they often resorted to images of violence, what one critic called a "necrology," a language of death. Journalists wrote on *deadline*, of course, and their old stories were stored in a library called a *morgue*. Editors would *cut* or *spike* stories or *bury* them inside the paper. With the coming of the computer age, such work was accomplished on a *terminal*.

While some of this seems old-fashioned, nothing is more real to writers than the power of the deadline. Writers come to see it as ally and enemy, an inspiration to get to work and the borderline that will keep the story from becoming great. The deadline helps kick in adrenaline, the journalists' drug of choice, the chemical that gets backsides moving toward chairs and hands moving across keyboards.

New information technologies have altered definitions of news and created a 24-hour news cycle, diminishing newspapers' power to break a story. With the exception of neighborhood news, newspaper readers are more likely to have first learned of a story from broadcast, cable or online media.

Such revolutionary changes in the way news is delivered have not diminished the force of deadline for writers. News writers and foreign correspondents write on deadline, but so do those who deliver features, analysis, sports, criticism and opinion. All journalists must learn to write quickly, blending the acts of thinking, reporting, planning and drafting into a single, continuous, efficient process.

Reporters cannot wait until they return to the office to find the focus of a story. By then it may be too late to gather the information. So reporters listen early for the distilling quotation or the fact that will become the lead. The ride back to the office can be used to rehearse and plan, saving precious minutes before deadline, time that can be used for clarification, revision and consultation with editors.

The journalists represented here learned all these lessons in the field. In the 1990s Richard Ben Cramer became well known as the author of book-length journalism, projects that were years in the making. But as a young reporter, in the late 1970s, he startled the journalism world with dispatches from the war in the Middle East that combined great reporting and narrative power.

Reporters act, in the words of British scholar John Carey, as "eyewitnesses to history." For Leonora LaPeter, this meant acting as the eyes and ears of readers. Her riveting account of a local murder trial and sentencing puts us in the courtroom to see and hear the testimony of witnesses. In this case, LaPeter also had the guts to ask why a person would commit such a crime. In journalism this is the Fifth W, the most difficult question for even a veteran reporter to ask on deadline.

In the face of fierce competition, David Von Drehle captured history on the run in his account of the funeral of former president Richard Nixon. It is an astonishing piece of deadline reporting and narrative writing that describes both the political legacy of a man and the passing of a generation.

Deadline writing need not mean conventional writing, as Francis X. Clines demonstrated with his dispatches from Northern Ireland. Clines writes for *The New York Times* and is known for his ability to find the fresh angle. For him and for the other great ones, writing begins with the legs, the ability to get out of the office; moves to the eyes, where the story becomes visible; and migrates to the heart, the head and eventually the hands.

The most important lesson from these writers is that fast writing does not equate with formula writing. Fast writing can be powerful and exquisite, full of history, context, motive and meaning—but only if the writer is prepared.

~ RICHARD BEN CRAMER ~

Richard Ben Cramer has written for newspapers, magazines and documentary television. He is also the author of *What It Takes*, focusing on the 1992 presidential race, and books about former senator Bob Dole and Yankee center fielder Joe DiMaggio. His reporting from the Middle East for *The Philadelphia Inquirer* in 1978 won the first award for deadline writing from the American Society of Newspaper Editors (ASNE) and swept most of the important awards for international reporting, including the Pulitzer Prize.

Cramer's reports for *The Philadelphia Inquirer* remain outstanding models of narrative writing, so vivid they unintentionally received one of the strongest compliments from cynics and reactionaries: accusations that anything this good must have been made up.

What the cynics failed to appreciate was the importance of *access* to great reporting and writing. Cramer walked across the no man's land between Palestinian and Israeli forces to gather the details needed to write a compelling story. That walk was no stunt. It was, instead, a journey toward understanding the violent distance between two peoples who cannot imagine a common ground.

What is the nature of Cramer's contribution to newspaper writing? Jim Naughton, his editor at *The Philadelphia Inquirer*, put it this way: "What he does is write about real flesh and blood human beings instead of nameless, faceless governments. . . . What Cramer did was to set out and consciously write about people, to find the people lurking behind the institutions, the people affected by government policies."

Consider how Cramer does this in his story of the Hadani family, who sit shiva for their slain daughter. He gives over much of the text to family members who speak powerful truths: a mother, who in her pain at the hospital can still recognize a "good Arab"; a child, who bravely escaped the violence; and an old man, who relates the violence to the history of the Jewish people. The piece is so tightly constructed and moves with such elegant symbolism that it seems the product of long, careful planning.

Cramer described how he wrote the story: "I got to Tel Aviv two days after [the bus attack]. I learn of this family outside Haifa, but I didn't know how hard it would be to get there. I had to pay a taxi driver a hell of a lot of money to drop me up there in the rain and just sit there waiting for me. He brought me down to a hotel in Haifa where I tried to write the story by telex, but they wouldn't send it without a censor seeing it. I was trying to write and trying to wake the censor up to read it. I can't tell too much about how the story was structured because it was written in a kind of white heat of frustration."

Such are the stories of the best reporters. If great literature can be said to be the best work created under *any* circumstances, then great journalism is the best work written under *these* circumstances.

Report from the Mideast

Shiva for a Child Slain in a Palestinian Raid

THE PHILADELPHIA INQUIRER • MARCH 15, 1978

HAIFA, ISRAEL — The Hadani family was sitting shiva. The house was filled with family and friends observing the ancient Jewish custom, a custom that surrounds the bereaved with the living so they will not dwell morbidly on the dead.

In the 48 hours since their daughter, Na'ami, who was 9, died in the Palestinian commando raid on the highway between here and Tel Aviv, Joseph and Levana Hadani have not been alone.

It was the same in a score of homes where the victims of the terrorists lived — neighbors and friends and family from all over Israel arriving to succor the survivors.

And it was the same, in a larger sense, throughout this tight little country, where everyone is touched by a single death and the death of 36 Jews is a tragedy both national and personal.

In English, the rite acted out by the Hadanis is called "sitting shiva for the dead." But shiva is really for the living. The women bringing food and the men bringing news, and the coffee and the self-consciously normal talk are all designed to keep the family thinking in the present and looking to the future.

There is strength in feeling so much life around, warmth in kissing and being kissed.

In the Hadani home, the treatment was working. Joseph and Levana Hadani, their brothers and sisters and fathers, had gathered in a small room at one end of the apartment for part of the night to quietly tell their story.

When the story was told, Joseph Hadani left the room for a moment, walking stiffly because of his wounds. When he came back, he was followed by four of his co-workers, who gathered behind him in the doorway.

Hadani drew to him Ayelet, 10, the daughter who remains, and he said in English he had obviously rehearsed:

"We are not broken."

It was to have been a festive occasion. Joseph Hadani's family and families of others in the national bus cooperative were on a sight-seeing tour. Joseph, for a change, did not have to drive a bus.

His wife began her story.

"I heard a shot and I didn't know what happened. All the people in the bus were singing, and with accordion. Everyone was so happy. It was the end of the outing for the Egged (bus cooperative) and we were going back to Haifa.

"I heard the shots and I heard someone fall down, and I heard crying. I recognized my husband's voice and I began to cry, 'Yosi, Yosi, my husband.' I ran to the front and shouted to them to open the door of the bus."

Levana Hadani was one of the lucky ones. She and Ayelet had been sitting in the back of the bus, away from the first bursts of machine-gun fire that came from the roadside.

The first bullets flying through the windshield wounded her younger daughter, Na'ami, who had been sitting in the little jump seat beside the driver, and her husband, Joseph, who had been standing just behind.

When the bus stopped, some of the other Egged drivers pulled Joseph onto the asphalt. Mrs. Hadani lifted her wounded daughter and ran toward the traffic to flag down a car.

"The man who stopped put his own children out of the car to take me and my daughter. Then he saw in his mirror the terrorists coming back toward the bus and his own children were around the bus with the shooting.

"He said he could not take me and he put me out on the road again. Then he went back to get his children."

The man was too late. He died trying to rescue his children from the machine-gun fire.

"So, I waited on the road and stopped a man and a woman who just saw the bus stopped on the side of the road, that's all. They didn't recognize what was going on. They started to pass it and they saw a man pointing a gun at the bus. They said they thought it was a soldier gone mad."

She got Na'ami into their car.

"The man (got out) and went to the other side of the road and began to stop the cars coming from Haifa. I was in the back of the car. And the woman turned it and put it across the road to stop the other cars.

"I felt so helpless. I saw my daughter's eyes close. Her head was open, here, at the top — so much blood. And I see here in her jaw a big hole. She doesn't move, but she breathes.

"I left my other daughter in the bus. I forgot everything. I cried in the back of the car, 'She's dying, dying . . . quickly, please . . . the hospital.' "

In the car, Mrs. Hadani found a piece of cotton, a little piece which she held ineffectually against the large wound in her daughter's head. With her other hand, she picked broken teeth and chewing gum from Na'ami's open mouth.

Crying, leaning over her daughter and dabbing at the large wound, Mrs. Hadani said softly over and over, "Rein yhi ye beseder — It'll be all right."

"I thought maybe she can hear me, maybe I can give her courage," Mrs. Hadani said.

At the hospital, they quickly took Na'ami away. The doctors gently told Mrs. Hadani they would do what they could, but she had seen the wound in the head and she knew. Ten minutes later, her husband was wheeled in.

"He spoke and I heard him: 'Where is my daughter? What condition is she in? Is she alive?'

"I took his hand. I wanted him to know that I am with him. I told him, 'Don't worry, she breathes.'

"They take him and a doctor comes. I hear him speak with a nurse, with instructions about my husband — 'Take him to the operating room.'

"The nurse answered, 'But doctor, we have so many and they need . . .' Then I started to scream. 'My husband before. First. Before everybody. I lost my daughter.' "

Three young men come into the Hadani home to find Joseph Hadani. They have just been to the hospital, where they visited Yosi Hochman.

Yosi Hochman and Joseph Hadani and the three young men in the small room of the apartment all are members of the Egged (bus cooperative) football team.

Hadani, his neck bent forward, rubs the stitches on his head meditatively while the three tell him about Hochman.

Hochman's wife and two children were killed in the attack. Hochman was wounded and lost a leg.

The three young men say that doctors at the Rambam hospital believe they can save Hochman's other leg.

"If he can learn to use it with a false one on the other side, he'll be all right," one of the young men says.

Hadani looks up at his three friends and says quietly, "Thank God."

"All I kept telling myself was, 'She still breathes,' and I waited outside the operating room in the hallway," said Mrs. Hadani.

"There was a man there, it was an Arab man. But a good Arab, you know? His wife was inside having a Caesarean and he was waiting for his child to be born.

"We smoked his cigarettes and all of sudden I wanted to talk.

"I ask him, 'Are you a Jew?'

"He tells me, 'No, but I'm a human being.'

"He said, 'Don't be worried, there'll be good news. They will save her.'

"I knew it was only words, but I was glad to talk to him. I needed to talk.

"Then, the nurse opens the door and told the man his wife was all right. I cried, 'What about my daughter?'

"The nurse comes to me and holds my arm and says, 'She won't leave. We did what we could.'

"I didn't say anything. I couldn't. I went to find my husband. They had him with shots in bed, but he spoke through the medicine. 'What happened, what happened to her?'

"I held his hand and I told him, 'She's being treated. It's all right. Don't worry.' "

Now Ayelet tells her story. At 10, she has poise and she knows it. Her bright green eyes shine, her cheeks are pink with the excitement of the telling. The adults urge her on with pride.

Hers is the one triumph in the Hadani household. She escaped from the bus before the terrorists took it over.

Someone yelled to get down on the floor—many did and became hostages.

"But I didn't," she said. "I saw the back door was open and I ran."

She hid in the bushes on a nearby hill, found a friend, Danni, also 10, and led him back to the road to flag down a police car. She led the police to where some of the wounded were waiting for help.

She and the wounded were driven to a hospital in Hadera, where she was examined and pronounced fit.

"There were so many people," she said. "They took one man right from the door into the operating room. An old couple came and wanted to take care of me. . . .

"Five minutes later, they released us and they took me to a restaurant. I told them I was a diabetic and they asked me if I knew when I had to eat. I decided to have some sugar so I wouldn't go into insulin shock.

"Mamma always told me to be brave. To be strong. Grandpa is very religious. He always told me to trust in God."

Then she showed a Donald Duck picture she had colored very neatly that day. And she told about the letters her 4th-grade classmates sent her Monday. One said she was like Steve Austin, the Six Million Dollar Man. Another boy wrote: "I want you to live for 500 years."

"That night, Ayelet slept with me. I just told her (that) daddy and Na'ami were having treatment, that everything was all right," Mrs. Hadani said.

"Yesterday, the next morning, when we woke up, I gave her breakfast and then, in the kitchen, I took her hand and I said, 'If you promise to be strong, I'll tell you.'

"I told her, 'You may have to be sister to an invalid.' I wanted to tell her little by little. Nobody else should tell her. We understood each other. She might have heard it on the radio.

"Then she promised to be strong. I hugged her and we cried.

"I told her, 'Don't wait for her, little Ayelet. She won't come any more. But don't cry. I need you to help me. I need you to be strong.'

"Then we listened together to the radio. They were announcing the dead. The first name we heard was Na'ami. I was just happy that I told Ayelet before."

Now Joseph and Levana Hadani have left the small room to take care of their guests. It is part of the shiva that they should do so, that they should be among the living.

Joseph's sister, Malka Meroz, remains in the small room. She leans back and sighs wearily.

"After the Sadat visit, we felt a little bit relaxed," she said. "We felt maybe the peace was coming to us. Now, it's a dream. It was too good a dream."

"Now the parents are every day guarding the kindergarten," said her husband, Michael.

"Something must happen," said Mrs. Meroz, leaning forward again.

"Something must happen—to them. Something dramatic, something to shock them, the Palestinians. Perhaps we must pay (back) in the same way. I don't think some Arab mother must cry, but something must happen. It is not heroism to kill children. The world must do something about it."

"Maybe the answer must be in the same way," said Itzhak Hadani. "I don't understand this killing of children in the middle of the day. But I don't know if I hate them. This will not bring me back my niece. I don't know if revenge is the answer."

Then from the corner, Moshe Kaski, 69, Levana Hadani's father, held out a hand and got silence in the room.

"I will say this and you will make a translation," he said.

"This is the Bible: We, the Jewish people, have to suffer all our lives and to sacrifice sometimes our lives, but those conditions bring us to be hard. And those who want to destroy us will themselves be destroyed."

And then he too rose to go out to the guests in the living room, and the telling of the story was over.

➤ LEONORA LaPETER ➤

Great journalists aren't easily dissuaded. Consider Leonora LaPeter's career path. She didn't decide on a life in the newsroom until her junior year at the University of Illinois at Champaign, not nearly enough time to build a file of clippings or win an internship, which is the typical route to a reporting job. She worked as a waitress and then made her way into newspapers via the back door, working in the circulation department of the *Seattle Daily Journal of Commerce*.

Two years after graduation, she had a few stories published in a weekly newspaper and then landed a job at the *Okeechobee* (Fla.) *News*, covering police news, the courts and city government. Reporting and editing jobs followed at *The Island Packet*, in Hilton Head, South Carolina, and the *Tallahassee* (Fla.) *Democrat*. In 1998 she took a job as court reporter for the *Savannah* (Ga.) *Morning News*, where her stories on a dramatic murder trial won the 2000 Jesse Laventhol Prize for Deadline News Reporting by an Individual. Today LaPeter works as a reporter for the *St. Petersburg* (Fla.) *Times*.

The hallmarks of good narrative — characters instead of sources, scenes instead of summaries, dialogue instead of disembodied quotes — distinguish LaPeter's trial coverage. From the opening statements and chilling testimony to the meting out of four death sentences described in the story reprinted here, LaPeter draws on the deadline storyteller's principal tools: exhaustive reporting that fills the reporter's notebook with detailed observation and a commitment to tell a story as well as report the news.

Whenever possible, deadline writers prepare in advance. For instance, the interviews LaPeter conducted before the trial paid off in this piece with information that deepens the reader's understanding of the case and the families affected by it. The other key is to "write while you're reporting," LaPeter says. "The second I got to the courthouse every morning, I would be looking for my lead. I'd be looking for details, quotes, for the transition, and I'd also be looking for the structure of my story." LaPeter didn't fall into the usual deadline trap, waiting until the last minute to write. Instead, she moved to the back of the courtroom in the afternoon, while court was still in session, to tap out a lead.

Reporting for story pays off when the clock is ticking to deadline, LaPeter says. "When court was out, I would go the hotel, and it wasn't, 'How am I going to write this?' It was, 'What am I going to write? What details am I going to use?' "

Good writers learn from reading words as well as writing them. LaPeter is convinced that the children's books she reads to her daughter have had a positive effect. "They have this rhythm and this pacing, and I actually believe that's improved my writing. . . . My pacing has gotten a lot better."

Detail and pacing are just two of the many elements in LaPeter's story that convey the trauma and tragedy of a murder case. Notice the variation in sentence and paragraph length, as well as the presentation of contrasting viewpoints that convey the competing interests present in any courtroom drama. These are deliberate choices, the products of preparation and an engaged mind, and they make all the difference between dry, lifeless journalism and news storytelling that leaves an indelible mark on the reader's mind.

Jury Sends Santa Claus Killer to Electric Chair

SAVANNAH (GA.) MORNING NEWS • SEPTEMBER 4, 1999

MONROE, GA.—The jury had left.

The sentence had been read.

Jerry Scott Heidler's face was still as stone.

Only when Superior Court Judge Walter C. McMillan Jr. actually sentenced Heidler to death for the murder of the Daniels family did Heidler break down for the first time and cry.

Sitting at the defense table surrounded by six guards, his hands and legs shackled, Heidler shook with the force of his tears. He didn't say anything but wiped his nose on his blue and green polo shirt and folded his hands on his lap.

Four death sentences, one each for Danny, 47, Kim, 33, Jessica, 16, and Bryant, 8, whom Heidler shot dead in their beds in Santa Claus on Dec. 4, 1997. Two additional life sentences for kidnapping one of the Danielses' daughters and sodomizing her by the Altamaha River. Another 110 years for kidnapping two other Danielses' daughters and subjecting one of them to witness the molestation of her sister.

McMillan gave Heidler the maximum sentence on all charges, saying the 22-year-old Alma man did not deserve mercy when he showed no mercy on the Daniels family. He set Heidler's execution date for between Oct. 1 and Oct. 8, although the sentence will be automatically appealed to the Supreme Court of Georgia within 30 days.

And McMillan expressed sorrow for the tiny town of Santa Claus, which must celebrate Christmas and remember Heidler in the same month for years to come.

Jurors seemed to take Friday's decision much harder than the guilty verdict they rendered on Thursday. They sent a note to the judge about an hour into their deliberations, saying they had prayed for everyone and wanted to read a statement when they gave their verdict.

About 45 minutes later, they emerged from the jury room, many of them overwrought with tears as jury foreman James Burrows read the death sentence.

"We have shared in this with you and like you, it has changed our lives forever," Burrows read from a sheet of paper. "Yesterday and today, we held hands and prayed for courage and guidance to do the right thing."

Asked after the trial about his decision, Burrows said he just couldn't talk about it.

"It's too soon," he said. "I'm just not ready. I don't even want to talk to my wife about it. It was very hard."

Friends and family of the Danielses said Friday's verdict finally gives them the closure they need, although they felt sorry for Heidler's family.

"It was the right thing, but I do feel sorry for his sister, because she's going through the same thing we are," said Connie Smith, Kim Daniels' sister. "It's hard to lose someone. But he did what he did for no reason, and I feel he needs to pay for it."

Brandy Claxton, Kim Daniels' 17-year-old daughter, worries about her sisters and brothers. Corey and one of the girls are with Kim Daniels' former foster parents. Two other girls are with Danny Daniels' sister. Gabriel, who was 10 months old when the Danielses were killed, has been adopted out of state.

"The only thing that keeps me sane is that the day before (she was murdered) I saw her and said, 'I love you,'" Claxton said. "That's what keeps me sane."

Defense lawyers had tried all morning to raise sympathy and compassion for Heidler, whom they characterized as a mentally ill man with a troubled childhood who needed help rather than a death sentence.

But the testimony of Heidler's mother, sister, junior high school teacher, foster mother, a psychologist and several social workers did not overcome the gruesome crime.

Heidler's sister, Lisa Heidler Aguilar, was the last witness to testify for the jury.

"I don't want them to kill my brother," said the 24-year-old mother of three, breaking into tears on the stand.

Aguilar, who works with her husband as a migrant worker, testified that both her father and her stepfather had been alcoholics over the years, but neither had ever abused Heidler. She denied that black magic or voodoo had ever been practiced in her mother's household, as other witnesses have testified.

A worker from the Department of Family and Children Services testified that Heidler's mother, Mary Moseley, had threatened to cast spells on the child protective services workers who visited her home and checked up on her children. One spoke of Moseley leaving a voodoo doll with a pin in it in her office a decade ago.

Heidler, who had open-heart surgery when he was 4 years old, was placed in two foster homes because of poor supervision by his mother, the DFACS workers said.

He had imaginary friends, a mouse that he carried around in his hand, said Sylvia Boatright, Heidler's foster mother when he was 11. He called her Boatright Grandma. She learned to love him, she said.

"All he'd ever say is 'come on lil' mouse, come on lil' mouse,' " said Boatright, who lives in Alma. "Scotty was also afraid of the dark. He was afraid a knife would come through the ceiling and cut him."

Later, when he returned to his mother, he attended a school in Baxley for children with learning disabilities. He mutilated himself by picking at his skin until he bled, testified Marilyn Dryden, his teacher at the time.

One time, Heidler didn't come to school.

"So I rode over with my supervisor and we stood outside his door and sang, 'You Are My Sunshine,' and that got him up and he came out," Dryden said. "He came to school. He had a big smile on his face."

DFACS workers said by this time Heidler was a troubled young man in need of some help. He tried to commit suicide a number of times, mutilated himself and landed at Georgia Regional Hospital twice for mental problems—once when he was 11 and another time when he was 13.

James Maish, a forensic psychologist from Augusta, testified Friday that Heidler suffered from a severe case of borderline personality disorder. He said Heidler had eight of the nine symptoms, including suicide attempts, outbursts of uncontrolled anger and "frantic efforts to avoid real or imagined abandonment."

About 2 percent of the population suffers from the disorder and 10 percent of those kill themselves.

His diagnosis was not different from the other three court-appointed mental health experts who examined Heidler. But he took it a step further, saying Heidler had no control over his actions because of his genetic disposition.

"Originally, we thought that every personality disorder was from a bad environment growing up," Maish said. "In other words, whatever was going to happen, you'd lose the battle by age 6."

"In either case, nurture or nature, did Scotty Heidler have any control over this?" asked defense lawyer Michael Garrett.

"No, he can't control that," Maish said. "It's something you're born with."

Moseley, Heidler's mother, acknowledged her son was troubled. But she continued to pledge his innocence on the stand Friday.

"I raised Scotty," she said. "Scotty did not do that murder."

"Even though a jury found him guilty of it?" asked District Attorney Richard Malone.

Moseley shook her head.

"He loved that family. He cared for that family. My family cared for that family," she said. "He's not that kind of person. You've got to know him to know if he's capable of that."

The evidence against Heidler—a confession, finger-prints at the scene, DNA evidence and witnesses—was so strong that defense lawyers Michael Garrett and Kathy Palmer did not try to put up a defense.

They did try to save his life, though.

"About 350 years ago, our ancestors would know what to do about Scotty Heidler, they'd say 'He's possessed by the devil, let's burn him,'" Garrett said. "It's the supreme irony that here we are in 1999 at the end of the third millennium, and we have the same mentally ill person and you are asking to burn him, literally. Have we not progressed as a civilization any farther than that?"

Malone, however, pointed out that Heidler knew right from wrong and was responsible for his own actions.

"What happened in that house is consummate evil," Malone said. "Jerry Scott Heidler had a terrible childhood, yes, but when are we going to expect him to take responsibility for his actions?"

⌐ DAVID VON DREHLE ⌐

David Von Drehle is a national political writer for *The Washington Post*. He won the ASNE award for deadline writing in 1985 and was a runner-up for the first Jesse Laventhol Prize for Deadline News Reporting by an Individual in 1994. He is the author of *Among the Lowest of the Dead: Inside Death Row* and *Triangle: The Fire That Changed America*.

Anyone who has ever looked from a keyboard to a ticking clock knows what David Von Drehle is talking about when he says, "Deadline always makes me shiver."

We live in an age when news and information surge from a media fire hose: All-news cable channels, live feeds and the Internet saturate us and make the newspaper writer's job more difficult than ever. When news is available, instantly, from so many sources, making sense of the deluge is the newspaper's most valuable contribution. Von Drehle's story, "Men of Steel Are Melting With Age," demonstrates how a skillful journalist can provide not only the news but the meaning behind it.

Like any good storyteller, Von Drehle provides setting, the weather and cast of characters, each vividly sketched, from "Henry A. Kissinger, who seemed small and somehow vulnerable," to the Rev. Billy Graham, once "the vivid, virile lion of God, with a voice like Gabriel's trumpet. Now . . . a frail old man who struggles to his feet."

Von Drehle uses the narrative's timeline and plot to move the story. It begins as the mourners gather, glad-handing like politicians at a "precinct caucus." The middle conveys the details of a state funeral that had all the trappings of a political rally, with some mourners wearing old Nixon campaign buttons and others lapel pins that separated the classes of celebrity in attendance ("generals mixed with corporate titans and international arms dealers mingled with movie stars").

Then comes the climax, that point in every good story when everything changes. Von Drehle re-creates that moment when "the mood of a political rally evaporated," with the once mighty statesman Kissinger cracking into a sob.

The weather, like the mood, changes, and the reporter notices the darkening sky, the sun's surrender to the clouds, the growing chill. The story closes quickly: "The cannon boomed; the rifles popped; the polished wooden coffin sank into the wet ground."

Notice how he ends with dueling images—the brave smiles of the mourners contrasted with the "end of power . . . down the path, beneath the trees, under the ground."

Through it all, Von Drehle is guided by the storyteller's compass: the theme. His reporting is a search, not only for quotes and details but also for meaning, the strand that will hold all the pearls he collects in his notebook. It comes as a moment of epiphany, he says, in this case when he sees Kissinger and Bob Dole "each burst into genuine tears" and hears Billy Graham preach about the "democracy of death."

Men of Steel Are Melting
With Age

THE WASHINGTON POST • APRIL 28, 1994

YORBA LINDA, CALIF.—When last the nation saw them all together, they were men of steel and bristling crew cuts, titans of their time— which was a time of pragmatism and ice water in the veins.

How boldly they talked. How fearless they seemed. They spoke of fixing their enemies, of running over their own grandmothers if it would give them an edge. Their goals were the goals of giants: Control of a nation, victory in the nuclear age, strategic domination of the globe.

The titans of Nixon's age gathered again today, on an unseasonably cold and gray afternoon, and now they were white-haired or balding, their steel was rusting, their skin had begun to sag, their eyesight was failing. They were invited to contemplate where power leads.

"John Donne once said that there is a democracy about death," the Rev. Billy Graham told the mourners at Richard M. Nixon's funeral. Then, quoting the poet, he continued: "It comes equally to us all and makes us all equal when it comes."

And here, the great evangelist diverged for a moment from his text to make the point perfectly clear. "We too are going to die," Graham intoned, "and we are going to have to face Almighty God."

Coming from Graham, the words were especially poignant. He is the only American who claims the place of honor in our solemn national ceremonies, even above the sitting president. And once he was the vivid, virile lion of God, with a voice like Gabriel's trumpet. Now he is a frail old man who struggles to his feet.

The senior men of the Nixon administration looked quite old: George P. Shultz, the all-purpose Cabinet secretary; the disgraced vice president Spiro T. Agnew, who emerged from his long seclusion clearly stooped; the foreign policy guru Henry A. Kissinger, who seemed small and somehow vulnerable.

And the junior men looked very senior: Nixon chief of staff Alexander M. Haig Jr., resembling a retiree at the yacht club; political legman Lyn Nofziger, still looking like an unmade bed but now your grandfather's unmade bed; muscle man Charles W. Colson, his crew cut replaced by a thinning gray thatch. G. Gordon Liddy, with his bullet head, looked the least changed of all.

"Let not your heart be troubled, neither let it be afraid," Graham said.

They arrived full of the old sangfroid, smiling and glad-handing for as much as an hour before the service began. Nixon's men and many of the other dignitaries worked the crowd like a precinct caucus; surely Nixon, the best pol of his era, would have approved. As a Marine band played Bach's ineffable hymn, "Jesu, Joy of Man's Desiring," Republican National Committee chairman Haley Barbour pumped hands with a broad grin on his face, and nearby David R. Gergen, the perennial presidential adviser, worked a row of mourners like a rope line.

And in the beginning, perhaps, the event reminded them of just another political event. A very small number of people attended, compared to the number who no doubt wished to honor Nixon, but even among the exclusive group, the crowd was separated by various shades of lapel pin. Purple was the best, the regal color—bearers of purple buttons could go right up to the front rows, where generals mixed with corporate titans and international arms dealers mingled with movie stars.

The band had shifted to "God of Our Fathers" when the congressional delegation arrived, and this ignited another flurry of politicking. A number of people had dusted off old Nixon campaign buttons, which they displayed proudly as they milled among old friends. Nixon speech-writer Patrick J. Buchanan caught sight of an old friend and stepped lively to meet him, while nearby White House Chief of Staff Thomas F. "Mack" McLarty chatted amiably with Colson. (They call McLarty "Mack the Nice." No one ever called Colson "nice" when he served Nixon; Colson was the one who offered to run down his grandmother. But that was a long time ago.)

It is possible to pinpoint the instant when the mood of a political rally evaporated. It was when Kissinger, almost invisible behind the bulky presidential lectern, quoted Shakespeare in speaking of Nixon: "He was a man, take him for all in all, I shall not look upon his like again."

And that great rumbling Kissinger voice—which once spoke of war and nations and nuclear strategy as if all these things were mere entertainments, mere exercise to tone his Atlas-like muscles—cracked into a sob.

The sky darkened just then. The sun gave up its hours-long struggle to penetrate the clouds. The day fumed cold, and after the shock of hearing Kissinger cry, moments later Senate Minority Leader Robert J. Dole (R-Kan.) was crying too.

It was appropriate, perhaps, that the funeral of the first U.S. president from California should be held on a parking lot, across the street from a strip mall. The Nixon Library and Birthplace stands on the spot where Nixon's parents raised a mail order house nearly a century ago.

This was the frontier then; now it is just another cookie-cutter suburb. Tough people settled this place — "Chinatown" tough. They diverted vast rivers, crushed powerful unions, and made this remote land of dry winds, hard ground, earthquakes, fires, droughts into the great postwar city. Richard Nixon was one of them, and he went farther than any of them: He remade the country through his unstinting use and abuse of power; some say he remolded the world.

But none of that kept him from the leveling end that awaits even the most vigorous and clever wielders of power. The cannon boomed; the rifles popped; the polished wooden coffin sank into the wet ground. Chilled, the mourners hastened across the green grass to a gathering where canapés were served by uniformed staff. And though their smiles returned, the end of power lay before them, down the path, beneath the trees, under the ground.

~ FRANCIS X. CLINES ~

During his four decades at *The New York Times*, Francis X. Clines has proved himself one of the most versatile and gifted writers in the paper's history. Now a Washington-based reporter, he was a London correspondent for the paper when he won the ASNE award for deadline writing in 1989.

In an age when reporters can cover meetings on C-SPAN, consult transcripts of news conferences they need not attend, and never leave the comfort of the newsroom, Francis X. Clines is a throwback to a time when shoe leather was the journalist's principal means of transport. His work demonstrates that there is no substitute for being on the scene.

Clines knows that only by being there can the reporter soak up the sensory details that bring a story to life and listen for the quotes that make it breathe. He needs this raw material to produce stories that, like the lead from a story about a Belfast funeral, have the gritty feel of reality and the lyricism of poetry:

"Beyond the coffin, out in the churchyard, red-haired Kathleen Quinn was full of fun and flirting shamelessly for all her eight years of life. 'Mister, I'm to be on the TV tonight,' she told a stranger, squinting up happy and prim. Kathleen had taken her brother's bike and skinned her knee bloody, all while people were praying goodbye inside the church to another rebel body in another coffin."

Reported from the land of James Joyce, Clines' story is more than a news account; it provides a portrait of the artist as a reporter. He delights in the detail, carefully observed and joyfully wrought.

After the reporting, of course, comes an equally challenging step: making the right selections from the multitude of details, voices and people that fill the reporter's notebook. The beginner who worries about leaving things out can take comfort from the lesson that Clines says he must keep relearning.

"If you're not careful, you can let too many people into the story, who will more or less make the same point, and eat up the story, so that you haven't told the story. It is, after all, a story first, and not a catalog of comments. I have to rerun that every time: Don't let a crowd in a story. I always feel guilty when I interview a lot of people and then don't use many of them. But you're interviewing them for your telling of the story, and not for their telling of the story, unless they were in some unique position."

From Ireland, Clines went on to report from the Philippines, London and Moscow. Today he still hits the streets—the reporter as witness, still mastering the craft, the writer as apprentice. "You read, and you know what you like when you read, and that rubs off. It's give-and-take, and you're always self-adjusting. It's a learning process, but it's self-taught."

The work of Clines has such texture that it deserves the most careful critical attention, which is why we have chosen to X-Ray his report about civil war in Belfast. This analysis reveals how the larger themes of political and religious conflict are represented on the level of language and syntax. Dualities are everywhere: in scenes, in imagery, in sentences and phrases.

In Belfast, Death, Too, Is Diminished by Death

THE NEW YORK TIMES • MARCH 20, 1988

BELFAST, NORTHERN IRELAND — Beyond the coffin, out in the churchyard, red-haired Kathleen Quinn was full of fun and flirting shamelessly for all her eight years of life. "Mister, I'm to be on the TV tonight," she told a stranger, squinting up happy and prim. Kathleen had taken her brother's bike and skinned her knee bloody, all while people were praying goodbye inside the church to another rebel body in another coffin.

Soon the cameras were watching the coffin being carried out from the windowless fortress of a church, down the curl of the street in the simple hamlet, and on to the ever-filling graveyard patch devoted to republican rebels.

As it turned out, the television ignored Kathleen and missed a classic Irish truth, a sight for sore eyes. She climbed back on the bike and headed off in a blur, oblivious of a piece of nearby graffiti that seemed about all of life's withering dangers: "I wonder each night what the monster will do to me tomorrow."

Eventually there was woeful monotony in what became a week of mourning and parading and dying. At a funeral for three slain republican agents Wednesday, a grenade-throwing intruder had killed three people. There was another republican funeral Thursday, then two on Friday, and three more on Saturday. The dead were produced by assorted violence — some were innocent victims, others were zealous aggressors. Yesterday, at a cortege for a victim of Wednesday's funeral, two British soldiers in civilian clothes drove

Alliteration emphasizes girl's innocence

Even the innocent can be bloodied

Literary phrase

Flyover paragraph: summary of recent news

Coffin, representing death, contrasts with innocent girl

Cinematic view: verbally evokes a movie shot

Death and innocence again contrasted; tension builds

into a crowd of mourners and were dragged from their car, beaten, and shot to death.

The best hometown poets wisely retreat from Northern Ireland once their sense of mortality is honed to piercing, so this dark progression was left to be described in the prosaic catchall "the troubles," as if Job had called his plagues "the unpleasantries."

Brilliant cultural analysis: euphemism hides the unspeakable

The deaths were handled by Gerry Adams, the eerily placid, black-bearded leader of Sinn Fein, the rebellion's political arm, as if he were the Osiris of his people, the king rallying souls to the underworld, to the plain slant of Belfast hillside called Milltown Cemetery. Mr. Adams, whom police officials suspect of being deeply involved in rebel violence, exhibited the demeanor of a parish curate in adapting almost instantly to expressions of fresh official grief for bodies freshly felled in Wednesday's attack.

Mythological metaphor shows Adams as shepherd of death

Great adverb: "eerily" modifies meaning of "placid"

The earth had not been closed on their predecessors before the newest victims went from praying for the dead to being dead. Asked what he thought of it—the brazen intruder exploding the grief—Mr. Adams replied rather gently, "It was one of those things." He cited it as a demonstration of the state of war he prefers as a description of life here, as opposed to the state of criminal terrorism the British government, trying to rule this place, attributes to the rebels of the Irish Republican Army.

Effective shift of meaning

Contrasting labels reveal how two sides frame reality

There is at least as much fighting over words and symbols as over flesh and earth. Most metaphysically absurd was the attempt by Mr. Adams's enemies in the paramilitary gangs of the Protestant loyalist majority to portray the grenade attacker as a genuine eccentric among the hundreds of modern Irish gunmen who have stalked their fellows in all imaginable lethal manner. The attacker was somehow being rated as beyond the bounds of the "normal" killers of Belfast, "rejected" by the main paramilitary organization, said one quasi-brigadier, as if denying the vendetta

Strong parallel

(CONTINUED)

Good Irish name

wildness of the historic gangs of Ireland—the Peep O'Day Boys and their nasty counterparts.

"You, the people of Belfast, have won the battle of the funerals," a Sinn Fein official told a graveside crowd. He spoke not of quantity of casualties but of the police's finally deciding to stay away from the cemetery and overlook the rebel rhetoric and paraphernalia. This victory of the funerals was proclaimed in a booming brogue across the gravestones by a speaker who seemed intent on listing each outrage in eight centuries of Anglo-Irish violence.

Ancient grievances live on

But this hoary tower of calibrated grievance seemed to crumble at the sight of placid Irish women suddenly made to suffer here and now. Here was a young woman, a Catholic nationalist, staggering back from a grenade, bleeding from her face onto gravestones proclaiming the certainty of final peace. "Why would anyone want to do that?" she asked so simply later. And there was an older Protestant loyalist woman asking virtually the same question the morning after as she stood with singed hair by the ashes of her house after it was gasoline-bombed in a random, retaliatory raid by nationalist vandals. "Some poor Catholic woman will get it done to her," she said of the vengeance.

Less effective the second time

Quotes reveal solidarity of women

One point of rare agreement among nationalists, loyalists, and the British authorities is that atrocity tends to be layered like slag here, not woven linearly. So the latest sensational deaths at a funeral instantly diminish the importance of the preceding outrage. Thus the Sinn Fein mourners, in feeling newly violated, could also feel freer of the pall of the rebel explosion last fall that killed 11 Protestant civilians.

Comparable rubrics seem to underpin the postmortem morning television news shows as they assemble the usual balance of partisan analysts. In this, the London government often leaves the nationalists livid by assuming the

News media coverage puts story in larger context

role of the sad, bewildered referee among these unruly Irishmen.

The same leaders from a score of civic and church institutions come forward each time to the television cameras with capsules of concern and recriminations that can seem, with each new funereal cue, as horrendous in their own good way as the inevitable deaths to follow. More was the hopeful comfort, then, in the death-defying sight of red-haired Kathleen as she happily skirted the latest funeral.

Kathleen is back, but what is her future?

Chapter 2

LOCAL REPORTING AND BEATS

An old-fashioned word describes some of the best kind of reporting in America. That word is *shoe-leather*. When reporters get away from their telephones and computers, hit the streets, talk to folks about their needs and concerns, listen and learn, they create special opportunities to discover powerful and useful stories. Walk and talk. Shoe-leather.

Rick Bragg wrote for *The New York Times*, but he grew up in the South and brings a distinctively local perspective to the story of a hardworking Southern woman who saved her pennies and donated a small fortune to a university.

Thomas Boswell reveals how the deep knowledge that comes from beat reporting—in this case, covering a baseball team—can lead to rich cultural insights that help readers see below the surface and understand.

Jonathan Bor shows that experience on a beat can be the best preparation for deadline writing, in this case the dramatic story of a heart transplant operation.

Mitch Albom, a best-selling author and sports columnist, takes his shoe leather into the community to tell the story of a young athlete who seeks to escape a world defined by guns.

Russell Eshleman proves that deep reporting, short writing, and sharp wit can combine to make the workings of state government accessible and interesting to citizens.

Finally, Dan Neil reveals how the beat can become the offbeat. Combining reporting and literary skills, Neil writes wildly unconventional critiques of automobiles. Although much automotive journalism in America reads like advertising, Neil understands the cultural and political influence of the car. He understands its power and poetry.

A debate has raged since the 1990s about the role of the journalist within the civic life of communities. The traditional model insists that the journalist be detached and independent, if not objective then at least neutral about how things turn out. Such independence, say the traditionalists, begets credibility. A new school of thought contends that the reporter must not be just a watchdog, biting the heels of official power, but also a guide dog, leading citizens toward solutions and the common good.

Smart reporters do not have to choose between these models, but can select the best methods and practices from the old-fashioned and the innovative. From either perspective, shoe-leather works: in the development of sources, in finding community listening posts, in the continuous learning that distinguishes the great reporters and writers from the ordinary.

Whether the beat is weather, politics, education, health care or sports, communities need writers with a distinctive vision and a powerful voice, one that speaks directly to readers.

~ RICK BRAGG ~

Growing up in Alabama, Rick Bragg soaked up the storyteller's approach to news "by watching the men in my family sit on the front porch. And these are men that never read a book in their whole life, but they sat on the front porch and told long, beautiful stories with drama and danger and great detail. . . . I knew how to tell a story long before I ever sat down to write one."

As a national correspondent for *The New York Times*, based in Atlanta in the mid-1990s, Bragg roamed his homeland, the South, going to "the places where the stories were the darkest and richest . . . where life is at its most tenuous." His assignments took him from the child murder trial of Susan Smith to an Alabama prison where aging inmates created a nursing home for felons.

His stories bring the storyteller's art and craft to the news. This requires an unerring eye for the resonant detail: the tape binding the ragged Bible of washerwoman Oseola McCarty "to keep Corinthians from falling out."

News storytelling doesn't get much better than Bragg's portrait of Miss McCarty, an 87-year-old black Mississippi woman who "spent a lifetime making other people look nice," taking in "bundles of dirty clothes and [making] them clean and neat for parties she never attended, weddings to which she was never invited, graduations she never saw."

Miss McCarty, he writes, "is 5 feet tall and would weigh 100 pounds with rocks in her pockets. Her voice is so soft that it disappears in the squeak of the screen door and the hum of the air-conditioner."

One of Bragg's editors was the legendary Gene Roberts. Roberts led *The Philadelphia Inquirer* to a string of Pulitzers and then ended his career as managing editor at *The New York Times*. As a young reporter, Roberts had an editor named Henry Belk who used to prod the beginner with this command: "Make me see." For Belk, that was a requirement; he was blind, and his wife read him the paper every day. To make readers see, to allow them to witness the world from their breakfast tables, is the challenge for every writer.

When you read Rick Bragg, he makes you see, and hear, and, most important, feel.

In addition to his newspaper journalism, Bragg is the author of three best-selling books — *All Over but the Shoutin'*, *Ava's Man*, and *I Am a Soldier, Too: The Jessica Lynch Story*.

All She Has, $150,000, Is Going to a University

THE NEW YORK TIMES • AUGUST 13, 1995

HATTIESBURG, MISS.—Oseola McCarty spent a lifetime making other people look nice. Day after day, for most of her 87 years, she took in bundles of dirty clothes and made them clean and neat for parties she never attended, weddings to which she was never invited, graduations she never saw.

She had quit school in the sixth grade to go to work, never married, never had children and never learned to drive because there was never any place in particular she wanted to go. All she ever had was the work, which she saw as a blessing. Too many other black people in rural Mississippi did not have even that.

She spent almost nothing, living in her old family home, cutting the toes out of shoes if they did not fit right and binding her ragged Bible with Scotch tape to keep Corinthians from falling out. Over the decades, her pay—mostly dollar bills and change—grew to more than $150,000.

"More than I could ever use," Miss McCarty said the other day without a trace of self-pity. So she is giving her money away, to finance scholarships for black students at the University of Southern Mississippi here in her hometown, where tuition is $2,400 a year.

"I wanted to share my wealth with the children," said Miss McCarty, whose only real regret is that she never went back to school. "I never minded work, but I was always so busy, busy. Maybe I can make it so the children don't have to work like I did."

People in Hattiesburg call her donation the Gift. She made it, in part, in anticipation of her death.

As she sat in her warm, dark living room, she talked of that death matter-of-factly, the same way she talked about the possibility of an afternoon thundershower. To her, the Gift was a preparation, like closing the bedroom windows to keep the rain from blowing in on the bedspread.

"I know it won't be too many years before I pass on," she said, "and I just figured the money would do them a lot more good than it would me."

Her donation has piqued interest around the country. In a few short days, Oseola McCarty, the washerwoman, has risen from obscurity to a notice she does not understand. She sits in her little frame house, just blocks from the university, and patiently greets the reporters, business leaders and others who line up outside her door.

"I live where I want to live, and I live the way I want to live," she said. "I couldn't drive a car if I had one. I'm too old to go to college. So I planned to do this. I planned it myself."

It has been only three decades since the university integrated. "My race used to not get to go to that college," she said. "But now they can."

When asked why she had picked this university instead of a predominantly black institution, she said, "Because it's here; it's close."

While Miss McCarty does not want a building named for her or a statue in her honor, she would like one thing in return: to attend the graduation of a student who made it through college because of her gift. "I'd like to see it," she said.

Business leaders in Hattiesburg, 110 miles northeast of New Orleans, plan to match her $150,000, said Bill Pace, the executive director of the University of Southern Mississippi Foundation, which administers donations to the school.

"I've been in the business 24 years now, in private fund raising," Mr. Pace said. "And this is the first time I've experienced anything like this from an individual who simply was not affluent, did not have the resources and yet gave substantially. In fact, she gave almost everything she has.

"No one approached her from the university; she approached us. She's seen the poverty, the young people who have struggled, who need an education. She is the most unselfish individual I have ever met."

Although some details are still being worked out, the $300,000 — Miss McCarty's money and the matching sum — will finance scholarships into the indefinite future. The only stipulation is that the beneficiaries be black and live in southern Mississippi.

The college has already awarded a $1,000 scholarship in Miss McCarty's name to an 18-year-old honors student from Hattiesburg, Stephanie Bullock.

Miss Bullock's grandmother, Ledrester Hayes, sat in Miss McCarty's tiny living room the other day and thanked her. Later, when Miss McCarty left the room, Mrs. Hayes shook her head in wonder.

"I thought she would be some little old rich lady with a fine car and a fine house and clothes," she said. "I was a seamstress myself, worked two jobs. I know what it's like to work like she did, and she gave it away."

The Oseola McCarty Scholarship Fund bears the name of a woman who bought her first air-conditioner just three years ago and even now turns it on only when company comes. Miss McCarty also does not mind that her tiny black-and-white television set gets only one channel, because she never watches anyway. She complains that her electricity bill is too high and says she never subscribed to a newspaper because it cost too much.

The pace of Miss McCarty's walks about the neighborhood is slowed now, and she misses more Sundays than she would like at Friendship Baptist Church. Arthritis has left her hands stiff and numb. For the first time in almost 80 years, her independence is threatened.

"Since I was a child, I've been working," washing the clothes of doctors, lawyers, teachers, police officers, she said. "But I can't do it no more. I can't work like I used to."

She is 5 feet tall and would weigh 100 pounds with rocks in her pockets. Her voice is so soft that it disappears in the squeak of the screen door and the hum of the air-conditioner.

She comes from a wide place in the road called Shubuta, Miss., a farming town outside Meridian, not far from the Alabama line. She quit school, she said, when the grandmother who reared her became ill and needed care.

"I would have gone back," she said, "but the people in my class had done gone on, and I was too big. I wanted to be with my class." So she worked, and almost every dollar went into the bank. In time, all her immediate family died. "And I didn't have nobody," she said. "But I stayed busy."

She took a short vacation once, as a young woman, to Niagara Falls. The roar of the water scared her. "Seemed like the world was coming to an end," she said.

She stayed home, mostly, after that. She has lived alone since 1967.

Earlier this year her banker asked what she wanted done with her money when she passed on. She told him that she wanted to give it to the university, now rather than later; she set aside just enough to live on.

She says she does not want to depend on anyone after all these years, but she may have little choice. She has been informally adopted by the first young person whose life was changed by her gift.

As a young woman, Stephanie Bullock's mother wanted to go to the University of Southern Mississippi. But that was during the height of the integration battles, and, if she had tried, her father might have lost his job with the city.

It looked as if Stephanie's own dream of going to the university would also be snuffed out, for lack of money. Although she was president of her senior class in high school and had grades that were among the best there, she fell just short of getting an academic scholarship. Miss Bullock said her family earned too much money to qualify for most Federal grants but not enough to send her to the university.

Then, last week, she learned that the university was giving her $1,000, in Miss McCarty's name. "It was a total miracle," she said, "and an honor."

She visited Miss McCarty to thank her personally and told her that she planned to "adopt" her. Now she visits regularly, offering to drive Miss McCarty around and filling a space in the tiny woman's home that has been empty for decades.

She feels a little pressure, she concedes, not to fail the woman who helped her. "I was thinking how amazing it was that she made all that money doing laundry," said Miss Bullock, who plans to major in business.

She counts on Miss McCarty's being there four years from now, when she graduates.

～ THOMAS BOSWELL ～

Thomas Boswell is a sports columnist for *The Washington Post*, where he started work as a part-time copy aide in 1969. He won the ASNE award for sportswriting in 1981. His sportswriting has been published in several book-length collections.

Boswell is a student of baseball. He is so studious, in fact, that when he covers a game, he not only records the performance of every batter but also makes note of every pitch.

The most devoted athletes are sometimes called "gym rats," which might make Boswell a "library rat." He likes to read and think before he writes. A graduate of Amherst College, Boswell reads 19th-century literature and literary criticism. Hence he writes an essay on the aging of athletes that mentions the likes of Willie "Pops" Stargell as well as John Keats.

That the sports section of a big-city newspaper could contain an essay that alludes to a poem by Dylan Thomas says something about the flexibility of the form. Boswell's writing strategy, whether conscious or unconscious, is to climb up and down the ladder of abstraction.

He begins with a down-to-earth image, "The cleanup crews come at midnight," but something immediately transforms it: "creeping into the ghostly quarter-light of empty ballparks with their slow-sweeping brooms and languorous, sluicing hoses." The language signals that something is up, that the story is about to gain altitude.

> All season, they remove the inanimate refuse of a game. Now, in the dwindling days of September and October, they come to collect baseball souls.
> Age is the sweeper, injury his broom.

With little effort, the physical has become the metaphysical, a contemplation on the mortality of athletes and the loss of youth within us all. But Boswell knows he must not keep readers at such a height for long, so down the ladder he slides: "Mixed among the burst beer cups and the mustard-smeared wrappers headed for the trash heap, we find old friends who are being consigned to the dust bin of baseball's history." Up and down readers go, not violently, as on a roller coaster, but as on a carousel, equally conscious of the up-and-down and the journey round.

The reader's journey comes from a coherent collection of anecdotes—some historical, others recent—on the aging of athletes. Boswell describes the process: "The most important thing in the story is finding the central idea. It's one thing to be given a topic, but you have to find the idea or the concept within that topic. Once you find that idea or thread, all the other anecdotes, illustrations and quotes are pearls that you hang on this thread. The thread may seem very humble, the pearls may seem very flashy, but it's still the thread that makes the necklace."

Losing It: Careers Fall
Like Autumn Leaves

THE WASHINGTON POST • SEPTEMBER 30, 1980

The cleanup crews come at midnight, creeping into the ghostly quarter-light of empty ballparks with their slow-sweeping brooms and languorous, sluicing hoses. All season, they remove the inanimate refuse of a game. Now, in the dwindling days of September and October, they come to collect baseball souls.

Age is the sweeper, injury his broom.

Mixed among the burst beer cups and the mustard-smeared wrappers headed for the trash heap, we find old friends who are being consigned to the dust bin of baseball's history. If a night breeze blows a back page of *The Sporting News* down the stadium aisle, pick it up and squint at the onetime headline names now just fine print at the very bottom of a column of averages.

Each year, the names change of those who have "lost it," and probably won't find it again. This year's list of those who are past 30 and into that inexorable stat slide includes Sal Bando, Lee May, Ed Figueroa, Gene Tenace, Fred Patek, Manny Sanguillen, Willie Horton, Bernie Carbo, Bud Harrelson, Bobby Bonds, Randy Jones, Dave Cash, Mike Torrez and Ross Grimsley. Not a bad season's haul, once you consider that, when the seine is finally culled clean, it may also hold Willie Stargell, Bill Lee and Joe Morgan.

"I like a look of Agony," wrote Emily Dickinson, "because I know it's true." For those with a taste for a true look, a glimpse beneath the mask, even if it be a glimpse of agony, then this is the proper time of year. Spring training is for hope; autumn is for reality. At every stop on the late season baseball trail, we see that look of agony, although it hides behind many expressions.

In Pittsburgh, "Pops" Stargell rides a stationary bicycle. A depressed giant sitting on a ridiculous toy, he pedals to rehabilitate an arthritic knee that has deteriorated for a decade. "Everything gets better slower each year," he says. "And, finally, it doesn't get better at all."

In Houston, Morgan helps the Astros with the sad bits and pieces of those skills that are left to him. The back-to-back MVP, a 240-ish hitter for the past three years, says of his last career stage, "I'm still a ballplayer, but you couldn't really call me Joe Morgan. . . . I'm used to laughing at other players. Now they're laughing at me."

In Montreal, "Spaceman" Bill Lee, in bullpen exile, spends these pennant-race days exorcising the nervous energy that consumes him. Lee spends half the game jogging just beyond the outfield fence, his cap and prematurely grizzled hair bouncing at the edge of view like a bobber on the water's surface being jerked about by a hooked fish. "I'm not through. They can't get rid of me," he says. "I pitched hurt for 'em for months. That explains the (bad) stats. But they don't appreciate it. Just wait. You'll see next year." It's an old litany. Lee's ERA is 5.47. Even Spacemen get jettisoned.

Finally, the towns become a swirl. The player's face is familiar with its look of wounded dignity, but the uniforms change. Jim Kaat, 41, has won 270 games, but his uniform gets harder to remember as he bounces from league to league, hanging on. "It's tough to love the game," says Kaat, now a Cardinal, "after she's stopped loving you."

To a ballplayer, the game is a seed he planted as a child, a kind of beautiful creeping ivy that he was delighted to have entwine him. As an adult, he felt supported in every sense — financial, emotional, psychic — by his green, rich, growing game, just as ivy can strengthen a brick wall. But ivy, given time, can overpower and tear down a house.

So, in a way, the aging player, whose life seems to be a mansion, knows that he is in a strong and even dangerous grip. In the end, he may not know how much of his strength, how much of his ability to stand alone, comes from the brick and mortar of his own identity and how much is borrowed from the vine that engulfs him more each year, even as it props him up. No wonder he is so fearful when the time arrives to hew through the root and pull free.

Mickey Mantle, retired a dozen years, still has a recurring dream that makes him awake in a sweat. In the nightmare, he is trying to crawl under the center field fence in Yankee Stadium, but something is snagged and he can't move. The PA system intones, "Batting fourth . . . No. 7. . . ." In the dugout, Whitey Ford, Billy Martin and Casey Stengel ask each other, "Where's Mickey?"

"And then," says Mantle, "I wake up."

This dream needs no interpretation. It epitomizes the nub of raw, disoriented fear, and the sense of nameless loss, that many fine athletes must feel if they were ever good enough to mesh their characters with their skills. How can we tell the dancer from the dance?

Even the most dignified and self-possessed of former stars occasionally shows a twinge of what haunts Mantle. Returning from a USO tour of Korea, Marilyn Monroe told her husband, Joe DiMaggio, then retired, "Oh, Joe, it was wonderful. You never heard such cheers."

"Yes, I have," was DiMaggio's clipped reply.

The desire for applause, for camaraderie, for the hard coin of indisputable accomplishment is a powerful pull. The green of the field has so many rich connotations that it even makes the green of a dollar bill seem faded by comparison.

In all baseball history, there is perhaps only one case of a great player who cut the vine, stepped free and tested his legs long before he lost it. When Sandy Koufax was 30, he won 27 games. And after the World Series, he retired.

"I was looking for time," he now says for explanation.

Only after 13 years of casual wandering—neither a recluse nor a public figure—did his nest egg run low. He returned to baseball, as a Dodger coach, because it was a painless way to make a buck as a pitching professor emeritus.

Koufax is simply the exception that proves the rule. Far more typical are Hank Aaron and Warren Spahn, the top home run hitter and winner in modern, lively-ball times. The former Brave teammates never faced each other in their careers, but they did this spring in San Diego when the 46-year-old Aaron came to bat against the 59-year-old Spahn. They weren't kidding.

Not since Babe Ruth faced Walter Johnson for charity when both were in their 50s have such legends met. The pretext for this time-warp freeze frame was a Padre-vs.-Pirate home run-hitting contest. But the real curiosity was watching Aaron and Spahn face each other from opposite ends of the tunnel of middle age. Aaron looked like he had spent his four retirement years locked in a bakery. Spahn might have spent 15 years prospecting in a desert, his skin weathered to rawhide, his bandy limbs and barrel chest shrunken.

The scene was elegantly set. Warming up, Aaron missed half-speed pitches. The crowd murmured its collective embarrassment and empathy as though an innocent prank had turned ugly. Meanwhile, thanks to aluminum bats and Japanese rabbit balls, Dave Parker, Dave Winfield and Stargell were having a tape-measure orgy. Aaron was mercifully forgotten.

Once the contest started, Aaron whiffed meekly twice against the Padre batting practice pitcher. Then, on the third of six allotted swings in the round, Aaron conked a homer. The crowd cheered with relief. Then, while their pitying applause was still in the air, the next pitch had already been dispatched even further into the left field bleachers. The crowd was rising and roaring. Reporters scrambled back into the press box just as players popped back out of runways into the dugouts to watch. The next pitch also went over the wall, delivered there by a sweet slash of the wrists. And, on his fourth consecutive swing—all this in 30 seconds or so, as emotions had gone from depression to glee—Aaron smashed his last pitch off the top of the center field wall 430 feet away, missing a fourth homer by a yard.

For the final round of the contest, Spahn pitched, lobbing in mush balls for the monsters to mash. Aaron hit last, needing just one homer to beat all the active stars. Spahn peered in, grinned and threw. Aaron swung and missed. He smiled back at Spahn. Spahn repeated the ritual and threw again. Aaron looked at the pitch as though it were a rotten mackerel. Although he was due five more swings, Aaron gently laid down his bat, turned his back on Spahn and walked away, ending the contest by fiat.

Back in the dugout, Aaron was asked "Why'd you quit? Hurt yourself swinging?"

"No," said Aaron brusquely. "Spahn was throwing screwballs."

And they say Walter Johnson threw sliders to Ruth.

In baseball, you see, no one ever believes he's really lost it. No American team sport is half so fascinated with the process of aging as baseball, perhaps because none of our games is so based on skill and timing rather than brute force. Nor does any sport offer prospects for an athletic old age that is so rich in possibilities for either humiliation or the greatest fame.

Every athlete in every sport deteriorates. But in baseball that battle against time—where a standoff means temporary victory—can be extended for as much as a decade by a dogged will and an analytical mind. Perhaps no sport encourages its men to rage so nobly against the erosion of their youth.

The ultimate cases in point are Aaron and Spahn, statistically the greatest old hitter and the best old pitcher ever. They alone among Hall of Famers actually got better after they turned 35. Aaron hit 245 homers and had his two best slugging-percentage years after that supposed watershed as he actually became a better pull hitter with age. After Spahn turned 35, and concurrently mastered the scroogie, he won 20 games seven times and won 180 games. No one is close to either mark.

Baseball, it seems, rewards stubbornness and indomitability, as long as those qualities are mixed with a basic humility, self-knowledge and willingness to adapt. Baseball's highest, and most appealing, type may be the veteran. No sport is so full of 10-, 15- and even 20-year pros, or is so defined by them.

"I disagree," John Keats once wrote in a letter, about the world as a "vale of tears. . . . Call the world, if you please, 'the vale of soul-making.' Then you will find out the use of the world."

Only with age do athletes discover that their playing fields have become vales of soul-making. Only as they become vulnerable, flawed and afraid do they seem truly human to us and most worthy of our attention. Nothing can stop the slow bleeding away of talent and confidence, but character is the best tourniquet.

"The player who ages poorly is the one who lets his vanity get in the way of his judgment," says Yankee Coach Charlie Lau. "Making 'adjustments' is another word for having the good sense to know you're getting older."

As an example, Lau cites those good friends, George Scott and Reggie Jackson. Each, with age, showed a hitting flaw. Scott, proud of his strength, could no longer manage his huge 38-ounce bat. Jackson had trouble with high and outside fast balls, popping them harmlessly to center. Scott, for three years, refused to use a lighter bat. Despite humiliating reverse shifts—with defenses playing him as though he were a weak lefty hitter—he persisted in his persona as "The Boomer." Now, he's out of baseball and doesn't understand. Jackson, on the other hand, worked with his stance and weight shift until that troublesome pitch suddenly became his bleacher meat. Now, at 34, he has his highest homer total since he was 23.

"Even after everybody else told Scott he needed to change, he wouldn't," summarized Lau. "But before anybody said anything to Reggie, he already had."

No better text could be asked to illustrate baseball's capacity for allowing age-with-dignity than the performance in the past month of the New York Yankees. Of all champions, they may well be the oldest, the most infirm and the most emblematic of what we mean by veteran fortitude.

If ever a team ought not bear inspection, it is these Yankees with a pitching rotation of Gaylord Perry (42), Luis Tiant (40), Tommy John (37) and Rudy May (37). Yet they are 20-3 in September. Autumn must be their proper season. More than half this team has, at one time or another, heard the words, "You've lost it." Names like Piniella, Nettles, Jackson, Watson, Murcer, Spencer, Rodriguez and Stanley have, among them, an average age of 35.

Look below the Yankee dollar signs and New York headlines. This is a team familiar with the look of Agony. Its players have been forced to look in the mirror. For most, their baseball world long ago became a vale of soul-making.

So, demands for September character have been within their reach. When the cleanup crews come to sweep out darkened Yankee Stadium this year, there will be no human refuse. All those aged expendables who were management's list for replacement with shiny expensive new parts have, by banding together, made themselves indispensable for at least a few months.

Age, with his broom of injury, will sweep them out someday. But, until then, these Yankees are a standing lesson of how old men, who are really young, can staunchly refuse to go gentle into that good night.

~ JONATHAN BOR ~

Jonathan Bor was covering the health and medicine beat for *The Post-Standard* in Syracuse, N.Y., when he won the ASNE award for deadline writing. He currently covers the medical beat at *The Sun* in Baltimore.

Bor wrote this heart transplant story in 90 minutes, after reporting for 48 hours without sleep. Even under less extreme conditions, Bor's story, a tightly constructed news narrative, would be an exemplar.

Notice the structure of the story, which falls nicely into an "hourglass" pattern, with the basic elements of news at the top of the story, a transition and a chronological retelling of events. This structure satisfies a time-starved reader's demand for important information and then offers the insight that comes from the vicarious experience of this dramatic event.

Bor witnessed the operation from a gallery directly over the operating table. He serves as the reader's eyes and ears, capturing the compelling and quirky moments that weave together a complicated news event. The larger news elements stand out:

- Bruce Murray is the first Syracuse resident to receive a heart transplant.
- Eric Rose may be the youngest transplant surgeon in the world.
- A travel-distance record is set for transporting the donor heart.
- The reporter witnesses the operation.

What remains in the memory are the smaller details: the diseased heart, a milky purple, dumped in the stainless steel bowl; the donor heart in a beer cooler; the young surgeon wearing a heart-shaped pin.

Even with less than two hours to write, Bor took his time with the lead, knowing it would convey the tone and theme of the whole story. "I tend to move very slowly for the first four or five paragraphs," he says. "In most cases that's the most difficult part of the writing. You have to deal with how you're going to bring the reader into the story. The lead also dictates what's going to happen from that point on. I recall spending a half-hour writing the first four or five paragraphs. Fatigue started to creep up on me, and I got a bit frustrated with the getting-off-the-ground process. Sooner or later, the first few paragraphs did take form, and everything else just flowed after that."

Both the medical and environmental beats have become increasingly important for newspapers and society, challenging the writer to translate complex issues for readers while, at the same time, crafting human stories that move readers toward compassion or outrage.

It Fluttered and Became Bruce Murray's Heart

THE POST-STANDARD • MAY 12, 1984

NEW YORK—A healthy 17-year-old heart pumped the gift of life through 34-year-old Bruce Murray Friday, following a four-hour transplant operation that doctors said went without a hitch.

Early Thursday morning, three surgeons at Presbyterian Hospital lifted Murray's flabby, enlarged heart from his chest cavity and replaced it with a normal heart that had been flown from St. Louis inside an ice-filled beer cooler. The operation lasted from 3:45 a.m. to 7:30 a.m.

As Murray's diseased heart sat in a stainless steel bowl at the foot of the operating table, doctors gradually weaned Murray away from a heart-lung machine that had kept him alive throughout much of the operation. The new heart, beating slowly at first, gradually took over the task of pumping blood through Murray's body. And by 5:25 a.m., Dr. Eric Rose emerged from the 19th floor operating room and proclaimed the procedure a success.

"It went beautifully," said Rose, who wore a heart-shaped pin bearing the inscription, "surgeon." At 33, Rose is said to be the youngest transplant surgeon in the world. "It was routine, nothing unusual. I do it every day, just as you hold that pad in your hand," he told a reporter.

Late Friday night, Murray was sleeping under anesthesia in the hospital's intensive care unit; spokesmen termed his condition critical but stable.

"His prognosis is excellent, at least in the short term. In terms of at least a year's survival, his prognosis is excellent." If Murray survives the first year, Rose said, his chances of living another five years are "at least 80 percent."

Within 24 to 48 hours, Murray could be expected to breathe on his own, unassisted by a respirator, Rose said. "He'll feel like his age then," he added. Within a few days, Murray should be able to sit up in bed and, within a week, pedal a stationary bicycle. Murray is the first Syracuse resident to receive a heart transplant.

Murray, of Kensington Place, has been taking an extended leave of absence from his job as manager of the mailroom at the Onondaga County Civic Center.

In 1977, a viral infection of his heart left the organ in an enlarged, weakened condition. Since then, Murray has suffered pneumonia, Legionnaires' disease, a stroke and congestive heart failure.

Doctors said his heart was pumping at 10 percent normal capacity. "His chances of lasting a year were zero," Rose said.

Murray originally planned to fly to New York City on April 23 for a transplant at Presbyterian, one of 18 hospitals in the country that perform the operation. But the hospital asked him to postpone the trip when another patient, whose condition had worsened, was given a higher priority.

Wednesday, Murray finally made the trip with Gladys Murray, his mother, and Lucinda Cawley, a personal friend and fellow stroke victim. She is also public relations consultant for the American Heart Association in Syracuse.

Murray had publicized his quest for a new heart through close contacts with the media to dramatize the need for organ donors. By signing organ donor cards, he said, area residents may someday provide "the gift of life" to others.

As it turned out, Murray's own wait for a donor proved remarkably short.

He met Thursday afternoon with a support group consisting of three recent transplant recipients and their wives. The patients included John Drohan, a Yonkers fireman, who received a new heart April 10 after waiting 2½ months.

"It was such a boost to see those guys," Cawley said. "One of them had his operation three weeks ago and he was up walking. He (Bruce) was buoyant, buoyant."

That same day, he met with his New York cardiologist, Dr. Ronald E. Drusin, and asked him to put his name in the national computer bank that matches transplant candidates with available organs.

Cawley remembered the meeting. "He said to Drusin, 'I'm here, put me on the computer.' Drusin smiled and said, 'I put you on the computer last night.'"

At about 5 p.m. Thursday, a donor was found: a 17-year-old boy, the victim of a car accident, who was declared brain-dead at St. Louis University Hospital.

Two hours later, a three-member transplant team from Presbyterian flew out of Teterboro Airport in New Jersey to pick up the new heart. The team traveled 850 miles to obtain the heart; the donor organ spent four hours in transit.

Both are records. "About four hours is the most I'm comfortable with, but the distance really didn't concern me," said Rose.

The team—consisting of a surgeon, a physician's assistant and a nurse—removed the donor's heart at about 11:30 p.m. They placed it inside a plastic bag filled with an iced-saline solution, and they placed that bag inside three outer bags. The package was placed inside a blue beer cooler that bore the stamp "Transplant."

By the time their jet landed at Teterboro at 3 a.m., Murray was in the operating room where he was being prepped for surgery. Anesthesia put the patient into a deep sleep. A respirator breathed air into Murray's lungs via a tube inserted in his throat. Doctors cut a slit the length of Murray's chest. As many as a dozen doctors, nurses and technical assistants hovered over the patient, passing instruments, attending to heart monitors and swabbing the patient's bleeding chest.

Meanwhile, a state police escort ensured swift passage from Teterboro, over the George Washington Bridge and to the hospital for the vehicle carrying the transplant team and beer cooler. Within 10 minutes after landing, the transplant team was rushing the beer cooler through the hospital emergency room and up an elevator 18 floors.

By the time the heart arrived in the operating room, Murray's chest was wide open. Doctors had used a power saw to cut through his sternum, and a clamp-like retractor spread his chest apart. Murray's diseased heart, about half-again larger than normal, was fluttering inside the exposed chest cavity.

Surgeons swiftly turned the task of pumping blood over to the heart-lung machine. Their hands moving with quick deliberation, surgeons inserted tubes inside the heart's major blood vessels and severed the vessels from the heart.

The tangle of tubes carried the blood to a cylinder that supplied it with oxygen. From there, the blood traveled to a large console, which performs the job of the heart. Three spinning disks pumped the blood through the clear, plastic tubes back to the patient's body.

In one careful, spectacular moment, the surgical team made the exchange.

At 4:33 a.m., doctors lifted the diseased heart—milky but slightly purple—out of Murray's chest cavity and handed it to attendants. They, in turn, placed it in the steel bowl. On a platform at the foot of the operating table, the spent heart rested for the duration.

"How many things do you know that work for 34 years," Rose quipped after the operation.

The beer cooler was opened, and the donor heart was placed inside the patient's chest. The new heart, about as large as a relaxed fist, was attached to the blood vessels.

It jerked and fluttered and became Bruce Murray's.

But for the next two hours, the heart-lung machine continued to do much of the pumping. Because the heart was cold, it could not pump vigorously. But as blood pumped by the heart-lung machine flowed through it, it contracted and expanded and gradually warmed. As it warmed, it pumped with more authority.

Probes carrying mild electric shocks were used first to speed up the new heart, and later to synchronize its beat. "His rate is slow, but that's not unexpected," a technician explained. "It takes time for the heart to come back."

At 6 a.m., most everyone on the operating room floor stood with arms folded, staring at Murray's new heart and at the monitors that recorded its activity. Murray had been weaned entirely from the heart-lung machine, and his new organ worked.

"He's on his own," the technician said.

~ MITCH ALBOM ~

Mitch Albom is the nationally syndicated sports columnist for the *Detroit Free Press*, a frequent commentator for ESPN, the host of a radio talk show and the author of the best sellers *Tuesdays with Morrie* and *The Five People You Meet in Heaven*. America's sports editors named him the number one sports columnist in the nation for nine straight years.

While Albom has covered most of the major sports celebrities of the late 20th century, he writes some of his most powerful stories about sports figures few know: a promising race car driver killed by a drunken driver; a high school girl whose dreams of success are threatened by illness; a community divided over a rape case that pits the victim against a popular football player.

In the story of Dewon Jones, Albom accomplishes the writing equivalent of a crossover dribble. First he crafts an upsetting story about a young man whose world is defined by the presence of guns. The flow of the narrative runs against a pattern so familiar it has become a cliché, the one in which the talented young athlete has a promising career cut short by a brush with crime. Albom turns that story on its head, for Dewon Jones is lucky to be alive, so deep is his immersion in the destructive element. In this case, sports redeems him, offering a lifeline out of a culture of violence.

Now comes that crossover from narrative to opinion, as Albom uses his license as a columnist to point readers toward a moral lesson and challenge them to action:

> They are high school kids who have fired on and been fired at and they swear they want nothing to do with guns anymore. "Guns are nothing but trouble," they say.
>
> They came to this conclusion the hard way.
>
> What's our excuse?

Albom admires the late Chicago columnist Mike Royko, especially the way Royko would leave the message of his columns until the end. Albom's column follows that structure.

But the power of Albom's final question comes only after exhaustive reporting and careful storytelling. The columnist is "still a reporter," says Albom, who likens it to getting "another stripe in the military. You don't throw out the other ones that you got on your patch. . . . You're still obligated to report, and you're still obligated to give people enough of the story that if they choose to disagree with you, there's the detail and the evidence in the column" that allows them to do that.

Along with being a columnist and reporter, Albom also wears the stripe of musician. When the writing is going well, he says, his body sways as his fingers play the letters on the keyboard. A variety of writing devices create the rhythm in Albom's work. Albom varies the length of his sentences to establish a pace for the reader. And short sentences punctuate the text, carrying powerful messages that echo throughout the piece.

Mackenzie Football Star
Another Gunplay Victim

DETROIT FREE PRESS • DECEMBER 22, 1995

"A person like me needs all the support he can get, because of all the things that happen to me."
— From a 10th-grade English paper by Dewon Jones

The first gun in his life was a gift from a relative, a rifle that had been snapped in half. "Let the kid have it," his step-grandfather said. So Dewon Jones took it and fixed the trigger and the barrel, and soon he had a weapon instead of a toy. One day, he was playing with his best friend James. Dewon put the gun in his pocket and danced like a cowboy. The gun went off.

"I'm shot!" he yelled. "I'm shot!"

At the hospital, doctors used tweezers to remove the bullet. Dewon and James made up a lie to police. They said they were on the porch when someone drove past and fired four random shots, and one hit Dewon's leg. The police wrote this down. It was not so unlikely, not where these kids live. No one was arrested. No one was charged.

Dewon Jones went home the next day, wearing the unofficial tattoo of his city: a bullet hole.

He was 10 years old.

*   *   *

The second gun came two years later. It was a starter's pistol, which belonged to an older kid named Cisco. Dewon, by this point, had been kicked out of several schools, his father was not around, so he looked up to older kids. When Cisco said, "We got something going down, you want in?" Dewon said yeah. He didn't even ask about his share.

A few days later, on a warm autumn night, Cisco brought a girl to a Coney Island near Eight Mile and Fleming. His crew—which included Dewon and James—jumped out and demanded the girl's money and car keys. One kid waved the pistol. Cisco acted frightened, which was part of the plan. Dewon, the youngest, was the lookout. He checked both ways, then jumped into the stolen car with the others.

A week later, when the police figured it out—Cisco wasn't too bright; he parked the car in front of his house—the helicopters flew overhead, beaming down spotlights. It was like something out of a movie. Dewon was scared. He hid in the attic. When the police left, he packed a small brown suitcase, planning to run away.

"Where you gonna run?" his uncle said.

"I dunno," Dewon said.

He went to a friend's house. An hour later, the police picked them all up. Armed robbery. Dewon and James—who pretty much went along for the ride—were considered accessories. They were fingerprinted. Put in a holding cell.

James got probation. Dewon was not as lucky. He was sent away to Starr Commonwealth, a residential treatment program for juvenile delinquent males—in Albion, 100 miles from home.

Dewon calls it "getting locked up."

He was 12 years old.

*   *   *

The third gun—we can only hope the last—came when Dewon returned from that treatment program three years later. He had calmed down. He had learned a lot. Out of the city, in a place where you can see trees and lakes and men without weapons, he had become a young adult, a certified lifeguard and a promising athlete, playing flag football and lifting weights. In group therapy, he spoke about his problems—no father, working mother, no money, no discipline—and he was even looked up to as a leader. One time, a kid named Darnell ran away. The whole class went looking for him, but it was Dewon who found him, hiding in a barn, sitting on a tractor behind bales of hay. Instead of turning him in, Dewon told the kid he should come back on his own.

"Where you gonna run?" he said, the way his uncle had once said it to him. "Where you gonna run?"

That night, when everyone was asleep, Darnell crawled back into his bed. Later he thanked Dewon for "saving him." Dewon felt good.

But good only lasts so long. When Dewon came back to the city, things were just the way he left them. Drugs. Guns. He had been home less than three months when, on a Saturday afternoon, he walked over to James' house to get a pair of pants. The same James who had been with him for the biggest trouble in his life.

"I got a heater," James said, greeting him at the door.

"Whose is it?"

"Ray's."

"You better give it back."

"You wanna see it?"

They went to James' room. They checked out the gun. It was a .22-caliber pistol that Ray, their friend, had gotten for protection.

"You should give it back to Ray."

"Nuh-uh."

"I'm telling you."

"Watch this."

James started twirling it, spinning it on his thumb. "I'm Robocop," he said.

Pow! The gun went off, a small blast followed by a ping. The two teens instinctively covered their faces. But Dewon felt something weird beneath his fingers. Warm. Then sticky. He couldn't open his left eye.

"I'm shot!" he yelled, for the second time in his life. James grabbed a towel to stop the blood. His mother screamed. Someone called an ambulance, and the police came, too. As he ran downstairs, Dewon glanced in a mirror. His face was already swollen and bruised. Everything he saw was red.

"Where else are you hit?" the ambulance people yelled. They were ripping off his clothes, searching for wounds.

"What are you doing?" Dewon asked, stunned. "Why are you ripping my clothes?"

"Where else are you hit?"

He was in a hospital for 10 days. They took X-rays, gave him IVs. The shot had ricocheted off a wall and entered just above his left eye. It had cut through several arteries and nerves and was lodged somewhere near the nasal cavity. They couldn't remove it without risking blindness in *both* eyes. The doctors shrugged. He would have to live with it.

Dewon went home with a bullet in his head.

It is still there today.

He is 16 years old.

Guns, Guns, Guns

Everyone should have a gun. That's what some people say, right? Protect yourself. It's in the Constitution. Dewon Jones, sitting now in his football coach's office at Mackenzie High, shakes his head and says those people "are fools. What you need a gun for? You ain't the police."

The kid sitting next to him agrees. That kid is James Montgomery, the one who shot Dewon in the eye. Maybe in another environment, you shoot somebody, you are no longer his friend. Not so in northwest Detroit.

"I knew he didn't mean to do it," Dewon says. "That's why I told the police I didn't want to press charges.

"To be honest, I blame myself for asking to see the gun. I should have known better."

Dewon Jones is a big, bruising kid, 6-feet-1, 250 pounds, with a broad neck and shoulders thick from lifting weights. He has an impish smile, a rolling laugh, and if not for the way his left eye droops, you would hardly be surprised that he plays football at Mackenzie, a middle guard on the defensive line. It was a guidance counselor's idea, the football. She thought it would give him direction. She was right. Dewon was depressed after the shooting. He had to wear a patch for six months and apply medication several times a day. His face was bruised and swollen, the left side partially paralyzed.

But football gave him focus. He loves it now. Dreams about it. Wants to be the first in his family to go to college and play ball.

If he has to take the bullet with him, so be it.

A Hit on the Field

"What do you see right now?" he is asked.

"I see you," he says.

"What do you see if you close your good eye?"

"I see a lot of red, and some black. You're kind of a blur."

"Doesn't that make it hard when you play football?"

He laughs. "I know where the quarterback is. And that's who I gotta find."

In the first game of this season, against Detroit Western, Dewon, a junior, sacked the passer on the opening play. He had three sacks against Detroit Henry Ford. He finished the season as the team sack leader and was named honorable mention All-Detroit by the *Free Press*. You have no idea what that means to a kid like Dewon, who has rarely heard a compliment from any voice of authority. Bob Dozier, his coach at Mackenzie, says Dewon's strength and quickness give him a good chance at a college scholarship. Dewon lights up when he hears that.

"I'm gonna make it out," he says. "I have no doubt."

James Montgomery, who shot him, looks at Dewon and nods in agreement. James, 18, is smaller, with a sad, round face. He also attends Mackenzie, when he feels like going. The two young men have known each other for as long as they can remember. They've been in church together and in a cell together. One summer, they were swimming in the high school pool when James tried a fancy dive off the board and tore cartilage in his knee. He panicked.

"I came up swallowing water and yelling for the lifeguard. He didn't hear me. But Dewon saw me and jumped in and came up under me so I could breathe. He pushed me to the side and got me out. . . .

"The fact is, Dewon saved my life."

Four years later, James shot him in the eye.

City Can't Be Ignored

If this doesn't sound like normal friendship, well, this must not be your neighborhood. The bullet life goes on every day in Detroit, right under our suburban noses, and so many of us act as if it doesn't matter, as if the city is just some place we pass on the Lodge Freeway, hit the gas, get it behind you.

But you can't get it behind you, because we are all in this together, geographically, economically and emotionally. Dewon Jones might have been shaped by his encounters with guns, but he is also a precious resource, a kid who has learned from the horror and wants to graduate and make a better life. He is doing well in school. He is serving as a mentor to some other students. He swears he wants nothing to do with guns, hasn't touched one since that day, "never want to see one again." He is adamant about this.

He is also a statistic, one of thousands of black youths to be shot before his 16th birthday. Bullet in his head. A permanent souvenir.

"How big a shock was it," he is asked, "when you told your friends you'd been shot?"

"Not so big. I know people been shot all over their body and they're still living."

"And James, how many guns had you fired before you accidentally shot Dewon that day?"

"Seven," he says.

Seven? No big deal. Guns are toys, guns are status, guns are everywhere here. Finding them is not the problem; avoiding them is.

"I don't want a gun," Dewon says. "I'm sick of guns. You got a gun, stay away from me."

He blinks hard. Sometimes, he says, his vision goes red, as if gazing through a veil of blood. You wonder if it's his eye or his perspective.

The Write Way

The bell sounds. School is out for the day. Students race through the halls, some screaming, others laughing. A few wave to Dewon through the open door. He nods.

He has taken to the staff at Mackenzie, especially Dozier, his football coach, and an English teacher named Ellen Harcourt. She encourages him to write, and one day, to her surprise, he gave her a composition called "Reflection on My Life."

"My life is moving on and there is nothing I can do about the problem that most changed me around. Guns are not toys, but I had to learn the hard way. That's the big reflection on my life. Or should I say, my unforgotten picture?"

It is a touching phrase, "my unforgotten picture." How can he forget? The world he sees every day is not the one shared by many of us. It is bloodshot, literally, but in that way it is much closer to what our city's children see every day, every night, everywhere. And it has to stop.

You look at these two high schoolers, you hear them talk about police and holdups, and you realize what a war it is for kids today. When Dewon was shot, a female officer told James, "If your friend dies, we're gonna charge you with some kind of murder."

"What were you thinking?" James was asked.

"I thought, 'I'm little, and I'm going to jail.'"

I'm little, I'm going to jail.

I'm little, I've been shot.

Who's little anymore?

Dewon Jones and James Montgomery pull on their coats and leave the school building out through the metal detectors and into the winter snow. One has a bullet on his conscience, the other wears that bullet in his head. They are high school kids who have fired on and been fired at and they swear they want nothing to do with guns anymore. "Guns are nothing but trouble," they say.

They came to this conclusion the hard way.

What's our excuse?

⚬ RUSSELL ESHLEMAN JR. ⚬

Because so many prizewinning newspaper stories are long, the American Society of Newspaper Editors has, on occasion, gone out of its way to honor great short writing. Russell Eshleman was so honored in 1992 for his brief, offbeat stories on state government. These bright news nuggets ran in *The Philadelphia Inquirer*, for many years the home of great stories, some of them so long they could be measured by the pound.

Eshleman's work in that environment offered readers some relief. His brevity, exemplified here by two stories, sent a message to readers that fine work could be expressed in small, tight packages. His wit let readers know that reporting on government and politics could be accessible and comprehensible, qualities too often lacking in standard coverage.

Eshleman graduated from West Virginia University with a degree in journalism and minors in political science and business. After stints at smaller Pennsylvania newspapers in Gettysburg and Lancaster, he arrived at the *Inquirer* in 1984 and became an expert on the coverage of state government.

"I don't believe that government writing has to be dry and stodgy and lengthy all the time," Eshleman told The Poynter Institute's Karen Dunlap. "I think you can do short stories and make your point and be just as effective and informative. A lot of times I'll write short, humorous stories that are actually about serious matters, and they can be effective."

One of Eshleman's former editors, Jim Naughton, wrote this appreciation: "His byline is almost as long as some of his sentences. He is terse. He writes short. But good."

Even for Trees, Age Could Have Its Privileges

THE PHILADELPHIA INQUIRER • MARCH 12, 1991

HARRISBURG, PA.—Everybody complains about deadwood in state government, but a Montgomery County legislator wants to do something about it.

The Senate Environmental Resources and Energy Committee is considering a proposal that's enough to make a lumberjack wince—a bill requiring anyone who wants to chop down a 200-year-old tree to get a permit.

It's called the Historic Tree Act, and the sponsor is—as you might suspect—Sen. Stewart J. *Greenleaf*.

The proposal would require the Bureau of Forestry to establish and maintain a state register of historic trees. Besides 200-year-old trees, qualifying timbers would include historically significant trees chosen with the help of the Pennsylvania Historical and Museum Commission.

Trees on the list would be protected from destruction or defacing unless the person felling the tree obtained a permit from the state. Permits would be issued only to protect the public health, surrounding property, or the tree itself or for a compelling public reason. Violators would be subject to fines up to $500 or imprisonment up to six months.

At a time when lawmakers wish they could make money grow on trees since they're far from out of the woods yet on important budgetary matters, Greenleaf's proposal might be just the sort of diversion that could make its way through the legislative thicket.

It does, after all, enjoy the backing of a Bucks County Republican who is a key member of the environmental committee—Sen. James C. *Greenwood*.

Domino's Bites Back at Tax

THE PHILADELPHIA INQUIRER • JUNE 13, 1991

HARRISBURG, PA.—Hold the anchovies, the green peppers . . . and the taxes.

That message was being delivered at the Capitol yesterday by the folks from Domino's Pizza, who are involved in a lobbying campaign.

Lobbyists for the pizza-maker distributed hundreds of pepperoni-size pins with the words "pizza tax" and a bar drawn through them to legislative offices. Their goal is to kill what they believe is a half-baked idea by Gov. Casey to eliminate a tax exemption they now enjoy.

"When we talk to our customers, they're surprised and disappointed by the proposal to tax pizza," said Bob Deak of State College, who owns seven Domino's franchises and is leading the no-pizza-tax campaign. "We don't think taxing food is a direction the state should be heading in."

Casey, as part of a $2.74 billion tax package, has proposed language that would reverse a 1989 state Supreme Court decision that said pizza, when it is either delivered or picked up to be eaten at home, is not subject to the sales tax.

The Casey administration estimated that the exemption costs the state $10 million a year.

Not surprisingly, the Casey administration is panning the no-pizza-tax pins.

"If the product is delivered ready to eat, there's no reason it should not be taxed the same as restaurant food," said Revenue Department spokesman Rod Snyder. "It's considered a luxury item."

But Deak doesn't buy that proposition. He said the proposal would generate just $4 million for the state and is simply the result of an angry Revenue Department trying to "get even" for the 1989 Domino's court decision.

"The reality of today's society is that having pizza delivered to your home is not a luxury," Deak said.

~ DAN NEIL ~

There is an outlaw quality to Dan Neil's life story that makes the reading of his brilliant and eccentric work as an automotive critic for the *Los Angeles Times* even more intriguing. A lover of fast cars from boyhood, Neil admits to a life of misrule. His personal wildness belies the rigorous discipline and intellectual dexterity that mark his work as among the most distinctive in American journalism.

Neil's first job in journalism was a classic: part-time obituary editor for his local newspaper, *The News & Observer* in Raleigh, N.C. In 1991, he moved to the classified advertising side of the paper, producing the weekly advertorial Real Estate and Auto sections.

On his own initiative, Neil began writing automotive reviews for the Auto section and continued to do so for six years, without benefit of an editor. During this time, Neil's often outrageous and frequently eloquent writing became a reader favorite. The paper's publisher often remarked that his best writer worked for the classified advertising department.

In 2003, the *Los Angeles Times* recruited him to be the "automotive critic." Along with winning an ASNE award, Neil won the 2004 Pulitzer Prize for criticism. The *Los Angeles Times* also has sent him to write dispatches from the Middle East.

We have chosen one of his prizewinning stories, "Caught Up in the Crossfire," for X-Ray Reading because it strikes many of the tones of Neil's authentic voice. The story is rich with allusions to both high art and popular culture. It follows its metaphors and analogies from beginning to end. It hits the mark on matters of design and engineering. It exudes American "auto"-eroticism. And it offers one unusual word after another, including "twee," a mild British insult applied here to the exaggerated style of Chrysler's PT Cruiser.

"If it's in the dictionary," Neil says, "it belongs in the palette of newspaper writing."

Caught Up in the Crossfire

LOS ANGELES TIMES • OCTOBER 1, 2003

Edgy lead persuades reader to "go along for the ride"

Like many great beauties—Marilyn Monroe, for instance—the new Chrysler Crossfire has a faintly tragic air about it. And like many consumers of beauty—Frank Sinatra, for instance—I'm only too happy to exploit it.

The 2004 Crossfire ($35,570 as tested) joins Chrysler's recent portfolio of low-volume, high-zoot production cars—including the PT Cruiser and the Prowler—that riff on the history of car design. The PT Cruiser and the hot-rod-inspired Prowler are not really serious cars but fun and frothy exercises in nostalgic styling, rendered with a kind of Toontown exaggeration that gives the viewer a winking nudge in the ribs. Alas, one's ribs get sore pretty quickly. These days, the PT Cruiser strikes me as insufferably twee. Both it and the Prowler look destined for the nearest Shriners parade.

Writer is riffing: Unusual words add style and set tone

More lighthearted teasing

British slang for overly precious offers funny contrast

The Crossfire, on the other hand, is deadly serious, a lighted fuse of polished elegance and high ambition. It's a small car, only 159.8 inches long sitting on a 94.5-inch wheelbase. But the Crossfire has tremendous visual presence, with its wide body raked over relatively huge 19-inch rear wheels and 18-inch front wheels. The glassed-in part of the car, the greenhouse, is low and narrowed, giving the car a sloe-eyed allure.

Specs enrich description for car nuts

Modifiers help reader visualize new model

The most distinctive part of the Crossfire profile is its boat-tail hatchback, formed as the edges of the roof converge into a kind of teardrop shape, leaving the rear fenders to flare out over the rear wheels. It's a wonderfully organized form—romantic and rational at the same time. But what makes the Crossfire work is its surface detailing: the Art

(CONTINUED)

Euphony—agreeable-sounding words

Deco fluting, polished strakes, raised spine and sculpted surfaces, which make the car look like a piece of precision-milled machinery. This is the kind of car that makes you set your alarm clock early so you can go stare at it in the driveway. It's gorgeous.

Analogy evokes car commercials

Auto reviewer as business writer

As a "halo" product, the Crossfire is crucial to the Chrysler brand's effort to move upmarket, to be a premium brand in the same league as Lexus or Cadillac. This is not an easy thing to do. Consumers have a pretty definite idea of how much they are willing to spend on a Chrysler, no matter how swell it is. The Crossfire argues its case well.

So what's so tragic? Only that it's not really a Chrysler. Under the artful skin of the Crossfire is the running gear of a Mercedes-Benz SLK, right down to the crankshaft in its 3.2-liter V-6 (the car is assembled by Karmann in Germany). This is the first car to come from the DaimlerChrysler merger that gene-splices Chrysler design and Mercedes engineering.

Wordplay draws on lexicon of another field

Automotive history builds case for author's wish

Although few could complain about the results, I confess to a little wounded nationalism; it would have been great for such a wonderful car to be American to the bone. Chrysler, more than any other American car company, could justify a revival of streamlined, Deco-flavored styling. Chrysler's Airflow sedan in the 1930s was America's first streamlined mass-production car and what it lacked in functional aerodynamics it made up for in the expressive, streaking styling of the Machine Age. The most exciting car of the year is made of leftover Mercedes.

A wry punch line—no longer evokes car ad

Pushes into realm of architectural criticism

And there is a degree of insincerity to the Crossfire. In the same way that Frank Gehry's Guggenheim Museum in Bilbao, Spain, is an elaborate titanium blossom surrounding more or less rectangular spaces, the Crossfire's exterior design, as beautiful as it is, isn't essential to the car.

Of course, a few laps around the neighborhood will wring such doubts from your mind. The Crossfire is wicked fun to drive. In the transition from the SLK's open top to a fixed roof, the chassis has become substantially stiffer. The car has all the flex of a cast-iron sink and that lovely feeling of deep soundness that Benzes, at their best, have. It feels as if you have a good leg under you at all times.

Teenage slang replaces highbrow architectural lingo

Commuters, be advised: The Crossfire's suspension tuning favors handling over comfort. The ride is pretty choppy in that short-wheelbase way, and there's a steady diet of zings transmitted through the steering wheel and seat from the huge Michelins.

Good for freeway driving? Author has Southern California reader in mind

On the other hand, the car handles far better than I expected, with a nice even balance in S-curves that gradually and gracefully transitions to understeer. Toss it from corner to corner and the Crossfire recomposes itself without fretting, with little body roll or ungainly rebound.

Thanks to the car's low weight and its yards of high-quality rubber, the Crossfire has lots of lateral grip. The car has anti-lock brakes and traction and stability control, but on dry pavement these systems allow enough slip and slide to have fun.

Ideal balance informative and entertaining

Our test car was equipped with Benz's five-speed automatic transmission mated to the 215-horsepower V-6 engine. A six-speed manual is available, though most Southern California commuters will shun it. The car was pretty quick, returning zero-to-60-mph times in the neighborhood of seven seconds, though adding more power would be a beautiful thing.

It's expected that Chrysler will avail itself of the supercharged version of this engine, which in the SLK produces 349 horsepower—a lot of ponies, by anybody's reckoning. I just don't see where Chrysler will put the supercharger. The Crossfire's hood is practically on top of the engine cover.

(CONTINUED)

One curiosity is the motorized spoiler that deploys from the cam-back at speeds above 60 mph. In mixed city driving, where one often goes above and below 60 mph, the spoiler cycles continually with a very low-tech-sounding motor whine. However, considering Audi's experience with the TT—the humpback car was quietly redesigned to include a spoiler after some Autobahn accidents revealed that the rear was lifting at high speed—the Crossfire's spoiler is probably a good idea.

History, trends and technology exemplify author's expertise

Life inside the Crossfire would be cozy. Tall drivers may have a little trouble getting comfortable because the car has limited leg room and little recline available behind the deeply bolstered seats. Yet for a car so closed in, outward visibility is quite good (you are never far from a window in a small car), and the sculptured rear fenders create open sightlines through the side mirrors.

Consideration of a range of readers

The car's instruments are sensibly arranged; indeed, given their vintage, they have a comforting simplicity: More fan? Turn the knob to the right. More volume? It's the knob on the left. Technophobes may like the car solely for its refreshing lack of digital interface. The central console and all the switch gear are coated with a shiny metallic finish, as in the less expensive Mercedes C-Series, a sort of acrylic that is strangely warm to the touch. The same material covers the shifter. The comforts of home include heated power seats, a 240-watt Infinity stereo with two subwoofers and six speakers, keyless entry and dual-zone climate control.

Tour is thorough

Composed and compelling, precise and polished, the Crossfire is a singularly appealing car. Unlike a lot of design-intensive cars, whose appeal is so perishable they ought to come with a "best-if-used-by" stamp, the Crossfire has a bearing that should hold up well over time.

Bottom line: Crossfire gets a thumbs up

The Shriners will have to look elsewhere.

Kicker brings review full circle

Chapter 3

OBITUARIES
AND FUNERALS

Fifty years ago, obituaries were a rite of passage for new reporters. Reporting and writing an obit was often the first task for journalism newcomers. Obits introduced neophytes to the basic story form, the absolute need for accuracy and the sometimes painful but necessary encounters with people at times of great stress.

Over the years, newspapers developed different reporting and writing strategies for different kinds of obituaries. On the most basic level, information was gathered from the family of the dead person at the funeral home. This could be passed along to the newspaper, where it would be assembled into prose and placed in the paper, sometimes in a single short block of type, perhaps with a photograph.

Prominent citizens and celebrities received different treatment, not the least of which was considerably more space in the paper. At times, obit files were compiled on the more prominent people while they were still alive, a nice bit of long-range planning. This allowed the newspaper to report a death—from Dr. Spock to Dr. Seuss to Papa Doc—promptly and with great detail about the life of the deceased.

Occasional experiments have been introduced to the obit over the years, including a British newspaper's efforts to publish more candid, less polite renditions of a person's life, such as information about bad habits, professional scandals and personal indiscretions.

The two writers represented here each offer a distinctive and unconventional approach to stories about the dead. At one end of the cultural spectrum is Ray Bolger, a famous figure in Hollywood culture, whose image as the Scarecrow in *The Wizard of Oz* has become iconic for generations of Americans. Tom Shales of *The Washington Post* understands the relationship between the words *celebrity* and *celebrate*. His obituaries celebrate the achievements and the humanity of those in the culture who always seem, even in death, larger than life.

On the other end of the cultural spectrum is a lady who worked in the Tastykake factory in Philadelphia. Jim Nicholson, formerly of *The Philadelphia Daily News*, is the master of the feature obituary. What would it be like, he once wondered, if we treated the common man and woman in Philadelphia with the same dignity and respect and space we accord the celebrity? His attention to detail and the distinctive characteristics that set each person apart—while also seeing that person as part of a family and a larger community—transform the mundane into the transcendent.

When journalists cover births and deaths, weddings and funerals, their work becomes more visibly an act of culture, and the newspaper comes to serve as the handbook of membership in a community. But writing obits has a practical side as well, for there comes a time in every reporter's life when an important source will refuse to talk. "Whom would I talk to," the reporter wonders, "if I were writing this person's obituary?"

~ TOM SHALES ~

Tom Shales writes for the Style section of *The Washington Post*. He was the paper's television editor and chief critic when he won the ASNE award for obituary writing in 1988. That year he also won the Pulitzer Prize for criticism.

Although Shales won an award for obituary writing, he thinks of his pieces on the likes of Ray Bolger not as obits but as "appreciations." The word *obit* comes directly from the Latin word "to die." But the word *appreciate* means "to value" and is related to similar words such as *price* and *precious*.

Perhaps we could say that Jim Nicholson's obits show us the value of the life of the common man and woman, while Tom Shales' show us the value of the uncommon person, the celebrity who becomes a cultural icon for many. At first thought, Shales' approach may seem undemocratic, an elevation of the famous for who they are rather than what they do. But Shales avoids the trap. Without using the word *I*, he speaks in the voice of Everyman, at least of every person who has delighted in a movie such as *The Wizard of Oz* or has clipped from a magazine a photo of a glamorous movie star. The voice is nostalgic and sentimental, refreshingly free of the cynicism that infects much commentary about the culture.

Speaking of *The Wizard of Oz*, Shales says, "It's one of those movies like *Casablanca* that has a huge place in people's hearts, and that place seems to get bigger and bigger over the years. . . . It's funny how these things get into your consciousness, and they're part of your basic life experience." This experience is not only individual but also cultural. Shales shows us how the passing of celebrities such as Ray Bolger marks the passing of a generation, even as their work and their images are immortalized on the screen for a new generation to appreciate.

Shales ends his tribute to Bolger with two lines from the movie: "To Oz?" "To Oz!" It may be the most idealized ending of any newspaper story ever written, a tribute not just to an individual performer but also to what is best and most innocent in our collective memories.

Ray Bolger, the Immortal Scarecrow

THE WASHINGTON POST • JANUARY 16, 1987

"I think I'll miss you most of all," Dorothy whispered in the Scarecrow's ear. We shared her sentiment. The Cowardly Lion was funny, the Tin Woodman was dear, but the Scarecrow had soul. Oz wouldn't have been the same without him. The rest of the world won't be the same without Ray Bolger, the lanky and vivacious vaudevillian who played the Scarecrow, his role of roles, in *The Wizard of Oz*.

Yesterday in Hollywood, at the age of 83, Ray Bolger died. He was the last surviving star of *The Wizard of Oz*—made in 1939 but never far from the public eye—and even if his appearances grew rare in recent years, you knew he was around, and you felt that, just like you and the kids, he might have been watching the movie during its annual telecasts.

Bolger never expressed anything but gratitude about being known best for this one part, despite the many others he played on stage and screen in his long and rambunctious career. In 1976, he looked back on the film and said, "It's a great American classic, and after I'm gone, it will be—and I will be—remembered. And very few people can say they were remembered for anything in life."

Ray Bolger can be remembered for even more than this well-loved triumph. He electrified Broadway, dancing George Balanchine's "Slaughter on Tenth Avenue" in the finale of Rodgers and Hart's *On Your Toes* in 1936. The dance was constructed to become more and more frenetic, and Bolger said later that he fainted "many times" after his nightly performances. It, too, is an American classic, and so, really, was he.

When he appeared in Frank Loesser's *Where's Charley?*, a Broadway musicalization of *Charley's Aunt*, Bolger had, and made the most of, another fabled showstopper, the song "Once in Love With Amy," so infectious and lilting that audiences began singing along with him. Sometimes, he later recalled, they demanded so many encores that he would finally bring the singing to a halt and announce, "This is a play. We have to finish it!"

"Amy" is a moonstruck anthem to a first love. "Once you're kissed by Amy, tear up your list; it's Amy," Bolger sang. In real life he was once in love with Gwendolyn, always in love with Gwendolyn—Gwendolyn

Rickard. They were wed in 1929 and the marriage lasted until Bolger's death.

In person as on stage, Bolger was the picture of ebullience. Even in his seventies, his eyes shined a buoyant, youthful, crystalline blue. He was not easily lured into racy gossip about the early days of Hollywood, and he denied stories that the older stars on the set of *Wizard* became irritated when they thought that young Judy Garland was upstaging them. He was, it appears, that seeming contradiction, a Hollywood gentleman.

He started dancing at the age of 16, saved from a life in the insurance business by the urge to perform. He learned some of his first steps, he said, from a night watchman who had once been a hoofer. For a time, he toured the vaudeville circuits as half of an act called "Sanford & Bolger, a Pair of Nifties." Roaming New England as a vaudeville performer was, he said later, "my education."

His comic dancing style was his alone, facilitated by a pair of legs that, he was once told, "seem to start under my arms." In films like *The Harvey Girls*, in which he starred with Garland again, he performed singular specialty numbers full of impish brio and gravity-defying displays worthy of the great silent-movie comics. He knew how to make people smile and how to leave them happy.

His efforts in television, in addition to 30 years of annual telecasts of *The Wizard of Oz*, included an early ABC sitcom called *Where's Raymond?* in which he played a Broadway hoofer much like himself. More recently, he popped up on the occasional *Love Boat* or even on sitcoms like *The Partridge Family*. He had tremendous energy, loved to work, and once wrote, "You can never stop learning in television; the medium is limitless."

Only last Sunday night, the Arts & Entertainment Channel, a cable network, reran a mid-'60s *Bell Telephone Hour* that Bolger hosted. Though in his sixties, Bolger reprised a taxing adaptation of "Slaughter on Tenth Avenue." When he danced lyrical passages, his arms floated in air, and they seemed just as much a part of the dance as his lengthy legs were. It was the juxtaposing of balletic slapstick and moments of elegant grace that made his dancing style his own.

One other Bolger television show was short-lived but memorable, a Sunday afternoon variety hour in the '50s called *Washington Square*. Bolger danced on a studio set made to resemble a Greenwich Village neighborhood. An Italian woman would sing operatic arias from her tenement window. And Bolger introduced a novelty tune, "The Song of the Cricket," that became a national hit.

In 1976, he returned to TV for a straight dramatic role in a remake of John Osborne's bitter play *The Entertainer*, cast as aged exvaudevillian Billy Rice. The production was poor, but Bolger was golden. He had a climactic dramatic dance routine that made it all worthwhile.

"People just don't know what entertainment is anymore," Billy Rice grumbled. Bolger said he didn't agree with that remark, but with his death, the era of vaudeville and all its dauntless, resourceful troupers fades still further into history. When *The Wizard of Oz* is shown each year, it really is a one-night stand of old pros, a two-hour vaudeville revival, a chance to see and share a form of magic rarely practiced today.

It is a cliché to say we shall never see its like again. But does anybody honestly think we will?

Every child knows that the Scarecrow played by Bolger asks the Wizard of Oz for a brain, not knowing he has had one all along, and is given an honorary degree at the end of his journey: "Th.D., Doctor of Thinkology." Delighted almost beyond words, the Scarecrow puts his finger to his head and declares, "The sum of the square roots of any two sides of an isosceles triangle is equal to the square root of the remaining side."

Then he exclaims, "Oh joy, oh rapture! I've got a brain!" He asks the Wizard, "How can I ever thank you?" and the Wizard replies hurriedly, "Well, you can't." No matter how many viewings are under one's belt, it's joy and rapture every time. How can we ever thank Ray Bolger? Well, we can't. But immortality, he felt, was thanks enough. It is his.

To Oz? To Oz!

⌁ JIM NICHOLSON ⌁

Jim Nicholson worked as an investigative reporter for many years, with brief stints as a political campaign manager and private detective. His "common person" feature-length obituaries for *The Philadelphia Daily News* won the ASNE's first obituary writing award in 1987.

Over time, the newspaper obituary desk has become the province of the very young and the very old among journalists. Some are sent there to cut their journalism teeth, to learn the basics about reporting, interviewing, accuracy and the needs of readers. For more experienced journalists, the reporting of the obit may seem like the most sedentary of journalistic tasks.

Those who think of the obit desk as the elephants' graveyard should consider the case of Jim Nicholson. When he won the ASNE award at age 45, he looked like an aluminum siding salesman or a guy who plays the corpse in a detective movie.

That's not why he earned the monicker "Dr. Death." It was his invention and mastery of a form of writing known as the feature obituary. Nicholson had to fight to accomplish this task, overcoming the old reputation of *The Philadelphia Daily News* as a scandal sheet, the skepticism of funeral directors and the cynicism of his fellow journalists.

"My God," they told him. "Fifteen inches for a guy that fixed toilets—in our newspaper?"

But Nicholson followed his instincts, checked the rival *Philadelphia Inquirer* obits for hints of an interesting life and then used his skill as a telephone interviewer to milk family members and cronies for wonderful details about the deceased, spoken in the working-class dialect of the Philly row houses. So we find out, for example, that Marie Byrne smacked her kids for "making the nuns upset" and that she had a "private prayer list with countless people on it."

It's an old ideal in American journalism: Everybody's got a story. But Nicholson put it to the test and proved it day after day. The astonishing body of his work also proves Scholar James Carey's theory that "news is culture," that the most noble of reporting goals is to chronicle the rhythms of life and the rites of passage—cycles of birth and death, of marriage and divorce, of achievement and failure.

"This stuff will outlive any kind of investigative work I ever did," Nicholson says. "It's hanging on walls. It's laminated. . . . With one old Irish guy I did, the family said, 'Well, Uncle Tommy can read this later,' and they put it in the casket right in his pocket."

Since winning his award, Nicholson has spoken about his craft at national and regional writing workshops and has been featured prominently in several textbooks about journalism. He helps other newspapers develop the form of the feature obituary.

For X-Ray Reading, we have chosen Nicholson's feature obituary of Marie Byrne, an Irish-Catholic mother who worked in a plant that produced Tastykakes. The obit is so easy to read, so direct and simple, that it seems devoid of craft. Nothing could be further from the truth. Our annotations make visible Nicholson's detailed reporting, his delight in language and names, and his love for the fondly remembered anecdote.

Edward E. *"Ace" Clark, Ice and Coal Dealer*

THE PHILADELPHIA DAILY NEWS • MARCH 19, 1986

Edward E. "Ace" Clark, who hauled ice through Port Richmond by horse-drawn wagon and by truck for nearly 40 years, died Saturday. He was 85 and lived in Port Richmond.

Clark also had been active in church activities and local sports teams since the mid-1930s.

"Ace," who got his nickname as a kid from the gang that hung out at Tucker and Cedar streets, quit school in the sixth grade because life on his father's ice wagon seemed more interesting than books. He took over the business—Pastime Ice & Coal Co.—when he was 17.

His favorite among his horses, which he stabled at Seltzer Street below Somerset, was one named "Major." He could go into a house with ice, through the back door, across the alley, and out the front door of the house in the next street, and Major, who knew the route, would walk himself around the block and be there waiting on the next street.

"We used to say that if us kids had of been horses, we'd have been the best-raised kids in the neighborhood because Dad knew more about horses than he did kids," said his son Bob Clark, with a laugh.

Powerful arms and shoulders atop spindly legs, Ace Clark was a man of many friends who had a zest for life and would toss out the old icemen's line: "Every man has a wife, but an iceman has his pick."

Bob Clark said his father had keys to many of the homes; if someone wasn't home, he would bring in the ice, empty the refrigerator, and then repack the food around the ice.

"Can you imagine someone doing that today for a quarter?" said Clark, adding that the only day's work he ever knew his father to miss was when he got loaded the night of V-J Day and couldn't get up the next morning.

In the winter, when the ice business dropped off by as much as 75 percent, Ace delivered coal.

Though he loved horses, getting a Ford truck in 1937 meant he didn't have to feed the horses on Sundays. And Sundays for Ace Clark were for the church.

He was a past president of St. Anne's Holy Name Society and the St. Anne's Men's Club. He also was one of the organizers and first president of the Icemen's Union in Philadelphia in 1933.

"We had the first telephone in the neighborhood," said his son. "I think it was a fringe he got for being president, to do union business. But I don't think he did much business on it."

Ace Clark loved sports. He was manager of St. Anne's softball team in the 1930s and '40s and the basketball team in the 1940s and '50s.

Normally an easygoing sort, Ace Clark turned rogue elephant when his team was on the court or field.

"People used to go to the games just to watch him," said Bob Clark. "He'd throw his cigar down and get on the referee's case. He always thought his team was getting shortchanged."

By 1950, the ice delivery business itself was going the way of the iceman's horse a decade before, and Clark went to work for A&M Beer Distributors in Frankford. His son said he believes his father enjoyed that job even more than delivering ice because he could pause for a "boilermaker" — a shot of whiskey chased by a glass of beer — to get him on his way.

After six years delivering beer, he went to work for Highway Express and was still loading and unloading trucks when he retired at age 68.

After retiring, he became involved with senior citizens' organizations.

His late wife was the former Agnes M. Bannon.

In addition to his son, Robert J., he is survived by two other sons, Edward A. and Francis X.; two daughters, Anna M. McMenamin and Agnes M. Conahan; 29 grandchildren; and 27 great-grandchildren.

Mass of Christian burial will be celebrated at 10 a.m. tomorrow at St. Anne's Church, E. Lehigh Avenue and Memphis Street. Burial will be in Resurrection Cemetery, Hulmeville Road below Bristol Road, Cornwells Heights, Bucks County.

Friends may call from 7 to 9 tonight at the Hubert M. McBride Funeral Home, 2357 E. Cumberland St.

X-RAY READING

Tastykake Retiree
Marie Byrne

THE PHILADELPHIA DAILY NEWS •
APRIL 2, 1986

Marie Byrne, a lovable Irish mother who took in neighborhood runaways but was tough enough to keep them and her own kids in line, died Sunday. She was 65 and lived in Havertown, Delaware County.

Raised in the Swampoodle section of Philadelphia, the former Marie Kelly was a 1938 graduate of John W. Hallahan High School. She worked at Tastykake's Hunting Park plant for more than 20 years.

Interesting names enliven basic facts

Her house was a gathering place for all of her children's friends and occasionally would be a refuge for the youngster who had a rip at home. The runaway might stay a few hours or a few days. But any youngster soon found out that "she wouldn't be soft on anybody," recalled Brian Byrne, a son. "They would get whacked by Mrs. Byrne, too. You could come home for supper and never know who would be there, sitting at the kitchen table for supper."

Down-to-earth language: fitting for feature obit on everyday person

Quote reveals character: a mix of caring and toughness

Kids and adults liked being around her. It wasn't the lure of her kitchen, noted Brian. "Her idea of a meal was opening three different cans." Nor was it her ability to tell a good joke; she usually popped the punch line first, if she remembered it at all.

Keeps it real: She's not perfect

"She was the adopted American mother for kids who came here from Ireland," said Jean Marie O'Neill, a daughter. "They all loved her."

One who loved her was family friend Mary Byrne. Since there were already two aunt Mary Byrnes in the family, the kids called her "Uncle Mary." After Marie died, "Uncle

Author uses family's method of handling confusing names

70

Mary" dropped off a letter to the kids which was written to Marie. In the letter she wrote:

Letter: good way to introduce another voice

It was 43 years ago we met. You were so full of life, so outgoing, so determined to make life easier for all around you. You were so smart at work, so quick to learn. You were the one chosen for all the special jobs. The rest of us were just part of the group. . . .

Perfect, focused paragraph

Strict about education, she drove all four of her children toward college degrees, which they all obtained, and two of them earned master's degrees. And she helped find them jobs to pay for their educations. Their careers were a great source of pride to her in later years.

Brian said that if he or any of the other kids got into trouble at parochial school and got thrashed by the nuns, "mother would give me another beating for making the nuns upset."

She was old school

For about 15 years, Marie Byrne played Santa Claus for the family, the neighborhood and at Tastykake. She donned the red suit, and her kids, who had jobs at the plant at various times to earn college money, would get red faces.

Nice parallel

"Mom would make everyone in the cafeteria sit on her lap and tell her what they wanted for Christmas," said Jean Marie, "even the president of the company. I think one year he told her he wanted a new Lincoln."

Anecdote shows her sense of equality

She retired from Tastykake in 1974.

A member of St. Bernadette's Church, the Legion of Mary and the Cavan Society, she was a regular churchgoer who had a private prayer list with countless people on it. She was always volunteering her service. When her own efforts didn't seem to be enough, she volunteered her children.

Names reflect her Catholic heritage

"She was always the boss," said Jean Marie. "She had written instructions on how everything was to be done when she died. She wrote what Irish songs were to be played after the Mass and at the open-bar gathering later."

Not just Catholic, but Irish Catholic

Despite two years of illness, she wouldn't give in.

(CONTINUED)

"One day she would be in intensive care and the next day out shopping," said Jean Marie.

"She loved to shop and spend money. The Saturday before she died, we shopped and she joked that she would 'charge up everything and if I die, you don't have to pay for it.'"

Her husband, Eugene Byrne, died in 1971.

She also is survived by another daughter, Margaret Byrne Campbell; another son, Kevin; three grandchildren, Maura Jean O'Neill, John Henry O'Neill, and Sean Andrew Campbell; a sister, Katherine Lenahan; and a dear friend, Tom McDonagh.

Another inventory of names, typical of obituaries, but now special because her life has been celebrated

Mass of Christian burial will be celebrated at 10 a.m. Friday at St. Bernadette's Church, Turner Avenue near Bond Avenue, Drexel Hill. Burial will be in Holy Sepulchre Cemetery, Cheltenham Avenue above Easton Road, Cheltenham Township, Montgomery County.

Friends may call from 7 to 9 tomorrow night at the Robert L. D'Anjollel Building, 8645 West Chester Pike, Upper Darby.

Chapter 4

CRIME
AND COURTS

For centuries, writers have used crime and courts to craft powerful stories. The first family described in the Book of Genesis has one brother murdering another. The Christian Gospels build toward the trial and execution of Jesus. These archetypal stories have powerful moral messages.

In newspaper stories about criminal justice, such messages never take the form of secret editorials. Instead, the story of the murdered child and the grieving parent, told with detailed dispassion, can inspire outrage, or fear for one's safety, or satisfaction with the system, or a desire for reform. Such stories, after all, are about breaches in the social contract, the ties that ensure civil order and freedom from fear.

Unfortunately, such stories can be used irresponsibly. They can be exaggerated and sensationalized, attracting readers in the quest for larger profits. They can fuel an irrational fear of crime, distorting the way governments use their resources. Jail cells suddenly become more important than schoolrooms.

The reporters included here all find ways to blend dramatic narrative with civic purpose. Cathy Frye and Anne Hull focus on crimes that were covered by their newspapers in conventional ways. Then, immersing themselves in the lives of their characters and using the serial narrative form, they weave dramatic stories to reveal the effects of crimes on victims, families and keepers of the peace. Linnet Myers steps back from her daily coverage to pull back the veil on the assembly-line justice practiced in the Chicago criminal courts.

Many young reporters begin their careers on the police beat, what in the old days was called the Cop Shop. Here is how one journalist in 1941 described this rite of initiation: "The [reporters] who cover Police Headquarters have the seamiest work in the business. But it's valuable work. . . . In this job you cover the murders and the fires and the suicides, and it's no place for anyone with a weak stomach."

Journalism teacher Melvin Mencher urged his students to be "counter-phobic," to report and write against their fears, not in foolhardy, swashbuckling ways, but with courage and persistence, and with the appropriate help from editors and gatekeepers in the community.

Beyond the depressing nature of crime, young reporters will also confront complex and volatile social issues on these beats: from matters of race and social class, to the changing role of women and families, to shifting demographics, to controversial crime statistics, to widely differing perspectives on the police. The quest almost always is to get beyond the official sources of information down to the street level where the action is.

The writing of Frye, Hull and Myers demonstrates that covering crimes and courts can provide an arena in which the best storytellers can elevate their craft and play a key role in creating a safe and just society.

"I wanted people on edge from the very beginning," says Cathy Frye, whose series "Caught in the Web: Evil at the Door" appeared in three installments in the *Arkansas Democrat-Gazette* in late 2003. Her success becomes evident in the first four paragraphs, an opening that introduces readers to a web of unseen dangers similar to the virtual trap an online stalker used to snare 13-year-old Kacie Woody.

The newspaper editors who selected Frye's work as the year's best non-deadline writing praised her ability to weave "the details of dogged reporting masterfully, pulling the reader through a journey despite a sense of dread about the ending."

Narrative can be reduced to a simple definition, argues Jon Franklin, the two-time Pulitzer Prize winner who has devoted his career to the art and craft of storytelling: "Chronology with meaning . . . the episodic revelations of our public (and sometimes private) lives." For journalist Frye, that meant marrying the reporter's skill at unearthing details with the writer's gift for arranging events in a specific order to convey an inescapable sense of doom about Kacie Woody's fate.

Narrative writing's greatest strength lies in the way it puts the reader somewhere—a home on an isolated rural road where a teenager innocently chats on her computer; the corridors, counselor's office and school buses where the tragedy also plays out.

"Vary documentation," advises writing coach Donald M. Murray. Frye's dramatic narrative relies on exhaustive reporting that included interviews, observation and records, both public and private, among them transcripts of the online chatter that reflect a new age of electronic communication. They enable readers to eavesdrop on the conversations between Kacie and her online "boyfriends," including the middle-aged California stalker who posed as a teenager and eventually abducted her.

For structure, Frye relied on the timeline, a tool of choice for many narrative writers, organizing material chronologically as a way to understand the facts as well as present them. But it was a combination of persistence and empathy that enabled Frye to persuade Kacie Woody's family and friends to share the details that make this a story that should be required reading for everyone with a personal computer.

"Caught in the Web" could have easily become one of those "every parent's nightmare" stories that are a journalistic staple, but Frye has written a story as fresh as it is horrifying. She credits a journalism teacher whose "favorite tactic was to stand up and bellow out a cliché when he read your story out loud to the class." After graduating from the University of North Texas, Frye's career began with a circuit of Texas dailies as a reporter and editor. She joined the *Arkansas Democrat-Gazette* in 1999 and has covered several national stories, including the execution of Oklahoma City bomber Timothy McVeigh and New York City after the 2001 terrorist attacks.

Caught in the Web: Evil at the Door

ARKANSAS DEMOCRAT-GAZETTE • DECEMBER 14, 2003

This series of stories is based on interviews with investigators and Kacie Woody's family and friends, as well as police reports written at the time and a transcript recovered from the Woody family's computer. All direct quotes in the narration are based on the recollections of those interviewed. The parents of Scott, a 14-year-old Internet friend of Kacie's from Alpharetta, Ga., asked that his last name not be published.

He could see his 13-year-old prey framed in the living-room windows—cozy in her favorite nightclothes and typing speedily at the family computer on this rainy, 39-degree December night.

As usual, Kacie Woody had switched on all the lights as she walked from room to room, and the small house now glowed against a backdrop of towering trees.

He stepped closer. Kacie was there for the taking—typing, distracted, her silhouette melding with that of the computer monitor before her.

She was right there, only a stretch of dark and the front door between them, and she had no idea he had come for her.

*   *   *

Meanwhile, police officer Rick Woody—Kacie's dad—was on patrol in nearby Greenbrier, cruising the swath of U.S. 65 that cuts through this central Arkansas town. The traffic was mostly 18-wheelers, headed either north toward Missouri or south to Interstate 40.

Like most nights in Greenbrier, population 3,042, this one had been uneventful. Rick, suffering from a sinus infection, almost had called in sick. The night was cold and rainy, and his chief had told him to take it easy. Rick still felt poorly, but he figured he could make it through his shift, which would end at 2 a.m.

Rick liked policing the sleeping town. He made few arrests, but that was OK. His idea of good law enforcement was to prevent bad things, not to step in after the crime. That's why he watched out for the young women making nightly bank deposits after Greenbrier's stores and restaurants closed. They often neglected to call for an escort, so Rick would just show up when they were due to leave work.

While on duty, Rick kept his cell phone close so he could check frequently on Kacie. He never really worried, though. Kacie had grown up motherless and had assumed much responsibility at home. She laundered her own clothes, cooked dinner for herself and did her homework without being told. If there were an emergency, Rick could get from Greenbrier to the house in 15 minutes.

Kacie didn't mind her dad's late hours. She had always lived in the little gray house on Griggers Lane, on the outskirts of Holland, population 597, a tiny community in the center of rural Faulkner County. The solitude didn't faze her. Nor was she disturbed by the seemingly impenetrable darkness outside.

Most nights, Kacie didn't even lock the front door.

One of her older brothers, Tim, 19, still lived at home and was usually there with Kacie at night. Tim's friend, Eric Betts, also 19, had taken up temporary residence at the Woody house. So he, too, was in and out. If the guys weren't around, there was always her Aunt Teresa, who also lived on Griggers Lane.

But on this bone-chilling evening of Dec. 3, 2002, a Tuesday, Tim had left for the University of Central Arkansas library at 6 p.m. Eric was at his electrician's class. And Aunt Teresa was in Conway, cheering at her daughter's basketball game.

Kacie was home alone.

Earlier That Day

For Kacie and her circle of seventh-grade friends at Greenbrier Middle School, the day had begun with an argument. At the heart of the tiff were Kacie and one of her closest friends, Samantha Mann, also 13.

The girls all normally agreed on pretty much everything—which guys were hot, which girls were popular and, of course, the belief that "school sucks." The group convened each morning before walking to class arm in arm. A sense of security pervaded these locker-lined hallways, where blue-and-white panthers prowled and pounced across cinder-block walls.

Kacie's social path at school was neatly paved. She had attended Greenbrier schools since kindergarten, and her sunny nature attracted new friends each year. She also was the younger sister of two former football stars.

Her days were plagued by little more than the usual teenage worries—weight gain, grades and guys.

Like her friends, Kacie was experimenting with eye shadow as well as boyfriends. But learning to put on makeup proved to be much easier than mastering the intricacies of teenage courtship.

In an e-mail sent to a male Greenbrier friend that autumn, she had confided: *My longest relationship was . . . i think 3 months. I am usually the one that gets dumped . . . I have really bad luck with guys. Dude I am like sooo totally confused about guys right now!! ARGH! Sometimes guys really bad suck ya know? It's like . . . idk . . . weird . . . lol . . . well I am gunna jet bc i don't have nething to say . . .*

*   *   *

Samantha, a self-assured, outspoken blonde, could relate to Kacie's frustration. What Sam couldn't understand was her friend's fascination with the boys she met on the Internet. So far, Kacie had found love twice online. Both of these relationships bothered Sam. She worried about how freely Kacie was giving out her phone number to strangers. Several times, she had warned Kacie: "You can't be in love with someone from the Internet."

The girls' long-running disagreement peaked Dec. 3. It stemmed from a comment Sam had made the day before about a photo of Scott, Kacie's most recent online boyfriend. The picture, which hung in Kacie's locker, was of a young, dark-haired guy in a football uniform. Sam had said he was "hot." Kacie thought she said "fat." They had exchanged barbs, and by the following morning, the girls' mutual friends had taken sides.

Sam decided it was time to involve an adult.

For moral support, she took a friend with her to Room 214, where school counselor Dianna Kellar spends her days treading delicately through seventh grade's hormonal minefields.

With her maternal demeanor and lavish use of endearments, Mrs. Kellar, a middle-aged woman with salt-and-pepper hair, is a comforting presence in this small world of constant melodrama. She handled Sam and Kacie's fight as deftly as any other.

After hearing Sam out, the counselor summoned Kacie to the office and let the girls muddle through their grievances by themselves. By the time Mrs. Kellar reappeared, Sam and Kacie had patched up their friendship.

But Sam feared the truce would be short-lived. Kacie didn't know it, but Sam had told Mrs. Kellar that Kacie was giving out her phone number online. Mrs. Kellar had promised to talk to Kacie again, and Sam wasn't sure how her friend would react.

As the girls left that morning, Mrs. Kellar asked Kacie about the matter. Kacie assured the counselor she had shared her number only with people approved by her dad. But Sam knew this wasn't true.

During fifth period, Mrs. Kellar called Kacie back into her office and warned her about dangers online, but Kacie clearly had no fear of anyone she had met on the Internet.

In the months to come, Mrs. Kellar would wonder: *What else should I have asked?*

*   *   *

When Sam and Kacie met after school, Kacie was her usual bubbly self. But she made an unusual suggestion that later would cause her friends to wonder if she had sensed the horror to come.

As the girls prepared to leave, Kacie asked if she could spend the night at Sam's house. Sam, knowing her mom would frown on a school-night sleepover, said no.

Kacie also asked Jessica Tanner, a slender girl with large, earnest brown eyes. Jessica also said no.

Kacie persisted, asking a third friend, but received the same answer.

Kacie didn't explain why she wanted to sleep elsewhere that night. She just didn't want to go home.

The refusals didn't upset her. She laughed—that goofy, honking guffaw for which she was known—and headed to where her bus waited, its engine thrumming. Before boarding, she hugged all of her friends.

"Bye!" she called out. "See ya!"

A Final Chat

Kacie spent the evening watching the weather, fervently hoping that the predicted sleet and snow might give her a day off from school.

She showered and put on what she always wore to bed—a favorite pair of blue sweat pants sporting the endearment "Baby Girl" and a gray sweatshirt. Then she returned to the computer, which sat in front of one of the two rectangular windows overlooking the Woodys' front yard.

Awaiting Kacie was an instant message from Scott, who was writing from his home in an affluent suburb of Atlanta.

Kacie loved instant messages, which, unlike e-mail, pop up on the screen as soon as they are written. Conversations are in real time.

Kacie had met Scott in a chat room in May 2002. He described himself as a 14-year-old boy living in Georgia. He liked football and wrestling.

Kacie and Scott had officially become boyfriend and girlfriend on Oct. 3, 2002.

Scott's online moniker was Tazz2999. Kacie's was modelbehavior63. Their rapid-fire conversation made abbreviations a necessity and misspellings inevitable:

> **Tazz2999:** Hey Sweetie
> **modelbehavior63:** hey
> **Tazz2999:** how are you my angel?
> **modelbehavior63:** ok . . . u
> **Tazz2999:** better now that ur on sweetie

And they were off, fingers flying across keyboards as they bemoaned troublesome classes like math and Arkansas history, and analyzed Kacie and Sam's reconciliation. They also discussed Kacie's two favorite extracurricular activities:

> **modelbehavior63:** GUESS WHAT . . . GUES WHAt . . .
>   GUESS WHAT
> **Tazz2999:** WHAT hehe
> **modelbehavior63:** 23 kids outta 130 were picked to sing in
>   frontof the school board and I AM ONE OF THEM . . .
>   ooo adn wednesday i have band practice and thursday i
>   have choir practice
> **Tazz2999:** Thats excenlant baby I told you You have the
>   most beutiful voice I have ever hears
> **Tazz2999:** *heard*
> **modelbehavior63:** ☺

As she instant-messaged Scott, Kacie was on the phone with another Internet friend named Dave.

Dave was upset. His aunt, in a coma since a car wreck, was about to die. Kacie hurt for him. Her mother, Kristie, had died in an accident when Kacie was only 7. Kacie was certain her beloved mama was now a beautiful angel, looking out for her from above. Still, heaven was so far away.

Kacie had met Dave sometime during the summer of 2002 in a Yahoo Christian chat room for teens. From the start, their friendship was full of romantic overtones, and even after Scott became her new "official" boyfriend, Kacie had continued her online friendship with Dave.

Scott knew all about Dave. Kacie had introduced them online. The two had even talked on the phone a few times, mostly about cars.

In his Yahoo profile, Dave described himself as an 18-year-old living in San Diego. His picture showed a young man with wavy, sandy hair that fell below his shoulder blades. With his tousled mane, square jaw and pouting mouth, Dave looked like a cross between a surfer and the lead singer of a 1980s hair band.

As Kacie consoled Dave on the phone, she kept Scott abreast of the grim situation:

modelbehavior63: tonight . . . Dave's aunt is going to meet my mommy

Tazz2999: ☹ Im so so sorry baby . . . atleast we know that she will be happy there with your mommy . . . I am sure she will look out for her . . .

modelbehavior63: yeah . . . i think they will be best friend . . . hehe

Tazz2999: . . . I hope Dave is alright

modelbehavior63: he is . . . i am on the phone . . . he has been laughing at me . . . bc he know it is the best . . .

Tazz2999: ☺ at least he is laughing

Kacie told Scott about her visit to the counselor's office:

modelbehavior63: so guess what i got . . . a lecture

Tazz2999: awww im sorry baby

modelbehavior63: . . . on how u could be a 80 year old rapest . . . lol

Tazz2999: lol

modelbehavior63: hehe . . . and that the picture was ur grandson

Tazz2999: how many times have u gotten that 1 hehe

modelbehavior63: um . . . i lost count . . . well . . . then . . . she is like . . . "do ur parents know u talk to ppl u dont know" i was like "yeah" and she was like . . . well be careful . . . and dont agree to meet them less ur mom or dad is with you i was like . . . okay . . . and she is like . . . well remember this lil talk . . . i was like . . . ok . . .

Tazz2999: uh oh. prolly means she is going to talk to u again . . .

modelbehavior63: i kno

The young couple moved on to more pleasant topics, like the fact that this day marked their two-month anniversary:

Tazz2999: I will always be your teddy graham and you will always be my angel and we will be together forever and always and longer

modelbehavior63: awww

Tazz2999: hehe what r u doing sweetie

modelbehavior63: eating and talking to dave and singing . . . Dave and i were crying together for a sec . . . i told him i loved him . . . and momma told me she did too . . . and that mommy talks to me . . . and that she said she would take care of his aunt

"R U OK?"

Kacie sent Scott a link to a weather Web site.

modelbehavior63: look at what it feels like outside!!

Tazz2999: awwww *holds her tight and rubs her arms to keep her warm*

Meanwhile, outside in the chilly darkness, someone crept across the Woodys' front yard—someone who had come for Kacie.

He had driven to the Holland community in a rented silver minivan, slowing down when he reached Griggers Lane, a narrow dirt and gravel road that dead-ends at the Woody home.

The house, illuminated by interior lamps and a single porch light, stood out in sharp relief against the blackness. Inside, Kacie still sat at the computer, reading Scott's fumbling attempts to wax poetic:

> **Tazz2999:** hehe ill always be with u my angel becouse ur all I want to be with
> **Tazz2999:** hehe i put my screen saver as the picture i have in my locker
> **Tazz2999:** ur the most beutiful angel in the world Kacie
> **Tazz2999:** r u ok sweetie?

When Kacie finally responded, her message was uncharacteristically brief:

> **modelbehavior63:** yah

It was 9:41 p.m.

Maybe the intruder knocked. Or maybe he just walked in.

Either way, he caught Kacie completely off-guard, covering her face with a chloroform-soaked rag and knocking her glasses onto her dad's recliner. He dragged the thrashing girl through the living room and hauled her out into the cold darkness, across the damp ground and into the waiting minivan.

Throughout the violent struggle, Scott's loving entreaties continued to pop up on the Woodys' computer screen:

> **Tazz2999:** r u busy baby?
> **Tazz2999:** . . . hehe guess so . . .
> **Tazz2999:** u there baby?
> **Tazz2999:** sweetie r u ok . . .
> **Tazz2999:** please talk to me baby . . .
> **Tazz2999:** ☹
> **Tazz2999:** when u r ready to talk sweetie ill be here . . .
> **Tazz2999:** r u mad at me sweetie? ☹
> **Tazz2999:** please talk to me baby . . .
> **Tazz2999:** r u ok sweetie

No response.

For the next 35 minutes, Scott filled the Woodys' monitor with increasingly frantic pleas:

Tazz2999: please GOD let her be ok
Tazz2999: Kacie please tlak to me
Tazz2999: please . . . please . . .

Still, no answer. Scott kept trying.

Tazz2999: Kacie Im so so scared I dont know what to do.
Tazz2999: . . . please . . . Say something

At 10:15 p.m., Scott called the Woody house.

Tazz2999: why isnt anyone answering the PHONE!
Tazz2999: UGH
Tazz2999: Please
Tazz2999: PLEASE PICK UP KACIE
Tazz2999: PLEASE
Tazz2999: GOD PLEASE LET HER PICK UP
Tazz2999: please be ok Kacie . . . GOD let her bo ok

Scott e-mailed Kacie's friend Jessica: *Jessica please let this be u something is wrong with kacie her s/n is still on and she all the sudden left during our convo but didn't log off and i tried to call her and no one answered and we weren't fighting or anything so i e-mail the cops to make sure she is alright i hop they get it soon . . . I'm going crazy I don't know what I would do without her please God let her be ok.*

But it was 10:44 p.m. on a school night, and Jessica wouldn't find the e-mail until the next afternoon.

Frustrated, Scott went back to instant-messaging the Woodys' computer:

Tazz2999: ERIC TIM DADDY DANNY ANYONE PLEASE
BE THERE TO HELP HER PLEASE I KNOW SOME-
THING ISNT RIGHT PLEASE PLEASE PLEASE

At The Woody Home

When family friend Eric Betts returned home from his electrician's class at 10:17 p.m., he assumed Kacie was already in bed. For more than an hour, he watched television, getting up periodically to do his laundry.

At 11:30 p.m., during one of his trips to the utility room, Eric noticed that Kacie wasn't in her room. He assumed she was out with friends or family.

Minutes later, Kacie's brother Tim arrived home.

"Where's Kacie?" Eric asked.

"I thought she was here," Tim replied. Concerned, he called his dad. The time was 11:40 p.m.

"Where's Kacie?" Tim asked.

"At home," Rick replied.

"No, she isn't," Tim said.

Rick had last talked to Kacie at 7 p.m. She had been practicing her saxophone.

Rick told Tim to call Kacie's friends. He also told him to check with Aunt Teresa next door. Meanwhile, Rick drove to the Greenbrier Police Department. When he arrived, he called Tim again.

"Nobody knows anything," Tim told him.

Rick notified the Faulkner County sheriff's office. Then he headed home. His little girl wasn't where she was supposed to be, and he was certain someone had taken her.

When Rick arrived, he noticed that both of Kacie's coats—a brand-new yellow one and her band jacket—were draped over a chair in the kitchen. Her tennis shoes and boots lay by the computer, where she always kicked them off.

At the time Kacie disappeared, the temperature had been 39 degrees and dropping. Heavy rains were moving through the area.

At 12:24 a.m., Deputy Dalton Elliott arrived at the Woody home. After looking around, he asked sheriff's investigator Jim Wooley to join him at the scene. Elliott also notified area law enforcement agencies that a girl was missing.

Meanwhile, phones rang all over Greenbrier as Rick, Tim and Eric quizzed Kacie's friends.

"Is Kacie at your house?" Rick asked Sam when a family member brought the phone to her at 1:11 a.m.

"No," a still-groggy Sam said. "Why?"

By the time Sam hung up, she was fully awake. "Pray for Kacie," she told her mom. "She's missing." Sam sat up the rest of the night, telephone in hand, repeatedly calling Kacie's house.

By now, Rick and the boys had noticed a phone call from Georgia on their Caller ID. The call had been placed at 10:15 p.m.

They made another discovery as well—a long dialogue on the computer between modelbehavior63 and Tazz2999.

At Scott's House

Scott checked his computer frequently. Every so often, he fell into a troubled slumber. Finally, five hours after the last message from Kacie, Scott's computer monitor flickered to life:

> **modelbehavior63:** hey scott ru there this is eric
>
> **modelbehavior63:** as soon as u get this ANSWER back PLEASE i have GOT TO TALK TO YA
>
> **Tazz2999:** im on . . .
>
> **modelbehavior63:** what happened with u and kacie tonight . . . did she just quit talkin . . .
>
> **Tazz2999:** yeah . . . just went silent
>
> **modelbehavior63:** did any thing seem like something was wrong?
>
> **Tazz2999:** nope not at all
>
> **modelbehavior63:** what was the last time that u talked to her . . . i need as close as a time as possible
>
> **Tazz2999:** 9:41 was her last message . . .
>
> **modelbehavior63:** ok . . . did she say anything out of the ordinary
>
> **Tazz2999:** no just quiet I can send you aour whole convo if u like
>
> **modelbehavior63:** no i already got it i just need to know if she has seemed like something has been bothering her or if she needed to talk to someone

Eric confirmed Scott's phone number. He also asked him for his full name, age and address.

> **modelbehavior63:** what was she saying bout the school consoler and this guy dave? anything wrong with her
>
> **Tazz2999:** well umm her ans Sam have been having a fight and they talked abot it with the consoler then Sam told the consoler that she was dating me and she got lectured . . . dont worry about Dave he is just a good friend I would have said something if i didnt htink he was a good guy but he is cool
>
> **modelbehavior63:** so has it just been tonight that she seemed quiet? . . . and did she talk about goin some where or with someone?

Tazz2999: Eric . . . can u tell me the [truth] now . . . where is Kacie

modelbehavior63: just tell me . . . i got to know it is VERY important

Tazz2999: ummm . . . i dont think so . . . not tonight . . . but she was on the phone . . .

modelbehavior63: do u know with who?

Tazz2999: Dave

Scott told Eric he didn't know when Dave and Kacie had ended their phone conversation. Nor did he know Dave's last name, only that he lived in San Diego. Scott promised to ask Dave for a phone number if he encountered him online.

modelbehavior63: i am going to get off of here but i will leave it connected just in case . . . thanks so much for the help

Tazz2999: anytime but can answer sumthing 4 me

modelbehavior63: whats that?

Tazz2999: what happen to Kacie . . .

⤚ LINNET MYERS ⤛

Linnet Myers was a feature writer for the *Chicago Tribune* in 1990 when she won the ASNE award for government reporting. Before leaving the paper in 1999 to write fiction, Myers covered the Gulf War and the war in Bosnia.

Myers' work illustrates one of the most important things reporters do: stand as sentinels at the gates of official power. In an ideal sense, they watch on behalf of citizens, alert to any misuse of the public's resources, to abuse and to corruption. The work is not easy.

While covering criminal courts for the *Chicago Tribune*, Myers was responsible for writing stories about Chicago's Violence Court, a place that revealed the city at its most grotesque and depressing. Chicago produced so many murders that the paper could not cover them all. Only the most bizarre, or ones involving more prominent victims, found their way into print. Myers would run from courtroom to courtroom, making sure she did not miss an important verdict or sentence. Sometimes she'd write four stories a day.

When Myers moved into features, she got the chance to do something she had wanted to do for a long time: take a step back from the episodic cycle of breaking news and look at the whole picture. Her series on the Chicago criminal courts won her an ASNE award. More important, it shed a cleansing light on one of the darker sides of the city.

Myers speaks directly to the reader, an unusual method of establishing a connection. This begins with "Step through the metal detectors." Then "walk down the hallway." Then "take the elevator." The voice is of a tour guide, but not one in an amusement park. It feels more like the poet Virgil, guiding Dante through the dark woods toward the gates of hell.

Inside the courtroom, readers are introduced to a strange assembly line of criminal defendants facing a cynical and overworked system of justice. This is by no means the best face of democracy. "On some days," she writes, "things are almost sedate at Violence Court. On others, 12 or 13 murder cases are heard in a single afternoon. Still others bring obscene parades of child molesters, rapists, or young gang members charged with killing one another over nothing."

Myers moves the reader skillfully from wide shots to tight ones, from gross statistics to human cases, from particular examples to overarching visions of what is wrong with society and the system. Just as Chicago is famous for its political corruption, it is also famous for dogged reporters such as Myers, who believe society and government can find a better way.

Humanity on Trial

CHICAGO TRIBUNE • FEBRUARY 12, 1989

Murderers walk these halls, and the mothers of murderers, and the mothers of the murdered too.

This is 26th and California.

Step through the metal detectors and enter the multicolored stream of humanity that flows through the Criminal Court building each day. It is the largest felony-trial system under one roof in the United States. In 34 courtrooms, nothing but felonies are heard: murders, manslaughters, sexual assaults, armed robberies, burglaries, drug cases. Last year, 19,632 cases were heard here.

Officially, it is the Cook County Circuit Court, Criminal Division. But those who work here refer to it by its near Southwest Side location, 26th Street and California Boulevard—known simply as "26th & Cal."

Outside, on the building's noble limestone walls, are carved the Latin words *Veritas* and *Justitia*—truth and justice.

Inside is a world the average Chicagoan never sees.

Walk down the hallway to the lobby of the building's old section, opened by Anton Cermak on April Fool's Day, 1929. With its imposing columns and ornate ceiling, this was the main lobby when, despite Prohibition and the St. Valentine's Day Massacre of that year, crime wasn't as rampant as it is today and there were only 15 courtrooms here.

The 19 new courtrooms and judges—added in 1978—cut the caseloads from a high of about 350 per judge, said Richard J. Fitzgerald, who was the building's chief judge until he resigned last month. "And that's what the judges have now," he said. "It's right back where we were."

From the lobby, take the elevator to the fourth floor, Courtroom 402. This is Violence Court, and only the worst cases—homicides and sex crimes—qualify.

Violence Court is the first stop for suspects who have just been arrested. There are no full trials here. Cases are quickly read and bonds are set during hearings that last only a few minutes each.

This courtroom gives a taste of an overwhelming fact: crime in Chicago. Observers here watch criminal after criminal come and go as if in some grisly surrealistic play.

Take a seat and watch as defendants are led in from the lockup, one by one. The deputies first bring in Nisi Nunzio, charged with sexually fondling a little girl at the Shedd Aquarium. "It was a setup," Nunzio begins.

"What's that?" asks Judge Michael Bolan, looking up from his papers. "Oh, it's a setup, okay."

The judge hears the evidence from Richard Stevens, an assistant state's attorney. "The 10-year-old victim, who was watching the fish, felt the defendant behind her," Stevens says.

Stevens reads the defendant's background: He has convictions for contributing to the delinquency of a minor and for public indecency. Security guards at the aquarium had noticed him there before, acting suspiciously, Stevens says.

Judge Bolan sets the bond at $10,000 and adds a condition: Nunzio can't return to the aquarium while the case is pending. "You're off aquarium duty," the judge says. "Do you understand?"

Nunzio is led away, and Antonio Balderos is led in. Prosecutor John Mahoney reads the charges: murder, armed robbery, burglary, theft.

"That's a mouthful," says the judge. It is a potential death-penalty case; Balderos is ordered held without bond and is led away.

Next, Reginald Morgan, charged with sexual assault. Defense lawyer Thomas Breen objects because Morgan has been indicted by a grand jury without a preliminary hearing, at which the defense could present its case. The objection is routine, but today Breen decides to add a little emphasis. "We're shocked," Breen says.

"For the record, he's shocked," says the judge.

On some days, things are almost sedate at Violence Court. On others, 12 or 13 murder cases are heard in a single afternoon. Still others bring obscene parades of child molesters, rapists, or young gang members charged with killing one another over nothing.

It is here that you hear of the crimes that don't make the news — the everyday murders, run-of-the-mill, the ones reporters call "cheap." In a saner place, they would be news — in some places, even big news. But not here. Here murder has somehow become part of everyday life.

There were 660 homicides in Chicago last year. In Violence Court, that statistic becomes real.

There are robbery murders, gang murders, domestic murders, insanity murders, arson murders, tavern-fight murders, child-abuse murders, contract murders, and rape murders.

There also are murders over things like a piece of banana pie, a girlfriend who turned out to be a boyfriend, or a feud about something nobody can remember — things that can almost seem funny, here in this strange and violent world.

One day a man named Andre Collins was brought in after being picked up on a warrant for an armed-robbery murder. The paperwork was in duplicate; Judge Bolan announced that Collins was charged with two murders.

Collins didn't react at all when the first charge was read, but he wasn't ready to accept two. "Uh-uh," he objected. "Wasn't no two." Spectators giggled, and Judge Bolan turned his chair around, broke into laughter, and turned back again a moment later, his face red.

"Sometimes you have to turn your chair to the wall so you don't laugh out loud," Bolan said in a recent interview. "Or I bite my hand because I don't want to lose my decorum. There's only one judge in the room, and if you lose it, the whole place loses it."

Yet there is a chill to the humor, and Judge Bolan sometimes wonders what he is accomplishing.

"It's frustrating, you know, that tomorrow there's going to be a whole new batch," he said. "It's of a continuing nature. You'd like to see some kind of reward, and there's no clear lines here of any reward. I don't build any buildings, I don't invent computer chips. Is the world any better for what I'm doing here? I ask myself, 'What are you doing, Michael?'

"You can get totally immersed in this building. . . . There's a Criminal Court personality: You become cynical as hell, nothing is taken at face value, you cross-examine everything. Nobody's innocent. Innocence is something that's lost in childhood.

"But when a person is accused of a bad act, that doesn't sum up that person. I still believe very much in the innate worth of all human beings. If you ever lose that, you ought to hang it up. Even if they've done a bad thing, that's a human being suffering there. . . . And the victims too are suffering. They're hurt. They're all hurt people."

Bolan finds that people always ask about his job.

"No matter who they are, they still want to know what's happening at the slime pit, at 26th Street, at slice-of-life land," he said. "It's human nature with all its pretenses stripped away. . . . Headquarters for tales from the dark side."

Along with the judge, the regular cast in Violence Court includes defense lawyers, a team of prosecutors, and various police officers, who wait in the front rows for their cases to be called.

Sitting in the otherwise empty jury box are the news reporters, paid observers of this uncommon parade. As the weeks go by, a young city news bureau reporter watches each day in growing disgust.

"What is *wrong* with these people?" she whispers to another reporter. "What is *wrong* with them? What is going on here?"

As another lively day comes to an end, an assistant public defender leans over and whispers to those near him, "Every defendant is a jewel in the crown of life."

Violence Court is only the beginning. From here, the defendants are arraigned and then prepare to go to trial.

Murder trials are heard every week in the Criminal Court; often several are going on at once in the building's various trial courtrooms. Watch for a while and you'll begin to understand the lawyers' jargon, the legal motions, the judges who get angry if you talk.

To begin, open the heavy wooden door to a sixth-floor courtroom and watch defendant Johnny Freeman on the witness stand.

He is testifying about the day 200 people surrounded him outside a Henry Horner Homes public housing building and angrily accused him of raping and killing a 5-year-old girl.

"Two boys jumped in front of me with baseball bats," Freeman is saying. "I started to run. . . . The whole crowd came at me."

Police saved Freeman from the crowd that day; they saved him for a Criminal Court trial.

Prosecutor William Hibbler now tells the jury that Freeman pushed Shavanna McCann from a 13th-floor window as the child clung to the ledge screaming, "Mama! Mama!"

"Shavanna McCann is still crying out," Hibbler says. "Not for Mama, but for justice."

Freeman got life in prison without parole. He was three months short of his 18th birthday when he committed the crime, three months too young for the death penalty.

Open another courtroom door on another day in another month.

Listen as the written confession of gang member Daniel Pena is read. "It was like—how you say—a payback," his confession says. "They kill one of ours; we kill one of theirs."

Stay in the Criminal Court awhile, and all gang-war murders start to sound alike. In another one, a friend of gang member Luis "Popeye" Toledo explains why Popeye died in a gang battle:

"I used to tell him it's stupid," she says. "It's all us Latinos killing each other. . . . Our own race is killing itself, and that sounds sad. It's really sad.

"But he said, 'If it's got to be, it's got to be.' . . . He had it in his heart."

In yet another gang case, Lawrence Taylor fired at a rival gang member and instead hit Laketa Crosby, 9, a girl jumping rope in front of the Cabrini-Green public housing complex.

Taylor rushed over and cradled her in his arms. "Please, Keta, don't die," he said. "I'll do anything . . . if she lives. I'll take care of her." Keta died, and Taylor got 80 years.

*   *   *

Lorenzo Molina is accused of murdering Humberto Sotelo, the man who allegedly killed Molina's father 15 years ago in a tiny Mexican town. It was the most recent killing in a decades-old feud, say police detectives Tony Jin and William Baldree.

The detectives say Molina doesn't know what started the feud; neither do other family members. "They usually start over something simple," Jin tells you. "We asked them, 'Did somebody steal a chicken or call someone's daughter a whore?' They said, 'We don't know.'"

Michele Schwartz sits on the witness stand, her arms outstretched, demonstrating how she shot her husband, the Rev. Charles Jones. The couple, both missionaries, had been arguing over who saved more souls.

Schwartz says she fired in self-defense and is acquitted. "I'm just a servant of the Lord," she tells you as she leaves the courtroom.

Mack Lewis was convicted of killing his girlfriend's father, Clarence Marshall, after Marshall failed to share some banana pudding pie on Easter Sunday. "He was saying how good the pie was and didn't bring any home," a prosecutor says.

Loveless Austin's girlfriend turned out to be a man. During an intimate moment, he discovered that "Stella Essie" was actually Jerome Brent. The next day, Austin came back with a sledgehammer and a knife, seeking revenge. He got 40 years in prison.

Lon Shultz, an assistant state's attorney, later tells you that Austin got the name "Loveless" because "his father insisted on him being named that."

The little girl standing outside a second-floor courtroom looks confused, her face twisted into a frown, as if trying to remember something.

During the trial she just attended, she noticed that someone "said my mama's name." The child, Leslie Morris, was 14 months old when a man named D'arthagan Sargent murdered her mother. Now she is 6.

Police arrived at the scene to find tiny bloody handprints on the refrigerator and little footprints of blood leading across the floor. "The girl is incredible," her father tells you. "She managed to open the refrigerator and eat the raw bacon and cake that was on the bottom shelf." She was found after two days, cuddled against her dead mother.

"The mind is a wonderful thing," says her father, Raymond Morris. "She doesn't remember that night."

Or does she? For years, no one could sleep in front of Leslie. "When you went to sleep, she'd raise your eyelids," says her aunt. Her father says she'd follow him everywhere, so closely underfoot that "I've stepped on her." She'd wake from nightmares, "hollering, crying, shaking," he says.

"Leslie doesn't know what it is. But we know."

The child's mother, Rhonda Barnes, was strangled by Sargent, an ex-convict who had committed six rapes by the age of 15, says Linda Woloshin, an assistant state's attorney. Sargent served five years for those crimes and then was released.

"Psychiatrists were pleased with his conduct," Woloshin tells you. "Eight days after his release, he raped again." He served eight years that time and again was freed. Two years after that, he murdered Leslie's mother.

As the prosecutor talks, the child is still frowning in that peculiar way. You wonder if she understands. Or if anyone does.

*   *   *

You've heard there's a murder trial going on in the courtroom of Judge Thomas Maloney. On your way there, you see a man and woman talking in the hallway. Suddenly the woman faints, falling flat, so that her face hits the floor.

You hurry over, touch her gently, and she opens her eyes. "I tried so hard," she tells you, still dazed. "I'm so tired. I'm so tired. . . . I got to be with my child."

The man she was talking to, Assistant Public Defender Michael King, feels terrible. He didn't know she'd take it so hard. The woman is the mother of the man on trial, who is accused of murdering his wife. She is also the one who discovered the body and was preparing to be a witness. She fainted when King showed her pictures of the corpse.

"It's got to be a dream," she is saying as the paramedics arrive. "It's got to be a dream."

*   *   *

With time, you begin to learn the rules of the Criminal Court. Some are rules of law and evidence. Others are unwritten rules.

There's the Criminal Court rule of motherhood: Mothers will lie for their children. A mother will swear to tell the truth and then testify that her son was with her, when he was in fact committing murder.

A mother will stand up for her son—unless he was a baby and was beaten to death by her husband or boyfriend. Then it is likely that the mother will be loyal to her lover, not to her dead son.

There are rules that say it's hard to get a murder conviction for a child-abuse killing, because the grown-ups often say they were "disciplining" the children and didn't mean to kill.

There are rules that say little children who are sexually assaulted better be old enough not only to say what happened but also to know what day it is, what time it is, what truth is, what a lie is. Because they have to prove they're "competent" before they can even testify.

Other rules say the rape of a woman deserves the same punishment as the sale of 15 grams of cocaine. Rules say a rapist can get out of prison and rape again — and again — before he is put away for good.

There's a rule that says a 40-year prison term is really a 20-year term and a 10-year sentence really means 5 because of the prison system of "day-for-day time off."

Rules say you may commit the same crime as someone else but your sentence may vary greatly, depending on which judge you have. Also, all judges here are officially competent, but some are never assigned "heater" cases — the big cases that make the news.

Rules say the murder of a "dirty victim" — like a gang member or a vagrant — isn't good, but it's not as bad as the murder of a "clean victim." Rules say there's no sexism, but it's easier to get off if you're a woman.

Rules say there's no racism, but if you want to escape the death penalty, statistics indicate it's probably better to murder a black person than a white person.

As the weeks and months pass, you find yourself getting used to murder. You no longer flinch at the bloody pictures; the details become facts instead of horror stories. Then you walk in on a child-abuse murder trial.

"This is a photo of the belt you used to strike Keith, isn't it?" asks Assistant State's Attorney Tom Gibbons, who is cross-examining defendant Edward Thirston.

"Looks like it," answers Thirston, who is on trial for murdering 22-month-old Keith Jones.

"Is that where you struck the baby with the belt?"

"No," the defendant says.

Why, then, were welts on the dead baby's back, legs, arms, buttocks, and stomach?

"I don't know," says Thirston.

"It's a mystery?"

"To me it's a mystery."

*   *   *

The families of the dead sit in rows in the courtrooms. They're here for justice.

As you watch the trials, you watch them too. The cases can be dramatic, intriguing, absorbing. But when you glance over at the families, you remember how real they are. And how horrible.

"It's not TV," Assistant State's Attorney George Ellison tells a jury during the trial of Michael Bryant, charged with a brutal rape and murder. "It's real life, and it is horrid and it is atrocious."

The pain is etched on the faces of those whose loved ones were killed. You see where most of them are from: They're poor, they're black or Hispanic. They live in the ghetto, and maybe they should be used to violence. They're not. Their pain is so real you could reach out and grab it. Their eyes haunt you.

You meet a young man in the hallway. You know you've seen him before—you recognize the anguish in his dark eyes. Then you realize: His mother was killed in an arson fire, and you watched the arsonist's trial.

You start to wonder: How many deaths have you heard about? How many killers have you seen? Day by day, the anger around you seems to build. Sometimes the horror slams down like a sledgehammer. The judges and lawyers try to fit it all neatly into the courtrooms, the proceedings, the scientific evidence. It doesn't fit.

A weeping mother runs from a courtroom. The crime-lab microanalyst on the witness stand is using technical terms, but that can't sterilize the bloodstains on her murdered daughter's clothes.

The who, what, when, and where of each case have been answered. Only the why remains.

～ ANNE HULL ～

Anne Hull was a national writer for the *St. Petersburg* (Fla.) *Times*, where she began her career as a copy clerk. She won the ASNE award for non-deadline writing in 1994. She has been a Pulitzer Prize finalist six times and a Nieman Fellow at Harvard. In 2000, she joined *The Washington Post*.

After a teenager in a public housing project put a gun to a policewoman's head on a hot July night in 1993 and pulled the trigger, Hull reconstructed the crime and its aftermath in a powerful three-part series.

"Metal to Bone" illuminates two often misunderstood cultures, the insular worlds of the project dweller and the police, with unflinching honesty and enormous dignity. Police reporting rarely goes beyond the official version of events. In the series' first installment,

"Day 1: Click," we see a literary detective at work, searching for clues to the multiple causes and documenting the rippling effects of serious crime.

Hull's work combines the tenacity of the investigative reporter and the novelist's eye for detail. She is a practitioner of in-depth reporting, the so-called "immersion journalism" of *The Washington Post*'s Leon Dash and *The New York Times'* Isabel Wilkerson, who tunnel deep into a story to deliver important revelations about our times and the people behind the events.

For weeks, Hull rode along with the special police squad that patrolled Tampa's Ponce de Leon project; interviewed Eugene, the teenage suspect, and his family; and then sat through Eugene's trial and sentencing.

Newspapers are full of mug shots of young criminals and brief accounts of crime that fuel fear and breed prejudice among readers who never learn the full truth behind the news. "I wanted to bring a mug shot to life and let them learn about the life behind this photograph, and the path that swept this person to the crime," Hull says.

Hull achieves her goal by consistently populating the page with flesh-and-blood characters. She does it with intensive reporting of specific details, which are the foundation of good writing.

To Hull, "details can help explain the sum of a person." She isn't content to say that police officer Lisa Bishop's feet were small. To convey the blend of force and womanliness that captures her personality and dilemma, Hull gives this rich description: "In uniform she was petite and muscular, like a beautiful action-figure doll, with piercing green eyes and size 4 steel-toe boots."

"Metal to Bone" contains many extraordinary scenes. Whether reconstructed, based on extensive interviews, or witnessed by the reporter, they are remarkable for their sense of people, sense of place, sense of drama, attention to detail and authentic dialogue.

Metal to Bone, Day 1: Click

ST. PETERSBURG (FLA.) TIMES • MAY 2, 1993

It was just the two of them, father and son, living in a tiny apartment where the only luster was a gold picture frame that held the boy's school photo.

Their neighborhood stole the young. The father clutched his son fiercely.

"I don't want you making the same mistakes I did," he said, the voice of a thousand fathers.

On July 4, 1992, at exactly six minutes before midnight, the son stepped from his father's shadow. "I just wanted to be known," he would later say.

For his cold-blooded debut, he picked a police officer whose back was turned.

The sound she heard from the gun would reverberate for months. Click.

It was the same sound the key in the lock makes as the father comes home now to the empty apartment, greeted by the boy in the golden frame.

A file at the Hillsborough County Courthouse Annex contains all the information pertinent to the case. But there is no hint of all the things that were lost one Independence Day.

Officer Lisa Bishop's secret to guarding a sleeping city was pretzels. The crunching kept her awake. She'd pull into a convenience store on Nebraska, say hey to the prostitutes near the pay phone and buy herself a large bag of Rold Gold for the long night ahead. Her shift was from 9 p.m. to 7 a.m.

Four nights a week, Lisa clocked in for duty at the Tampa police station on the frayed outskirts of downtown. In uniform she was petite and muscular, like a beautiful action-figure doll, with piercing green eyes and size 4 steel-toe boots. She kept her hair back in a French braid. Even under a streetlight, her skin seemed carved in pearl.

Her beauty was a curse when she joined the force. She knew what the other officers were thinking: paper doll with a 9mm. Don't break a nail, honey.

After three years of working midnights, her walk got a little tougher and her language a little saltier. Schooled by one too many mean nights, Lisa developed a habit for watching hands. She lost count of all the traffic stops where the driver had a sawed-off shotgun on the floorboard and an outstanding arrest warrant in the computer.

"Take your hands out of your pockets," she'd shout. "Don't get squirrelly on me, and we'll both go home tonight."

Lisa, 30, wasn't unshakable by any stretch. Her biggest fear was rounding a darkened corner. Well, Bishop, she'd tell herself, *somebody's* gotta check behind that building. The hair still rose on the back of her neck.

Funny that she worked nights. As a child, the dark frightened her. Her mother would send her to the corner store at dusk, and she'd run all the way home to beat the falling light. As a cop, she grew to like the night. She drove along the deserted back roads of the Port of Tampa, where the warehouses and giant ships dwarfed her police car. To keep her company, the FM radio was usually turned down low to a country station, her ears perked for a Dwight Yoakam song.

Lisa did not come from a family of cops, never dreamed of being a police officer. She was a varsity cheerleader and star gymnast in high school before entering the University of South Florida. College lasted only a year.

"In my haste, I withdrew to go out and tackle the world," Lisa said. "I ended up working the mall."

She became pregnant when she was 21 and single. Her daughter, Morgan, was born with her mother's same startling green eyes. For years, Lisa bounced from job to job, "bored to tears with my life." She was 27 and struggling to pay the bills when a firefighter friend suggested she put her athletic skills and sense of adventure to use. Apply to the Tampa Police Academy, he said. Lisa had never handled a weapon before.

She was among 28 cadets who were sworn in with the Tampa Police Department on Oct. 1, 1989. She was issued a badge, a gun and a midnight shift.

Lisa got married the same year she became a cop. Her new career did not always complement her new marriage. "I found something in my life I enjoy," Lisa told Mike, her husband, over his objections. She learned to do what a lot of cops did: She stopped talking about work. All the images of her 10-hour shift—the way a wife's broken jaw hung down, the nightgown worn by a molested child, the beer bottle imbedded in a dashboard of a crumpled car—were filed away in some remote place in Lisa's mind and summed up in one word when her husband asked how the night went:

"Fine."

Her worry revealed itself in other ways. The first thing she did when she arrived home at dawn was strip off her bulletproof vest so she could hold her two young children.

Morgan was 7, and Cody, her new son, was 18 months old.

The Fourth of July was a 93-degree scorcher, with strips of clouds rolled out against blue sky. By early evening, as Lisa buttoned her police uniform, she thought how nice it would be to have a beer and watch the fireworks with the kids. Maybe next year.

As Lisa kissed everyone goodbye, she barely heard her brother-in-law call out to her. The minute he said it, he wished he could take it back.

"Don't get shot."

And she was gone.

Three times a day, a different shift of police officers gathered for roll call in the windowless squad room of District 2. For 20 minutes, a sergeant reviewed the recent tragedies and outstanding warrants before releasing the class of fidgety officers to the streets. On the Fourth of July, the officers were warned to keep their riot helmets ready and be on the alert for flying missiles and gunshots.

Lisa left the station by 9:30 p.m. and drove the short distance into Oscar 8, the zone she patrolled just northeast of I-4 and Ybor City. She and her partner drove in separate cars but answered calls together. One always followed the other for backup. At 10:49, while finishing a domestic dispute complaint, Lisa's radio squawked: Signal 41—shots fired—at 2003 Cano Court in Ponce de Leon public housing project.

Lisa, who was writing on her clipboard as she stood outside, looked over to Teresa Greiner, her partner. "Wanna go ahead and take it? We're right here," Lisa said, reaching for the radio holstered in her belt to let dispatch know they would respond.

Ponce is usually patrolled by a special squad of Tampa police officers known as the X-ray squad. But if X-ray is busy or off-duty, uniformed officers—such as Lisa—frequently respond to calls there.

Ponce has the highest crime rate of all public housing projects in Tampa. An 8-foot steel fence wraps around the 700 apartments, laid out in flat rows like grimy military barracks. Poverty, drugs and violence have made the neighborhood feel like a bombed-out combat zone. Cigarettes go for a quarter apiece at the corner convenience store, where everything is sold in small quantities that hint of a day-to-day survival.

Some cops in the department avoided taking calls in Ponce. The neighborhood frightened them. Or worse, it didn't seem worth saving. But not Lisa. She jumped at the chance. She always remembered the advice of one of her early mentors: You gotta chill, and the people will respect you. Don't come on all macho or defensive.

As Lisa drove through the streets, the sound of firecrackers and gunshots ricocheted around the treeless, hollow courtyards. Glass flakes glimmered on the sidewalk from a streetlight that had been used for target practice. So many people out tonight, Lisa thought, I bet one of every three is armed.

By 11 p.m., the police had responded to 24 calls to the Ponce area. Among the complaints were car thefts, several domestic disputes, two aggravated assaults and possession of drugs. Lisa's call was nearly the last of the day.

"What's goin' on?" she asked, walking up to the resident who had called the police. The woman told Lisa that a young man threw ignited bottle rockets underneath her boyfriend's parked car, then pumped it full of bullets, just for kicks. He ran when the police were called, but not before threatening some of the neighbors with the gun.

As Lisa listened and took notes on her clipboard, someone shouted, "There he goes."

Lisa looked up and glimpsed a figure cutting through a row of buildings. She bolted. Sprinting through the darkness, dodging the wire clotheslines that hung in back of most apartments, she reached for her radio and gave out an alert.

Other officers captured the suspect a block away. Lisa and her partner walked back to finish the investigation.

As they rounded a corner, they used their flashlights to illuminate the sidewalk. Passing a group of teenagers, one of the officers shone the powerful beam in a young man's face. Police flashlights are a familiar form of intimidation to many residents here, especially young men, who often find themselves in a spotlight for no apparent reason.

"I'll kick your ass," the young man yelled. Someone else in the group called one of the officers a whore and a b----.

This is bulls---, Lisa thought. She spun around to face the group.

"Look," she said, walking toward the teenagers, "you can say all you want, but I'll have more units down here than you can shake a stick at. Don't bother with it. Just go on about your business."

Back at Cano Court, Lisa needed to interview a few of the residents who witnessed the suspect shoot at the parked car. Her partner returned to the sector office to finish the report on the captured suspect.

That left Lisa alone on Cano Court.

She could have radioed for backup. Most officers considered it too risky to be alone in Ponce, particularly on a night as unpredictable as the Fourth of July. Lisa didn't.

Though it was nearly midnight, many residents were still on their porches or hanging out on cars, escaping the stultifying heat of the poorly ventilated apartments. Clouds of sulfur from firecrackers drifted through the humid air. Lisa began interviewing William Merrell, one of the people who had had a gun pointed at him. He was still jittery.

Lisa scribbled Merrell's statement, using the hood of her police car to steady her notepad. Merrell stood next to her.

Maybe it was the way Lisa was leaning over. Maybe it was her skin color. Perhaps it was because she was alone, without another officer to cover her. Maybe she had angered a group of boys by shining her flashlight in their eyes earlier in the night.

But there was no way Lisa could have seen it coming.

In an instant, someone forced her down over the hood of the car. A hard object was pressed to the back of her skull, just below her right ear, next to her hair ribbon. Metal to bone: She knew it was a gun. She froze.

"Don't move," the voice behind her ordered.

Maybe it was some other sort of weapon at her head, a lead pipe or something. But a voice in the distance confirmed what she feared.

"He's got a gun."

*   *   *

The car hood underneath her hand was warm and chalky. It was the only sensation she felt. The rest of the world shut down. Lisa held very still.

If I move he's gonna kill me, Lisa thought.

And then she heard the metallic sound.

Click.

Suddenly, a struggle erupted behind her. The pressure at her skull was gone. She could move. Lift yourself up, she ordered herself. Lift up.

In one sweeping glance, like a movie camera panning a scene, Lisa saw Merrell standing next to her with a terrified look on his face. Just beyond him, someone in a brightly colored outfit was running through a tunnel of screaming neighbors on the sidewalk.

She felt a flash of recognition. She had seen the outfit earlier in the night.

Lisa ran to the back of her car and crouched low for cover. She kept one hand on her holstered weapon and used the other to raise her corporal on the radio. She couldn't see the gunman. Most of the neighbors had fled into their apartments. She was out there alone.

Feeling exposed, she made the 15-yard dash into Merrell's apartment. Inside the small, neat apartment, Lisa was shaking. Merrell was just as panicked. He wondered why Lisa had come into his home. He feared she would draw the gunman inside. Watching her tremble, Merrell could not ask her to leave.

Lisa's corporal screeched up 30 seconds later. Lisa flew out the screen door to meet him.

"Somebody just put a gun to my head," she told him.

"Okay, just hang on," he said, hurrying out to the sidewalk.

Merrell followed Lisa outside. "Did you see a gun?" she asked him.

"Hell, yeah," he said. "I slapped it out of his hand."

Lisa suddenly realized what happened. This stranger had reached out and grabbed the gunman's hand, risking his own life.

"Thank you," she said, stunned. "You saved my life." She hugged him tightly. He could feel her shaking.

Lisa walked over to her corporal. He was bent over a gun on the sidewalk in front of 2005 Cano Court. The gunman must have dropped it as he ran away. Lisa stared at the pistol. Then she looked up at her corporal.

"Oh, my God, Jay, my kids, my kids," she said, beginning to unravel, "What the f--- am I doing out here? My kids."

Her corporal, a burly man with a silver crew cut, put his arm around her tightly and guided her back toward his police car. There was little time for comforting.

"It's okay. It's okay," he said, easing her into the front seat of his car. "Is he still around? Is anybody still around? Tell me what happened, quickly."

Lisa could not give a description of the gunman, only that he wore brightly colored clothes with a bold pattern.

The corporal rushed to the sidewalk to keep an eye on the gun. Police units were everywhere, sirens wailing, lights flashing. The neighbors stood on the sidewalks and their porches. Some disappeared inside their apartments, not wanting to be interviewed as witnesses.

An officer looked at the gun. It was a scrappy, black Colt .25-caliber semiautomatic. He slid the magazine out of the gun. It was empty. Next, he checked the chamber, the small compartment where the bullet rests when ready to fire.

He pulled the slide of the gun back, so he could see inside the slender chamber.

There was a bullet.

Lisa was driven downtown. She could give little detail of the assault. It had all happened behind her. One thing she was positive of was the click she heard from the gun at her head. It had sounded to her like a dry fire, as if the trigger was pulled but the gun did not discharge.

Near dawn, Lisa left the police station and drove home. It was Sunday, and the roads were so eerie and deserted they reminded her of the ending of a Clint Eastwood movie when he walks out of town alone. The adrenaline of the night had worn off. She felt empty and alone, wanting only to be held.

At home, she looked in on her kids and walked numbly into her bedroom. Michael was in bed, sleeping. He rarely woke up when she came home.

Lisa stood by the dresser and stripped off her gear. Moving in slow motion, she took her radio from her belt and set it in the charger. She unholstered her gun. Michael stirred at the noise and sat up in bed. Something wasn't right. He saw his wife standing at the dresser, gazing blankly at him.

"What's wrong?" he asked.

"Someone tried to kill me tonight," Lisa answered.

Finally, she felt safe enough to cry.

* * *

Officer Gilberto Mercado heard the details at roll call the next afternoon: Someone had crept up behind a police officer last night and placed a loaded gun to her head, execution-style. According to the report, the gunman pulled the trigger but the gun misfired.

Happy Fourth of July.

Gil drove his marked cruiser by the faded pastel buildings of Ponce de Leon. The sun drummed down on the broken sidewalks. Gil wiped sweat from his brow. Bulletproof vests weren't made for Florida summers.

He thought about last night. No mystery how the suspect got a gun. Guns were everywhere. Hell, he'd arrested a 12-year-old with a semiautomatic tucked in the waistband of his Ninja Turtle underwear.

But putting a loaded weapon to a police officer's head? Maybe the walls really were crumbling.

If the suspect was hiding here, Gil and the X-ray squad had the best chance of finding him.

The X-ray squad patrols two neighboring public housing projects — Ponce de Leon and College Hill Homes. The Tampa Police Department created the special unit in 1987 as a last-ditch effort to save the neighborhood from street-level drug dealers and "shootings that were as common as passing transit buses," according to one captain. Residents complained that police officers were rude — at times even physically brutal — and rarely came into the neighborhood unless there was trouble.

The TPD decided to give the two housing projects their own small police force — a handpicked and racially mixed group of 16 officers, called the X squad.

Over the years, the name grew into X-ray. It was a good name. X-ray hinted of a mysterious, special way of seeing things.

To outsiders, even to other police officers in the city, Ponce and College Hill must all look the same: 1,410 residential units stacked side by side like concrete boxes. Best seen through the rolled-up windows of a passing car.

But to Officer Gil Mercado, each apartment has a story, a life behind the screen door that hangs by a loose hinge.

At 31, Gil is a stocky man with thick forearms and the shoulders of a linebacker. He's been on X-ray almost two years. His skin is the color of light coffee, his eyes a shimmering green. Rods of silver streak through his close-cropped hair. He is constantly at war with a 5-pound spread around his middle. Too many plates of *palomilla* and black beans.

Gil keeps a picture of his son on his key ring. "That's my heart, right there," Gil likes to say, tapping the small photo. Before his wife leaves for work each morning, she takes the baby from the crib and lays him next to her husband, so the two Gils can wake up together.

Gil could be brooding or sunny, depending on his mood, but never volatile. Fair. Patient. Not the type to go ballistic with a nightstick. He has earned the respect of many residents in College Hill and Ponce. A hard thing to do if you are a cop.

Gil knows what it's like to live in poverty. He grew up in a New Jersey housing project. He was a 16-year-old street fighter when a high school teacher saw promise and intelligence behind the bloody nose and helped him get a football scholarship. It was his ticket out.

All it takes is one helping hand, is Gil's theory. He has reached out to many residents in College Hill and Ponce.

"You can't be a good officer just taking people to jail and putting them down," Gil said. He was a good listener, but he chastised himself for preaching too much.

One day, walking the beat in Ponce, he saw a teen mother he knew, pregnant with her third child. "You need to close those legs and go back to school," he scolded.

"Tell her, Gil," said the girl's friend, in playful agreement.

He later brought the woman a sack of diapers.

Gil never fooled himself into thinking he was a hero here. Old memories run deep. Too many residents remember Melvin Hair, a mentally retarded man who died in 1987 in a police choke hold outside his home in College Hill.

Some residents feared the police more than crime itself. A man was pulled over on a minor traffic violation one night, and as the X-ray officer approached the car window, the driver raised his trembling hands in the air and begged, "Don't shoot, don't shoot."

"Man," the officer said later, walking back to his police car, "someone must have f - - - - - with him."

There was no denying the everyday tensions here. Everyone — cops and residents — was on guard.

When riots broke out in Los Angeles in 1992 after the Rodney King verdict, College Hill had its own disturbance. X-ray officers in riot gear were on a sidewalk when bullets whizzed by their heads and into a bus stop sign. For months afterward, the officers stopped to touch the jagged holes left by the slugs.

But no bullets came as close as the one intended for Lisa Bishop on the Fourth of July.

Gil wanted to find who did it. He and Lisa graduated from the police academy together.

On the day after the Fourth of July, the temperature creeped up into the mid-90s, soaking Gil's dark blue polo shirt. The words X-RAY and POLICE were stenciled on the back. A wall of cool air hit him as he walked into the Sector E office, a police substation squarely on the dividing line of Ponce de Leon and College Hill. This is home base for X-ray, complete with lockers, bad coffee, a typewriter, file cabinets and a holding cell.

Inside the sector office, Gil's corporal, Chuck Blount, was flipping through a giant spiral notebook of information on people in the neighborhood who have been arrested or are suspected of criminal activity. A yearbook for offenders. "Courts female rockheads" are the words listed under one man's mug shot, describing his penchant for romancing crack addicts.

The most solid lead Gil and Chuck had to go on was a description read at roll call. Police had canvassed the neighborhood until dawn, interviewing witnesses. This was the composite they came up with:

Suspect is a B/M, 16-17 years old, 5'9", 145 lbs., med bld, dark complexion, nickname of "Eugene" who lives with his father in College Hill. He is driving a full-size Bronco, drk blu w/white panels.

Gil and Chuck tossed names out. Who was bad enough to put a gun to a cop's head? Who had a street name of Eugene? In this neighborhood, lots of young people had nicknames. The two officers came up with a list of possibilities, most of them long shots. They walked outside into the heat and began the hunt.

Riding together, they cruised down each block of Ponce and College Hill. It's a small area, less than a square mile total, but dense with people.

A sleeping bag was rolled out on a second-story roof where someone slept at night to stay cool. Children played makeshift tetherball by stringing a bag of garbage to the top of a pole. Teenage boys with gold teeth and Malcolm X hats pedaled small bikes to nowhere. Because of the holiday weekend, several block parties were humming, with music and cold drinks flowing. When the breeze blew right, like today, it was easy to get a whiff from Caldonia Red Bar-B-Q, a tiny, pink, hot shack where Mr. Caldonia worked his cleaver over a small rack in two seconds flat, good to go.

Gil had the windows in the police car rolled down. He always patrolled that way, to hear things and talk to residents. He drove by 2003 Cano Court, where Lisa Bishop was attacked. He could still see chalk on the sidewalk where the crime scene had been paced off. Everything else looked normal. Almost peaceful, in soft sunlight.

Gil and Chuck passed Cano Court and continued their search. While it was still daylight, they would ride the streets in search of Broncos. After dark, they'd start knocking on doors, making a few surprise visits.

* * *

By Sunday afternoon, William Merrell was tired and agitated. He hadn't slept all night. He didn't even undress for bed. A detective had been by to interview him. One neighbor teased him sourly about being a hero. Merrell knew what the neighbor really meant—he had helped the enemy.

Another neighbor commended his bravery. "You saved that police lady's life," the man said.

Merrell didn't feel courageous. He felt low. And he was afraid. Merrell wanted out of this dangerous place. The event last night only crystallized how life here had disintegrated.

The apartment Merrell and his girlfriend shared was an oasis. Silk flowers were arranged in a vase on a coffee table. Framed paintings of Nelson Mandela and Malcolm X hung over the color TV set. A mesh basket of fresh fruit was in the center of the kitchen table.

But no matter how nice they made the place, Merrell could not escape the gunshots at night or the violence outside his front door. He had to move away from here.

A wiry man with light skin and a close beard, Merrell lived 22 of his 28 years in Ponce de Leon. He moved here with his mother when he was 3. The trim landscape and quiet nights of his childhood vanished long ago.

Under the Housing Act of 1937, Congress directed all states to create low-income housing for urban residents. Ponce de Leon, one of the first properties the Tampa Housing Authority built, opened in 1941. It was occupied by white and Hispanic residents. College Hill was completed in 1945 and occupied by black residents.

Both were beacons of hope. Many older residents remember air that was fragrant with mango and lemon. "We used to suck the nectar out of the hibiscus," said one woman, 42, who spent her childhood in College Hill. "It was like heaven to us."

Public housing originally was conceived as temporary low-income shelter. But over the years, it evolved into a permanent community for the poor. The annual family income of Tampa's public housing residents is less than $5,000 a year. Less than 14 percent of the residents are employed. Nearly 80 percent are black.

Some residents, particularly older ones, will never leave public housing. Despite the crime and physical decay of their neighborhood, it is home.

But others, like William Merrell, are desperate to get out.

Each morning, Merrell waited by the phone to hear if he was needed at work that day. He had a part-time job as a truck driver and was hoping to get on full time. His girlfriend took care of their three small children. They paid $105 a month for their three-bedroom apartment in Ponce. Merrell felt caught in a trap. He could never quite save enough for his family to leave.

Merrell thought about it. People were saying he had saved the life of a police officer. He acted instinctively when he reached out and slapped the gun away. He risked his life for a stranger.

Maybe he could turn his act of valor into a new start for his family.

Maybe the police would give him some sort of reward. He would ask.

* * *

Lisa Bishop's phone was ringing by late afternoon, mostly cops who heard through the grapevine what happened. One of the callers was an officer who used to be on her squad. She considered him a mentor, a "policeman's policeman." He listened as Lisa recounted the sequence of events, the way she held still when the gun was pressed to her head.

"I thought if I moved he would have killed me," she told him.

The officer was supportive, until the end of the conversation. "Lisa," he said, "the next time, think, If you *don't* move, he's gonna kill you."

Another officer told Lisa the same.

"Kick, elbow, do *something*," the officer said.

Others called, offering their support and outrage. "You should have pumped his ass full of lead," a fellow officer told her.

Lisa couldn't shake those words. They ate at her. She sensed the criticism. There was nothing at the academy that had prepared her for that moment in Ponce. What happened last night was all about guts.

She didn't feel guilty for not taking a shot at the suspect. She could have accidentally hit a bystander. For all she knew, the weapon against her head could have been a toy gun. And she wasn't 100 percent sure the man running away from her was the gunman. It had all happened behind her back.

On the hood of that car, she thought, it was just me and him. That was my chance.

She wondered whether the gunman specifically targeted her. Had she angered anyone lately? Were there any outstanding vendettas against her? Hundreds. No one liked getting arrested. She arrested a 12-year-old who shot a man over a $10 rock of cocaine, and the boy was furious at Lisa for interfering with his business deals.

Maybe the gunman didn't care which cop he took down, and Lisa was just the unlucky one.

She didn't tell her kids what happened. What would she say to Morgan? Someone tried to kill Mommy last night? Morgan thought Mommy gave people speeding tickets. Lisa wasn't about to tell her differently. "I'm her Rock of Gibraltar," Lisa said. All those years as a single parent, it was just the two of them.

Lisa's sergeant called to tell her to take the night off, but she needed to work.

In a few hours, she would be back on the street. Where would the gunman be?

*   *   *

Around 7:30 p.m., Gil and Chuck were cruising through College Hill when they noticed a faded black Bronco with white panels parked on the side of the street. The two officers had pulled over Broncos and Blazers all afternoon, but after running the tags and checking the drivers' identification, they kept coming up empty.

They could see a young man sitting on the passenger side. The windows were rolled down. Chuck parked the police cruiser behind the Bronco so that it could not escape. Coolly, the officers walked up to the car. The Bronco had a temporary tag, which made it impossible to check against the computer. Many cars in the projects had paper tags or no tags. License plates and adhesive expiration stickers were always being ripped off from cars and used on uninspected or stolen vehicles.

"This your car?" Chuck asked the passenger.

"No," said the young man, who was about 16 and had his hair styled in a fade.

Gil hoisted himself up on the hood of the car so he could read the vehicle identification number stamped near the dashboard.

"Who's it belong to?" Chuck asked, watching the kid's hands.

"Eugene," he said, unfazed.

Chuck, wearing dark Ray-Bans, flashed his eyes at Gil when he heard the name Eugene. Feeling the rush of a catch, they knew the gunman had to be close by.

Just then, a strapping man in his early 30s walked toward the truck. He had been playing dominoes on a card table with some other men when he saw the officers around the Bronco.

"What's the problem with the truck?" the man asked.

"Is it yours?" Chuck asked.

"It is, but my son is driving it," the man said. "Why?"

"Do you have a son named Eugene?" Gil asked.

"Yeah," he answered. "Why?"

Gil knew this man. He was well known in the neighborhood. His name was Carl Williams.

Years ago, Carl served time in prison. When he got out, he scrubbed floors and earned his money the hard way. Now he was raising a teenage son by himself. He was best known for coaching Little League baseball teams. He coached Dwight Gooden and Gary Sheffield when they were after-school phenoms. All the young athletes in the projects knew Carl Williams. The X-ray squad even played softball against his teams.

"We need to get to Eugene as soon as possible," Gil told him.

Carl was courteous but asked why they wanted his son.

"I can't explain right now," Gil said. "It's about an incident that occurred last night. We just want to talk to him about it."

Carl sensed the finality in Gil's tone. He said he would find his son.

Carl thought Eugene was at his grandmother's apartment, a short distance from the truck. With the officers following, Carl walked to the apartment and checked inside. No sign of Eugene.

By foot, he led the officers to his own apartment, in another part of College Hill. Eugene was not there, either. Carl and the officers returned to the Bronco. Several other police units had arrived. Some officers were going through the truck. A crowd had gathered on the sidewalks and under the mossy oak trees.

Gil could see the worry on Carl's face. Raising a child in this neighborhood was not easy. Gil couldn't remember the last time he dealt with a father. This was the land of mothers, grandmothers and aunts. It was the land of tired women.

Again, Carl asked, what did Eugene do?

A sergeant pulled him aside. He told Carl that someone tried to shoot a police officer and his son matched a description of the suspect.

Carl couldn't believe it. He was sure the police had Eugene mixed up with someone else. Trying to shoot a police officer? That wasn't Gene.

"If you want your son alive," Gil told Carl, "you bring me your son. We need to take him in."

Carl didn't take Gil's warning as a threat; he took it as good advice. All he could think about was the police drawing their guns on Eugene in a case of mistaken identity. Carl had to hurry.

"I'll bring him to you," Carl said. "Give me 10 minutes."

Chapter 5

BUSINESS REPORTING AND EXPLANATORY JOURNALISM

Some of the best and most creative journalism in America can be found on the front page of *The Wall Street Journal*. Page One, especially the story in the center column, is worth a look every day.

For more than 20 years that column, known as the A-Head, has served up a daily dose of delight, even on days when the stock market has plummeted. The history of Camel cigarettes, the popularity of Spam, why the McDonald's french fry is the world's most popular food—all these have been the subjects of stories crafted by talented reporters and sometimes reshaped by a talented desk of rewrite editors. The goal of the *WSJ* reporters is to submit a draft of a story so solid that editors keep their mitts off of it. One story featured a language club whose members communicate in words of only one syllable. The reporter wrote the whole story, until the last sentence, in monosyllabic words, and the editors described the reporter not with the usual "staff writer," but with "staff scribe."

The work of William E. Blundell appeared many times in this special column, and during a distinguished career at the *WSJ*, he coached younger writers to excellence. His story about the life of real cowboys in an era of cowboy hype contains some of the finest contemporary writing about business: constructed upon a strong narrative line, reported from the field (on horseback!), connecting economics, popular culture and American mythology.

The first cousin of business reporting is explanatory journalism, a term made popular in the early 1980s by editors such as Gene Patterson of the *St. Petersburg* (Fla.) *Times*, who argued that a new range of complex issues called for a new kind of reporting. Talented reporters such as Peter Rinearson took up the challenge. His story on the engineering of a new airplane uses all the tools on the workbench of the explanatory journalist: translation of technical language, careful use of numbers, pacing of information and, most of all, close attention to the needs of readers.

Most journalists are at least somewhat afraid of numbers. They came to reporting and editing because of their language skills. But literacy and numeracy are not incompatible. Michael Gartner demonstrates the power of bringing them together. His editorial explaining a civic problem concerning property taxes, written for a small newspaper, is a model of watchdog vigilance and concern for what citizens know and understand about their community.

~ WILLIAM E. BLUNDELL ~

William E. Blundell spent three decades as a reporter and editor at *The Wall Street Journal*, where he won the ASNE award for non-deadline writing in 1982. He is a writing consultant at newspapers in the United States and Canada. His book, *The Art and Craft of Feature Writing*, is a standard text in journalism classrooms and newsrooms.

Blundell gave us a first look at his working methods in a 1982 interview: "I use a six-point outline for every story. It is not even an outline. I categorize my material. (1) I deal with history. (2) I deal with scope, what I am talking about. (3) I deal with the central reasons behind what is going on, political, economic and social. (4) I deal with impacts, who's helped or hurt by this, and to what extent, and what's their emotional response to it. (5) I deal with the gathering and action of *contrary forces*. If this is going on, is somebody trying to do anything about it, and how is that working out? (6) And at the very end I deal with the future. If this stuff keeps up, what are things going to look like five or 10 years from now, in the eyes of the people who are directly involved?"

It is fun to trace the results of such a process in Blundell's story on cowboys. The theme emerges quickly: There are few real cowboys left in an era of cowboy hype. He uses that theme as a sword to slice irrelevant materials from his notes and research. And he does so relentlessly. Everything left reinforces the theme, which he restates in what journalists sometimes call a "nut graph," the paragraph or sentence that captures the essence of the story:

> Finally, there is a little band of men like Jim Miller. Their boots are old and cracked. They still know as second nature the ways of horse and cow, the look of sunrise over empty land—and the hazards, sheer drudgery and rock-bottom pay that go with perhaps the most overromanticized of American jobs. There are very few of these men left. "Most of the real cowboys I know," says Mr. Miller, "have been dead for a while."

Says Blundell, "I try to teach reporters that if they have an important point they want to make, make it repetitiously but in different ways. Make it with a figure, make it with an anecdote and then maybe wrap it up with a quote." Find the theme. Hammer it home.

He adds: "The formula I teach is to tease the folks a little bit in the lead. They don't mind it. You are simply trying to get them interested. . . . Then somewhere near the top you have to tell them what you are driving at. Then you have to show them. And along the way you do things that help them remember it. Then you try and put an ending on the story."

The Life of a Cowboy: Drudgery and Danger

THE WALL STREET JOURNAL • JUNE 10, 1981

RAFTER ELEVEN RANCH, ARIZ.—The lariat whirls as the man on horseback separates a calf from the herd. Suddenly, the loop snakes around the calf's rear legs and tightens. Wrapping a turn of rope around the saddle horn, the rider drags the hapless animal to his crew.

The flanker whips the calf onto its back, and the medicine man inoculates the animal. Amid blood, dust and bawling, the calf is dehorned with a coring tool, branded in an acrid cloud of smoke from burning hair and flesh, earmarked with a penknife in the ranch's unique pattern (cowboys pay more attention to earmarks in identifying cattle than to brands) and castrated. It is all over in one minute.

Jim Miller, the man in the saddle, smiles broadly as the released calf scampers back to his mother. Mr. Miller is 64 years old. Born and raised nearby, he has been working cows in Yavapai County since he was five. He will keep on until he can't throw a leg over a horse anymore. "It's all I know and I like it," he says.

The marks of his trade are stamped into his body: broken legs, a broken ankle, dislocated shoulder and elbow, a thigh torn open by a broken saddle horn. The fingers of the right hand are grotesquely broken, and he can't flex them fully. It is the roper's trademark, the digits that have been caught in the rope and crushed against the saddle horn, but Mr. Miller still wins roping competitions with that hand.

Jim Miller is a cowboy. There are still many cowboys in the West. Some wear black hats with fancy feather bands; they tear around in oversize pickups with a six-pack of Coors on the seat. These are small-town cowboys. They don't know anything about cows, and the only horses they know are under the hood.

Others become cowboys at sunset, shucking briefcases and three-piece suits for designer jeans, lizard-skin boots and silver buckles as big as headlights. Then they go to Western nightclubs to see what everyone else is wearing. They are urban cowboys, and the only bulls they know are mechanical ones.

Finally, there is a little band of men like Jim Miller. Their boots are old and cracked. They still know as second nature the ways of horse and cow, the look of sunrise over empty land—and the hazards, sheer drudgery and rock-bottom pay that go with perhaps the most overromanticized of American jobs. There are very few of these men left. "Most of the real cowboys I know," says Mr. Miller, "have been dead for a while."

Hype and Illusion

A big man with a ready laugh, he is both amused and exasperated by all the cowboy hype. "It almost makes you ashamed to be one," he says. "You've got doctors and lawyers and storekeepers runnin' around in big hats and boots." None, he intimates, would want to step into a real cowboy's place today; their image of the life is an illusion.

The typical ranch hand in this traditional cattle county, he says, is in his late teens or early 20s—so green he often doesn't know how to shoe his own horse—and must do all sorts of menial chores. Nobody can now afford the "horseback men," aristocrats of the saddle who spurned all ranch work that they couldn't do from the top of a horse except branding. Most hands are local boys who commute to work from nearby towns, as does Mr. Miller himself. With few exceptions, the bunkhouses full of "bedroll cowboys," wanderers from ranch to ranch over the West, are no more.

Some things haven't changed, though. Punching cows, says Mr. Miller, "is still the lowest-paid job for what you have to know and do." In the '30s in Yavapai County, cowboys made $45 a month plus bed and board. The standard wage now is around $500 a month without bed and board. There is Social Security and the usual state coverage for job-related injuries, but there are no pension plans, cost-of-living adjustments, medical and life-insurance packages, or anything else.

Mr. Miller is one of the elite. His salary from Fain Land & Cattle Co., the family concern that operates the ranch, is $1,150 a month, but that is because he is the cowboss. The cowboss is the master sergeant of the ranch; he leads by example, works along with his men, and is in charge of day-to-day cattle operations. At various times the cowboss, or any other top hand, has to be a geneticist, accountant, blacksmith, cook, botanist, carpenter, tinsmith, surgeon, psychologist, mechanic, nurse and a few other things beside rider and roper. "There just isn't any point in a young fellow learnin' to be a top hand when he can make so much more today doin' practically anything else," the cowboss says sadly.

Then why do some still follow the life?

* * *

It is early morning on Mr. Miller's domain, more than 50,000 acres of rolling semi-arid dun hills and mountain slopes. The cowboss and two full-time hands work this country by themselves. They are going today to 7,800-foot Mingus Mountain to collect strays missed in the recent spring roundup. Mr. Miller surveys the land critically. Here and there the grama grass is greening up, but good summer rains will be needed to get the range in condition.

There is absolutely nothing that the cowboss can do about it except pray. The land is just too big. In almost every other occupation, man seals himself off from nature in factory or office tower, struggles to bend a little patch of it to his will, or tries to wrest away its riches by force. But the cowboy knows he is only a speck on the vast plain, his works insignificant, his power to really control the land almost nil; nature herself is the only manager of the Rafter Eleven or any other ranch. So the cowboy learns to bow humbly before the perils and setbacks she brings, and to truly appreciate her gifts.

A big buck antelope squirms under a fence and sprints over the plain, hoofs drumming powerfully. "Now that's one fine sight," murmurs a cowboy.

The party is not sauntering colorfully over the hills on horseback. It is bouncing over them in a pickup. The cow ponies are riding comfortably behind in a special trailer; they, too, commute to work now. Though he grew up in the days of chuck wagons, line camps, bunkhouses and the great unfenced ranges, Mr. Miller is a strong believer in modern methods. He uses an electric branding iron because it is faster, and he will even use a trailer to take small groups of cattle from place to place on the ranch rather than drive them on foot. One pound sweated off a steer costs the ranch about 67 cents.

But he and every other experienced cowman draw the line at replacing the horse. There is a strange chemistry between horse and cow, a gentling effect, that he declares irreplaceable. "Some dummies around here tried motorcycles once. Didn't work worth a damn," snorts the cowboss. No machine, he adds, can ever duplicate the instincts and balletic ability of a fine cutting horse dancing into a herd to separate steer from heifer.

At Mingus Mountain the horses go to work. There is no glamorous dashing about on the plain, only a laborious, slow plod up a mountain canyon that is rocky, steep-sided, clogged with brush. Jagged tree branches jab at the riders. It is grueling, hazardous work, but a nice piece of high country is a valuable asset to any ranch here. In winter it is actually warmer for the cattle because the cold air settles in the valley below, and the nutritious scrub oak and other bushes are available year-round and grow above snow.

In a high clearing fringed by oak, juniper and pine, 18-year-old Troy Tomerlin pauses awhile, chewing on a twig, to consider his future. He can operate a backhoe and could make almost twice as much doing that as the $500 a month he gets now. "But I don't know how I'd like diggin' septic tanks day after day," he says. "Here I can see animals, work with animals, move around a lot of country. In an office you can't see nothin' but a desk, and I don't like people lookin' over my shoulder. Jim tells us what to do, and how you do it is up to you. I like that."

Suddenly, dark clouds begin to boil up over the mountain. Last week the cowboys were pelted by hail the size of golf balls, but that is just part of the job. Lightning, however, is much feared by any mounted man caught on the open plain, and many cowboys have been killed by it. Last summer a bolt barely missed Troy and knocked him unconscious. Other cowboys have been killed or crippled when their horses fell on them and leaped back up to gallop in panic with the rider entangled in rope or stirrup. "I've had three real good friends dragged to death that way," Mr. Miller says softly.

Lariats Used Sparingly

The clouds pass over harmlessly and 18 head coaxed out of the rocks and brush are driven toward the plain. Tommy Stuart, a fine rider with rodeo experience, crashes through brush again and again to divert straying animals. The men cry out to the cattle in a strangely musical series of yips, calls and growls. Tommy has to rope a balky calf, the only time anyone uses his lariat; the cowboy who does so frequently doesn't know how to drive cattle, Mr. Miller says.

The trick, he says, is to watch the way their ears are pointing and so anticipate their direction. Mr. Miller also rests cattle frequently on drives to let cows and calves "mother up" so they're more easily driven, or to calm trotty (nervous) animals. "If you don't rest them," he says, "they'll start to run, they'll get hot, then they'll get mad. Then there's no turning them. You've got to keep your cattle cool."

The fall weaning is a particularly sensitive time. Separated from their mothers until the maternal bond is broken, the calves, now sizable, are under stress that can cause pneumonia. When the animals finish days of bawling and finally lie down, the sound of a car, a dog's bark, even the cry of a night bird, may set them back on their feet and running in stampede, mowing down fences, crushing each other in the pileup of bodies. This happened to Mr. Miller twice when he was cowboss on the big Yolo ranch.

Nothing untoward happens on this drive, and the riders finally reach the plain. No chuck wagon rolls up with a bewhiskered Gabby Hayes type ready to ladle out son-of-a-bitch stew—classically, a concoction of cow brains, tongues, hearts, livers and marrow, with a handful of onions thrown in to conceal the taste. Instead everyone rumbles back to the ranch house and the cowboss himself fixes lunch for his men: steaks, beans, bread smothered in gravy, and mayonnaise jars full of iced tea.

How to Get Fired

By tradition, the cowboss looks out for his cowboys and hires and fires them himself. Besides incompetence, two things will get you fired by Jim Miller: abuse of horses and bellyaching. The latter is a breach of a cowboy code still in force. For $500 a month, the ranch expects and almost always gets total and uncomplaining loyalty to the outfit. Unionism is an utterly alien concept to cowboys; if a man doesn't like his boss, his job or anything else, he quits on the spot.

Firing is as simple. There are no hagglings over severance pay, no worries about employee lawsuits. "I just tell them, 'This is it,' and they go," says Mr. Miller.

Once, when a cowboss needed good hands, he would just drop in at the Palace Bar on Whisky Row in Prescott. This was the hiring hall and water hole, full of men who had been on the range for months and were "getting drunker'n seven hundred dollars," as Mr. Miller puts it. He doesn't go there anymore. "Now it's full of hippies and such as that, people who don't know a horse from a cow," he says. Instead, cowboys call him at home when they need work.

Lunch is over, and the men get off their rumpsprung old chairs and go out to nurse a young heifer internally damaged when calving. If they don't get her up to walk she will die.

*   *   *

At the offices of the Rafter Eleven, Bill Fain has been told by his computer that the cattle he soon will sell will have cost about 68 cents a pound to raise and fatten. He expects to get 67 cents for them. That's the cattle business today, says Mr. Fain, vice president of Fain Land & Cattle and the third generation of his family on this ranch. And such thin margins make men like Jim Miller particularly important.

The cowboss is considered one of the canniest judges of livestock in the area, and buys the registered bulls and replacement heifers for the ranch. It is he, more than anyone else, who maintains the quality of the herd. He coaxes an 80 percent calf crop out of the 700 mother cows here, a good ratio. He does not overburden the land, letting it rest and renew.

"Our product isn't cattle. It's grass," says Mr. Fain, "and Jimmy knows that. A lot of people can rope and ride and love the life, but there are damned few left who can do all the things he does."

Outside, cars whiz by on the road that crosses what used to be called Lonesome Valley. Some 6,000 people live there now because the Fains, trying to diversify out of an increasingly risky reliance on cattle, sold a piece of the ranch to a developer who built a town on it. The Fains developed another piece themselves.

This has made the cowboy's job harder. Cattle have been shot and cut up on the spot with chain saws by shade-tree butchers who throw the pieces in the back of a pickup and drive off, leaving head and entrails. People tear down cattle feeders for firewood, shoot holes in water tanks, breach fences to maliciously run down calves. "People and cattle don't mix," concedes Mr. Fain. "It's a sick thing," says Jim Miller, and there is icy anger in his blue eyes.

Meanwhile, the old family ranches are being sold, most of them to investors who don't know one end of a Hereford from the other and are more interested in tax shelter than running a good spread. This has driven ranchland prices so high that a young man who really wants to raise beef either can't afford to buy or has no hope of getting a return on his investment. "I really can't see much future in the cattle business," Mr. Miller says.

Cougars and Grasshoppers

Perhaps not. But around Yavapai County the cycle of ranch life continues unchanged on the surviving family spreads. In Peoples Valley, cougars have taken 15 calves this year and lion hunter George Goswick is tracking them through the Weaver Mountains. In the pastures, mares are heavy with foals; in time, some will find their way into the gentling hands of Twister Heller, the horse breaker. On the Hays ranch, owner John Hays is stabbing a wild-eyed Hereford bull in the rump with a needle full of antibiotics and fretting about the grasshoppers that are all over the property. There is too much ranch and too many hoppers, so he must simply accept them.

At evening, Jim Miller comes home to a house and five rural acres with horse corral outside Prescott. He and his wife, Joan, have lived here 10 years; for the first 27 years of their marriage they lived on the local ranches he worked, raising four sons and two daughters, teaching all to rope and ride. None has followed in his footsteps because there isn't any money in it.

Next year, when he's 65, Mr. Miller plans to quit as cowboss at the Rafter Eleven and start collecting Social Security. But he says he will never stop working. Few men around here who have spent their lives on a horse seem able to get off. Jim's friend Tom Rigden still rides roundup and castrates calves on his ranch, though he has been blind for almost eight years.

Mr. Miller doesn't expect any trouble finding day jobs on ranches. At a time when there are so few real cowboys left, he says, there is always work for a top hand.

～ PETER RINEARSON ～

Peter Rinearson was an aviation reporter for *The Seattle Times* when he won the ASNE award for business writing in 1984 and a Pulitzer Prize. Since then, he has started a software company, turned it into an Internet company and co-authored *The Road Ahead* with Microsoft founder Bill Gates.

How does a writer keep a reader interested in a story, especially one filled with technical information? Writing teacher Don Fry helps his students figure this out by telling them the parable of the gold coins. Imagine, he says, you are walking through a forest and come upon a gold coin. You pick it up and put it in your pocket. Down the trail you find another, and then another. You would keep walking until the coins ran out. In the same way, readers who are rewarded with interesting nuggets will move down into the story.

One of our favorite "gold coins" appears in Peter Rinearson's series "Making It Fly," a great explanatory saga on the creation of the

Boeing 757. The section on engineering, reprinted from *The Seattle Times*, is richly detailed and carefully reported, combining the best aspects of business, technology and feature writing.

No detail is funnier, or more revealing of a corporate culture, than the revelation that engineers used to fire live, anesthetized chickens into the windows of airplanes to test them against puncture.

"Here's an example of how public relations people are not necessarily the journalist's best friend," said Rinearson in 1984. "Boeing did not want the chicken tests written about. Period." Rinearson avoided the flacks, pursued the chicken story doggedly, retrieved it and wrote it well.

Simple and clear prose is no accident. It is, at best, the product of craft, requiring disciplined effort and tireless revision. "The door is an example," said Rinearson. "I had more trouble writing that section on the door. I must have completely rewritten that section a half dozen times. I'd just throw it out and start all over again. . . . What I wanted to do was to get the writing to a place where it seemed effortless. . . . The goal was to make it so that the reader would have no sense of the fact that it was difficult to write."

In the heat of the story, Rinearson worked 70 hours a week for months. "I worked on Christmas Day." The result of this effort was more than 2,000 pages of raw material. "Right now," he said back then, "I have four shelves of notebooks. . . . I have four legal-size filing cabinet drawers stuffed to overflowing. . . . I'm putting all this stuff up on a database so I can keep track of it. . . . I have 325 major classes of sources of information. Interviews with 70 or 80 different people."

During the whole process, his goal was to understand so that his readers would understand. "One thing I learned early on as a reporter, that it's a lot better looking stupid to your sources than looking stupid to your readers."

Making It Fly: Designing the 757

THE SEATTLE TIMES • JUNE 19, 1983

Boeing's newest jetliner, silvery metal with the blue numerals 757 emblazoned on its tail, turned heads like a celebrity as it taxied into Montreal's Dorval International Airport last September.

It came to rest at an Eastern Airlines gate where top Boeing officials were waiting to give the airline's president, Frank Borman, his first ride in the airplane he had helped launch with a $900 million order four years earlier.

A gate agent stepped up to the 757's door, popped out a butterfly-shaped handle and turned it clockwise. Grasping the door firmly, while the top brass of Boeing and Eastern looked on, she pushed and pulled.

The 323-pound door moved only a few inches. It wouldn't budge beyond that. Try as she might, she couldn't get it open.

"See?" said Paul Johnstone, then Eastern's senior vice president for operations.

Johnstone chuckled later and explained that he had purposely chosen a small woman to open the heavy door—or try to—so Boeing executives could see firsthand that something was wrong. "I mouse-trapped 'em," he said.

Although the 757 passenger door met elaborate engineering criteria and reliability tests, in Eastern's view the airplane at Dorval International was a flawed product.

The airline was to take delivery of the first airplane in December, just three months away, and it wanted a door every gate agent, regardless of his or her weight or strength, could open.

The 757 door took about 70 pounds of strength to open, twice as much as a 727 door. There were several reasons, including that it weighed more because the 757 sits higher off the ground and the door must contain a longer escape slide for emergency evacuation.

Boeing hadn't ignored the question of how much strength was necessary to open the door, said Jim Johnson, 757 director of engineering. On the contrary, engineers had calculated everything from the door's weight to the viscosity of its oil to the effects of friction on the door's bearings and rollers.

D.P. Tingwall, chief project engineer for engineering computing, said door loads were examined by computer and the design of cam parts was modified on the basis of the computer's findings.

And yet an error was made.

"We didn't give proper consideration to a small-framed woman with light weight," Boeing's Johnson said. A small person didn't have enough leverage to move the door, he said.

Boeing first encountered the door problem last July 8, when Nancy Ballard, a 115-pound Eastern gate agent at Seattle-Tacoma Airport, had enormous difficulty opening a 757 door in a test at Boeing Field.

"This young girl damn near got herself a hernia trying to open the damn door," said Johnstone, now retired from Eastern. In fact, Ballard came away from the test with a muscle bruise the size of a baseball on one arm, where she had repeatedly leaned for leverage while trying to push the door open.

"I was able to open the door, but believe me, it was a strain," she said.

It took a dozen engineers eight 56-hour weeks to solve the problem by designing a dual-spring mechanism, but the solution hadn't yet been installed when Johnstone sprung his mousetrap in Montreal.

The door problem wasn't the only thing discovered relatively late in the development of the 757 that required re-engineering.

In the fall of 1981, an anesthetized 4-pound chicken was loaded in a pneumatic gun and fired at 360 knots head-on into a stationary 757 cab.

The expectation was that the chicken would deflect off the cabin's sloping metal roof. Instead, it pierced the airplane's skin.

"It looked like you had thrown a shotput through it," said Ed Pottenger, a Boeing engineer.

This shocking result, and the realization that it might be repeated if the 757 hit a bird in flight, led to some urgent redesigning of the cabin roof of both the 757 and 767. The challenge was great because several 767s already were flying and had to be cut apart.

The changes were particularly painful because beefing up the cab added 70 pounds to the weight of each airplane, and saving weight is an aeronautical engineering objective pursued with almost religious intensity.

"There are people in the Boeing Co. who kill their grandmothers for five pounds. I'm dead serious," said Leroy Keith, the Federal Aviation Administration official who oversees certification of jetliners and other transport aircraft.

Overcoming those obstacles was only a small part of the engineering that went into the door and cabin of the 757—and the door and cabin represented but a fraction of the 65,000 "engineering events" involved in creating the airplane's detailed design.

At its peak, 1,500 engineers and a like number of assistants were involved in the 757 project. Although it was building two new airplanes simultaneously, Boeing didn't want to swell its engineering ranks temporarily, so it imported engineers from subcontractors around the country.

Often using computers (which helped design 47 percent of the airplane's parts), the engineers tackled large questions such as what shape the tail should be and how far back the wings should be swept, and such seemingly small questions as whether a piece of hardware should be hollow and how many inches wide a restroom should be.

Along the way, the engineers helped contribute to a dramatic change in the nature of the airplane: The 757 Boeing started to build is far different from the 757 it actually built, largely because of improvements in the airplane's cockpit and electronics.

The 757 has 95,000 different part types and a total of 3 million separate parts. Engineers selected or designed each one. Other engineers decided when material would be needed to make the parts and when the parts themselves would be needed.

Phil Condit, who held the top two engineering posts on the 757 project before being named its vice president and general manager in January, said he didn't make important engineering choices so much as designate times when they must be made by rank-and-file engineers.

"I couldn't absorb enough data to possibly make these kinds of decisions," he said.

Although the engineering details of the 757 far exceed the grasp of any single human mind, the problems involved in the design of the passenger door and cockpit offer some insight into the complexities of conceiving and creating a new airplane.

A Boeing 757 passenger door doesn't attract attention, which is just fine with its creators.

"A door looks simple," Condit said. "That's the way you want it to look. You don't want the passenger worrying about whether it's going to work."

In fact, the simple-looking passenger door contains about 500 parts, held together by 5,900 rivets. Its mechanical systems were designed by a battalion of engineers and fashioned by custom-made tools that cost millions of dollars.

The curving 4-inch-thick door must contain highly reliable mechanisms, including a system to control the speed at which it rotates on elaborate hinges and a system that enables the door to power itself open and deploy an escape slide in an emergency.

The slide is stored in the door, but whenever the door is closed and "armed" the slide automatically attaches to the sill of the doorway. In an emergency, the slide is pulled out of the door as the door opens. The slide inflates automatically.

The slide must reach the ground in an emergency even if the airplane is resting noseup and taildown, or is listing to one side with a broken landing gear. And the slide must inflate rapidly and reliably, even in 25-knot winds.

The complexities of the 757 passenger door are all the more remarkable because of the utter simplicity of the door's basic concept. The door is, in essence, a plug not unlike a bathtub stopper or a bottle cork.

But unlike a cork in a bottle, which is wedged in from the outside, the 757 door is wedged from the inside. The pressurized cabin air helps hold the door in place.

With the first turn of the door handle, internal mechanisms unlatch the door and reduce its height and wedge shape by folding in "gates" at the top and bottom. The door swings into the cabin briefly, unplugging the doorway, then slides back through the opening at a 25-degree angle and swings wide to fold against the outside of the airplane.

But to think of the door only as a piece of hardware is to overlook what is perhaps its most telling characteristic: compromise. The door, like the whole airplane, is as much a collection of engineering trade-offs as it is a collection of parts.

"To the last detail, everything we do is a compromise," Johnson said. Boeing engineers refer to these compromises as "trades," and there are lots of them in a door.

For example, the door must be wide enough to provide passengers comfortable entry, yet not so wide it robs seating space. Its window must give adequate vision of what is outside, and yet not use up too much of the space needed for its mechanical innards.

The door must be strong enough to hold out an alien environment of sub-zero temperatures, low air pressures and speeds approaching the sound barrier. And yet, like the rest of the airplane, it must be as light as possible to maximize fuel efficiency.

"I can't overstress the complexity of this set of trades that are continually going on," Condit said. "How much off am I? What happens if I put a little more wing area on? How does that balance?"

Engineers have different concepts of what is important. "You get a hydraulics guy, and he thinks the airplane ought to have 80 million miles of hydraulic lines in it," said John Armstrong, chief test pilot of the 757 program. "And the propulsion guy thinks that the airplane's just a vehicle to carry his engines around."

"Weight is the all-important driving force behind almost everything," said Keith, the FAA official. "You can build something that is totally safe, fire resistant and fail-safe, but it would be made out of titanium and it would be heavy and it would be prohibitively costly. So you've got a series of trades.

". . . It's just one series of compromises. In performance, handling qualities, systems, reliability, comfort, economy, structure, fabrication."

That all the trades are made and an airplane is created and tested in just four or five years is remarkable, Keith said. "You've got a magnificent flying machine out of the deal in a relatively short time period. It just never ceases to amaze me."

Early in 1978, a cockpit designer named Tom White made a pie-in-the-sky suggestion—a suggestion that, if accepted, would fundamentally change the future of Boeing's new family of jetliners.

The 757 program was a year away from its eventual launch and the proposed configuration of the airplane kept changing. "Semifluid," one designer called it.

But Boeing was certain of one thing: Although much of the 757 would be new, including its engines, wings, and interior design, to save development costs it would use updated versions of the 727 cockpit, tail and body cross-section. In short, it would be a 727 derivative.

In a one-page memo dated March 23, 1978, White asked why the company shouldn't forget about making the 757 a derivative. Instead, he proposed putting the all-new Boeing 767 wide-body nose and state-of-the-art digital electronics on the narrow-body 757. It would be a challenge, since there was almost four feet of difference in the diameters of the two airplanes, but he thought it was possible.

White was suggesting more than just a nose job for the 757. It would be a complete personality change. It would make the 757 a sister to the 767, which was a 1980s airplane, rather than a half-sister to the 727, a 1960s airplane. But it also would cost Boeing a fortune in additional development costs and add substantial weight to the airplane.

White argued the updating would make the 757 attractive to airlines for years and might result in the FAA eventually approving a common pilot rating for both airplanes. This would cut operating costs for airlines flying both the 757 and 767.

The idea of creating a common cockpit for the 757 and 767 wasn't new to White's boss, Del Fadden. It had come up every few months. But never before had a designer developed the idea so imaginatively or made it seem within the realm of possibility. Fadden encouraged White.

But the suggestion went nowhere. It just wasn't what Boeing had in mind.

Over the summer of 1978, the 767 program was launched with United Airlines as its first customer. The 757 program was announced in late August, although it wouldn't get the official go-ahead from Boeing until the following March.

During that summer it dawned on Boeing management that the 757 was looking less and less like a 727 derivative. There was talk about using a non-727 tail for improved aerodynamics, and the latest cockpit design called for an advanced safety-and-maintenance monitoring system that could reduce the flight crew from three to two. Without a formal policy decision having been made, the 757 was evolving away from the 727.

In October, Ken Holtby, a Boeing vice president who had run the 747 division for four years, took charge of coordinating development of the 757 and 767. Management felt the two programs sometimes were plowing the same ground.

"One of the things that became immediately obvious was that many of the decisions that had been made on one program or another really should have been applied across the board," Holtby said. "We found a lot of differences between the airplanes that really couldn't be justified."

Holtby told the product-development organization to study ways to increase the commonality of the two airplanes. Much of the job fell to Doug Miller, a chief designer.

One of the first things Miller did was call Tom White. Together they went to Boeing's Everett plant to look at a mock-up of the 767 cab, which used a new design Boeing had been developing for years. They set out to prove the cab could be used on the narrower 757.

Soon there were a lot of people working on the common-cockpit idea, and excitement grew. Pete Morton, senior project engineer on the 757, became a powerful advocate. H.G. Stoll, Morton's counterpart on the 767, remembers a phone call in which Morton spelled out the common cockpit idea.

"At first I thought it looked like it was way out as far as an idea," Stoll said. "After all, (if) somebody says you're going to take the front end off a Cadillac and put it on your Datsun, your first reaction is that it's not a good idea."

Morton and Miller approached Condit, who, as chief engineer, was impressed with the idea of common parts between the airplanes, but thought a common FAA pilot rating was "pretty elusive, a pretty high-risk thing to be going after."

Eventually, the idea worked its way up the corporate ladder to Holtby, the vice president who had urged greater commonality between the airplanes.

"I had to be persuaded," Holtby recalls. "There are a lot of factors that go into that kind of a decision, including our capability. Quite a few of the guys were recommending against it because they didn't feel we had the resources to do it. So there was quite a bit of debate."

Boeing decided to take the gamble.

Today, both airplanes have identical cockpits, developed jointly by 757 and 767 engineers; Boeing perceives the evolution of the cockpit as a triumph; White still seeks new design ideas; Condit, who is only 41, has risen from engineering to become vice president and general manager of the 757 division.

And hanging on Condit's office wall, framed and signed, is one of White's original renderings of how he thought the 767 cab could be fitted to the 757.

Inside and out, the cab is the most expensive part of a jetliner's fuselage to engineer and manufacture.

The cab's exterior is of irregular shape. None of the metal is flat; even the contours are not uniform. Inside the cab, an impressive number of electronic and mechanical devices must be sandwiched into a small area.

Morton estimates 120 to 150 engineers were involved in creating the cab and cockpit on the 757 and 767, including those who designed the exterior, crafted the interior and figured out how to fit in all the instrumentation.

Cab design is based on the position of a pilot's eyes, hands and feet. The 757 and 767 cockpits are designed for people from 5-foot-2 to 6-foot-3. The shorter height was included in the design in the expectation that women pilots will become numerous during the useful life of the airplanes.

Boeing selected earth tones of brown and beige for the interiors because a NASA study found those colors reduce anxiety in high-stress environments. Sheepskin-covered seats were installed.

Boeing ran tests on how computer screens should offer information, seeking answers to such questions as whether pilots might be distracted if screens automatically changed displays. (Answer: yes. So Boeing designed systems so that nonessential screens would update displays only when requested to do so or in emergencies.)

Boeing engineers also used computers in wind-tunnel studies to simulate the airplanes' handling characteristics long before they ever flew. Test pilots expressed their preferences, and engineers changed computer software and the airplanes' control surfaces until they found configurations that gave both airplanes desirable flying qualities.

The goal, which Boeing says it achieved, was to build two airplanes that seemed similar to pilots, even though they are quite different. "Cockpits are the place in the airplane that have the most compromises that I know of," Morton said. "Everything comes together there."

"For example, if I want a good view of a panel, I don't want a big control column there," he said. "But the guy that's responsible for the control column would like a good meaty one that a guy can wrap his hands around and really pull. And he doesn't care if it blocks my instruments.

"And then I want a nice compact cockpit. I don't care if there's a quarter of an inch behind a panel. But the guy who has to go buy the equipment wants 18 inches behind there. And there's another guy with the responsibility to cool it. He puts ducts in the back of that thing. . . ."

The 757's front window, or "No. 1 windshield" as it is called, demonstrates the compromises that can be involved in a single jetliner component.

A big window gives a pilot good outside vision, but leaves less room for instrumentation. Glass contributes nothing to the strength of the cabin, so big windows mean big posts, which block vision. Structural engineers would just as soon have portholes as picture windows.

Glass must be strong enough to withstand the impact of a large bird at high speed. But thick glass doesn't transmit light as well as thin glass.

Glass is a poor insulator, so large windows can chill a cab at night and let in excess sunlight by day. Big windows can mean glare problems, too.

The aerodynamics of the cabin are crucial, both for fuel efficiency and to keep noise levels low. Curved windshields help aerodynamically, but can create optical distortions, including double light reflections.

The No. 1 windows, which are made in England, are the same for both the 757 and 767. There are two of them, one on the right side and one on the left. They are flat. The side windows, known as Nos. 2 and 3, are curved and differ between the two airplanes because their fuselages have different shapes.

The narrower 757 has smaller No. 2 and 3 windows and they are closer to the pilots' shoulders. But Boeing shaped and positioned them so that they give essentially the same field of view as the larger and more distant side windows on the 767.

The reason? Again, to make the airplanes feel alike to pilots.

In some places, engineers could not resolve differences between the two airplanes, but the variances aren't major. For example, the No. 2 windshield opens in both planes to allow an escape route for pilots, but the mechanisms differ due to fuselage shapes.

After its stop in Montreal last September, the 757 flew on to England with a load of Eastern and Boeing officials.

On the way, a duck hit one of the cockpit's No. 2 windows, not an unusual incident.

"It's usually not a big deal," said Les Berven, an FAA pilot who was co-piloting the flight. "All it did was just to make him into jelly and he slid down the side of the window."

The window didn't break — but then Boeing knew it wouldn't because the window had gone through a series of "chicken tests."

Boeing is a little touchy about the subject of chicken tests, and points out they are required by the FAA. Here's what happens:

A live 4-pound chicken is anesthetized and placed in a flimsy plastic bag to reduce aerodynamic drag. The bagged bird is put in a compressed-air gun.

The bird is fired at the jetliner window at 360 knots and the window must withstand the impact. It is said to be a very messy test.

The inch-thick glass, which includes two layers of plastic, needn't come out unscathed. But it must not puncture. The test is repeated under various circumstances — the window is cooled by liquid nitrogen, or the chicken is fired into the center of the window or at its edge. "We give Boeing an option," Berven joked. "They can either use a 4-pound chicken at 200 miles an hour or a 200-pound chicken at 4 miles an hour."

The British government requires that the metal above the windows also must pass the chicken test. This was the test the 757 failed. It had not been conducted on the 767, which has no British customers.

The 757 failure meant both airplanes had to be modified, since the metal overheads are structurally identical. Sixteen 767 cabs already had been completed, and had to be cut apart so reinforcing metal could be installed.

Mort Ehrlich, an Eastern Airlines senior vice president, said he watched Airbus Industries conduct chicken tests in Toulouse, France.

"A few of us who were there uttered the classic remark about how hard it is to be a chicken in Toulouse," he said. "I guess the same is true in Seattle."

⁓ MICHAEL GARTNER ⁓

Michael Gartner, the son and grandson of Iowa newspapermen, started out in journalism taking sports dictation at *The Des Moines* (Iowa) *Register*. For more than 40 years, he helped run newsrooms: as Page One editor of *The Wall Street Journal*; as editor of *The Des Moines Register* and *The Courier-Journal* in Louisville, Ky.; and as president of NBC News. He won the 1994 ASNE award for editorials in *The Daily Tribune* of Ames, Iowa, which he edited and co-owned until 1999. He also won the 1997 Pulitzer Prize for editorial writing.

Gartner says the greatest insult he ever heard was when an editor at *The Wall Street Journal* handed back a story to a reporter with this comment: "All of the words, but none of the music."

Words without music are sacrilege to Gartner, who composes editorials that are lyrical, clear and meant to be read aloud.

Gartner is not shy about delivering his opinions, but he relies on facts, as well as arguments, to make his case. His goal is to inform as well as persuade.

He has a formula for editorials. Bear in mind that there are formulas for executing a triple gainer over a diving board or a triple axel on ice; that doesn't mean everyone can do one. "The editorials that I like best are . . . stories with lots and lots of facts and a viewpoint that builds either through repetition or an alliteration or word play, and then culminates with an ending that's not a whack over the head with a two-by-four. . . . Rarely do I get so outraged I call somebody a jerk."

He doesn't need to. Instead, he marshals a symphony of facts—culled from the fine print of the city's tax rolls—and orchestrates them to make his case. "Property Tax Exemptions: Legal but Terribly Unfair" was the opening salvo in a series that attacked property tax increases, including the break given his own newspaper. Numbers can numb, Bill Blundell cautions writers, but here they illuminate, surprise, provoke.

A lawyer as well as a journalist and one of the nation's staunchest First Amendment defenders, Gartner champions speech and press freedoms with blistering logic and passionate style. He knows that editorials can be better than sleeping pills. So he keeps readers on their toes, changing the pace, slowing down, speeding up. His tools: one- and two-word sentences, and a refrain that echoes through the editorial.

"Should be, but isn't."

"Could make, but doesn't."

"Would be, but isn't."

"Would."

The power of repetition.

"But—for the fourth time—it's terribly unfair."

All of the words, and all of the music.

To see and hear the music in Gartner's work, we have chosen to X-Ray his editorial rather than merely reprint it. Our comments reveal the variety of strategies he brings to the creation of "civic clarity." These include the setting of a comprehensible pace, the artful repetition of words and arguments, and the careful use of cases and statistics. The result is a piece that sounds as if it's spoken—or sung—to a curious audience.

Property Tax Exemptions: Legal but Terribly Unfair

The Daily Tribune • August 2, 1995

Have you ever driven by that terrific piece of wooded land on Mortensen Road near Elwood? It's a great plot—about three acres—and city assessor Richard Horn values it at $196,900. Dr. Massoud Shahidi owns it, and at the new Ames tax rate for residential land it should be taxed at $4,228.

Specific case and concrete figures provide base to build on

Short couplet begins a pattern — Should be, but isn't.

Dr. Shahidi pays not a penny on that land.

Have you ever stopped in to visit the folks at the Iowa Poultry Association's headquarters? It's that nice-looking little building at 535 East Lincoln Way. Assessor Horn puts its value at $128,400, which could make its tax bill, as a business, $4,085.

Second couplet — Could make, but doesn't.

The Iowa Poultry Association pays not a penny on its building.

Have you ever stopped in the Elks Club? It's on Douglas, across from the library, and Assessor Horn says the building is worth $317,000. The property tax on that, at the business rate that other restaurants pay, would be $10,087.

Third couplet completes the pattern: Three is a magic number — Would be, but isn't.

The Elks pay not a penny on their club.

Dr. Shahidi, the poultry people and the Elks own just three of 116 buildings or sites in Ames that have applied for total exemptions from the property tax—and gotten them.

Courage to include his own company — Owners of another 114 homes or buildings—including *The Daily Tribune*—have received partial exemptions. All told, these 230 exemptions have taken off the tax rolls property valued at $52,974,895. The annual taxes that would produce—at the business rate for

Key numbers give perspective

The power of one word

businesses and the reduced residential rate for homes—would be $1,676,936.

Would.

It's all perfectly legal—and terribly unfair. What's more, this $53 million of untaxed property is just a small fraction of the total tax-free property in Ames, but it's the only amount you can put a precise figure on. These 230 homes and businesses had to apply for their exemptions, so they were first assessed. But other property is tax-exempt by statute, so assessors never even bother to value it. This includes the Iowa State University campus, the state-owned headquarters of the Department of Transportation, the city-owned Mary Greeley Medical Center, the federally owned Animal Disease Lab and all other land and buildings owned by the city or county or area or state or federal governments. The total is easily in the hundreds of millions of dollars—and would produce tens of millions of dollars in taxes.

Easy pace clarifies background

Repeated like a drumbeat

Would.

What this means is that the 8,846 homeowners and the 1,250 business owners and the 32 factory owners pay extra to provide the police and fire and roads and parks and other city services for the people who live and work in these tax-free spots.

It is, as we said, terribly unfair.

So why doesn't Assessor Horn make those people pony up so taxes can be cut for those who pay the full amount? He can't. He must grant exemptions to some people who seek them. Those include churches and the church-owned homes of ministers (that takes $20,771,650 off the tax rolls), religious schools ($80,300 for the Grand Avenue Baptist Church school), fraternal organizations ($633,900), agricultural societies ($3,427,900), nonprofit retirement homes ($7,017,900, which is the assessed value of Northcrest up on 20th Street), and other charitable and benevolent societies ($2,090,350).

Argument builds on strong reporting details

(CONTINUED)

And he must not tax—not a penny—the so-called forest reserve land in the city, which can be any plot of two or more acres on which the owner has no house and on which he plants some trees and bushes. The land remains private—only the owner can enjoy it. That's the exemption that frees Dr. Shahidi from taxes on Mortensen Road.

There's more. If you own undeveloped but unforested land in the city, you can plant a crop on it and have it valued as agricultural land, which is taxed at less than half the tax on residential land and which, by a quirk, is taxed even less than agricultural land outside the city. There's more than 1,700 acres of this so-called agricultural land within Ames, and probably half of it is really land being held for the bulldozer rather than the plow, land valued—and taxed—far below its worth. An example: the land on Airport Road where Sam's Club will be built was taxed at $1,000 an acre; it sold for $45,000 an acre.

Finally, you can have your taxes rolled back if you are in an urban revitalization district and improve your home or building. You can petition to have the taxes on those improvements forgiven for three years or reduced for five to 10 years. It's this exemption that allowed *The Daily Tribune* to escape paying taxes—about $3,100 a year—on $100,000 of improvements for three years.

All of this is, as we've said three times now, terribly unfair. It's also, as we said, absolutely legal. "There's nothing in the law that says it has to be fair," Assessor Horn notes. And he's right.

But there's also nothing that says the law couldn't change. And it should.

Why shouldn't the Iowa State Memorial Union—in effect a restaurant and hotel—pay the same rate as the Holiday Inn/Gateway Center?

Why shouldn't the Elks Club pay the same rate as Aunt Maude's?

Not afraid to look in the mirror

Repeated again—picked up in title

Move from "would" to "should": closes the persuasive argument

Why shouldn't Rev. Scott Grotewold of Collegiate United Methodist Church pay the same rate for his $138,000 house as Ted Tedesco pays for his home?

Why shouldn't *The Daily Tribune* pay the same rate for its new facility as the Red Lobster, which is not in an urban revitalization district, pays for its?

In case you missed it the first three times — The answer is, they—and we—should.

It may be legal that some people don't pay taxes.

But—for the fourth time—it's terribly unfair.

Chapter 6

OPINION
AND PERSUASION

W riters talk about "finding their voice," a term of craft both common and mysterious. What is this elusive quality called "voice," and how can something called voice exist when most readers experience the text in silence?

Writing teacher Don Fry offers a helpful definition: "Voice is the sum of writing strategies that creates the illusion that the writer is speaking directly to the reader from the page." Voice turns out to be one of many metaphors of sound used to describe the writer's art: from tone to rhythm to cadence. We say a story "sounds" good. Writers sit at a keyboard and try to make the story "sing." They hope their editor has a good "ear."

While all writers have voice, that voice is often muted, especially in news writing that seeks a level of principled detachment. Traditionally, it has been the columnist, the critic or the opinion writer who has been licensed to write with voice. In fact, the column was created to offer readers relief from the routine, sometimes dreary news of the day. The columnist could be clever, whimsical or unconventional. The editorial writer, on the other hand, wrote with the institutional voice of the newspaper but often revealed touches of individual brilliance.

The writers here offer readers strong voices. They are young and old, male and female, black and white. In each piece, the writer's voice is modulated by a set of specific writing strategies: the level of language from concrete to abstract; the use of first person or third person; the source and range of allusion; the high or low use of metaphor; the length and complexity of sentences; the distance from neutrality; the choice of conventional or offbeat perspectives; the preference for information or experience; the tone, from outrage to humor to sarcasm to sorrow.

Donna Britt's voice is outraged as she argues against a language of popular culture that denigrates women. Richard Aregood's voice is characteristically acerbic, both amazed and disgusted at politicians' nervy dissembling. Murray Kempton, who leads off this section, writes in a voice that outlives him, a voice both jazzy and literary, stretching the newspaper form to its limit.

New writers in this chapter include Bailey Thomson, who writes in the voice of the dedicated reformer; Cynthia Tucker, who holds the powerful accountable in the city of Atlanta; Andrew Malcolm, who is the master of erudite humor on the editorial page; and Leonard Pitts, who writes with passion, wit and irony, especially about race.

Young musicians sometimes develop their own styles by imitating those they admire. So it is with writers. They read for form and content, but also for voice. Imitation is the next step, a trick of language borrowed now and again. Eventually those little moves get absorbed, become unconscious, and something new emerges—an authentic voice.

～ MURRAY KEMPTON ～

The late Murray Kempton won the ASNE award for commentary in 1985 for his columns in *Newsday*, which he joined in 1981. His death in April 1997 ended a distinguished career as a graceful, insightful observer of American political culture.

Of all the ASNE award winners, Kempton was the most advanced in years and the youngest at heart. He won at the age of 67 and declared that he was old enough "to have found his way" as a reporter. An important part of his responsibility, he said, was to write for the next generation of writers.

The column presented here shows what a craftsman can do with 612 words. Kempton could move easily from a jazz memory to a police story with the same distinctive writing voice that made him the most idiosyncratic of newspaper columnists.

Among a generation of gruff urban voices, his was elegant. Among a cohort of straight shooters, his sentences wandered, sometimes looking desperately for a period. Among those who favored the gritty Anglo-Saxon, he feared no abstraction or literary allusion.

He used words never seen before in an American column. From his metaphors, readers could tell that he read a book. And from his historical references, readers could tell that he lived a life.

And, ah, those sentences, long and meandering, echoes of a bygone, more literate generation of writers and thinkers. What other journalist of his generation would begin a sentence, "I should not be surprised to be told," or write "after life was well along in its withering"?

In the end, Kempton marshaled his words to expose corruption and strive for social justice: "He spoke in the cold tones of a government whose gelid habits make understandable its alarm that, whatever the law says, a jury might hear such a story and run wild in its outrage." The storyteller cannot contrive such an ending, Kempton argued, or even imagine it in advance. It can only be reached.

"I've never found out whether anybody ever finishes my pieces or not," he said, "but I try to keep the person reading to the end. It's a story. You begin the story with some effort to make it interesting in the beginning, and then you get to a narrative line as fast as you can, and then you go through that narrative line. And then the best part of the piece ought to be in the last three paragraphs."

Kempton died at the age of 79. *The New York Times* wrote of him, "Despite his renown as a thought provoker, he believed that a good columnist does not forget how to be a reporter. And so he could often be seen on the streets of New York gadding about on his three-speed bicycle, usually attired in a conservative business suit, his spare white hair flopping gently or, in inclement weather, tucked under a black beret."

A Woman Burned While Police Had Their Danish

NEWSDAY • NOVEMBER 9, 1984

It is six years since the morning Nathan Giles Jr. accosted the car that Bonnie Anne Bush was driving to her Mount Sinai Hospital nursing post, forced her out with a gun, dragged her screaming into an abandoned West Side building, shot her and set her body afire.

Bonnie Bush's death did just about as much damage to the good name of the New York City Police Department as Kitty Genovese's did to Queens's reputation for conscientious citizenship. Kitty Genovese also screamed in the street through a protracted struggle with her murderer, and nobody who heard her called 911.

Kitty Genovese has been dead more than 20 years, and her ghost is still evoked whenever some moralist feels moved to arraign the callousness of this city's residents.

In Bonnie Bush's case, several citizens did their duty and the police botched theirs. The difference may be why Kitty Genovese's name has lasted so much longer than hers as a symbol of reproach to New Yorkers. Government is distinctly more efficient than the average citizen when it comes to erasing occasions for shame from the public memory.

Nathan Giles had a long struggle with Bonnie Bush before he got her to the killing floor. The first 911 call came at 8:03; there were four others, the last at 8:11. Antonio Reyes later swore that he ran up to a patrol car not many yards from the building into which the murderer had just dragged his victim. The two officers heard his story and went on eating their breakfast.

Meanwhile, back at 911, the headquarters operator had taken a succession of calls from witnesses to Bonnie Bush's peril and made such a hash of the information that the police details were scouring Manhattan Avenue for a criminal who had been identified as working his will at 15 West 102nd.

Bonnie Bush had been dead an hour when the Fire Department came to put out the blaze Giles had set, and reported a possible homicide to the police. It would be only speculation to suggest that she would still be alive if the police had done their job, but then, after all, Kitty Genovese might still be just as dead if any of her neighbors in Queens had dialed 911. The point is that each of these women deserved even a small chance of rescue and survival, and Kitty Genovese was cheated of her chance by private citizens and Bonnie Bush by official servants.

The two policemen who had tarried over breakfast were put to a departmental trial and found guilty of having failed to "take fundamental police action." The punishment in each case was suspension for 30 days of vacation time, with the option to make up the loss with extra work. Thus does the department define its sensitivity to the standards of police conduct: Two patrolmen who refuse to bother with a call of mortal distress lose their vacations and Cybella Borges loses her job because she posed in the buff before she was even a patrolman.

Bonnie Bush's parents sued the city for the neglect they claimed had caused her wrongful death. Kenneth Besterman, plaintiff's counsel with Richard Winer, said yesterday that he had entered the case with minimal hope, because "the law is 103 percent against us." And the law is indeed clear-cut—a citizen cannot expect the police to protect him from felonious assault unless he gives them advance notice of its threat. If the police do not learn of the crime until after it starts, no subsequent negligence on their part adds up to a legal tort.

Yesterday it was announced that the City of New York had agreed to settle the claim by paying $150,000 to Bonnie Bush's estate. Assistant Corporation Counsel John Ryan credited this unheard-of generosity to "the prejudicial nature of the facts," even though they were "irrelevant." He spoke in the cold tones of a government whose gelid habits make understandable its alarm that, whatever the law says, a jury might hear such a story and run wild in its outrage.

～ RICHARD AREGOOD ～

Richard Aregood was the editorial page editor of *The Philadelphia Daily News* when he won the ASNE award for editorial writing in 1991. He is a three-time winner of the award and also a winner of the Pulitzer Prize for editorial writing.

An effective editorial has two ingredients, according to Aregood: a position and a passion. Aregood should know. His many awards honor a style that leaves readers no doubt where he and his newspaper come down on the issues of the day, as in the following editorial. It's a quintessential Aregood diatribe, this one aimed at what he considered a fraudulent 1990 plan to reduce the nation's deficit.

This story retains relevance in the first years of the 21st century: Record deficits are being debated in the context of a new administration, and a strong stance coupled with concrete information make for compelling editorial writing.

In a genre known for its contemplative nature—why else would editorials be called "thumbsuckers"?—Aregood is a self-described "wild man." His pieces are always overspiced, loaded with invective, sarcasm and scorn. But even the tartest opinions need the meat of substantial thought and research. "Reporting has always been the most important part," says Aregood, who was a police reporter, rewrite man and editor before turning to editorials. "Even jokes need context."

Likening federal budget politics to the Wizard of Oz may seem over-the-top to some, until he points out "one of the more interesting irrationalities of tax law, mega-incomes are now taxed at 28 percent, while middle- and upper-middle incomes pay 33."

Aregood learned his craft from the newspaper rewrite specialists who were his generation's writing coaches. Economy is his grail, the legendary columnist Jimmy Cannon his model: "He could absolutely devastate a topic in eight words, and the fewer words you use, the more impact you have.

"Editorials in a lot of newspapers are just 24 inches of harrumphing, and I don't have time to waste on harrumphing. It's just like the rest of the paper. If you're going to have good writing in your newspaper, you should have people telling stories, and not just spitting out data."

Writing for a blue-collar tabloid in a northeastern caldron of ethnic politics, he is an equal-opportunity basher, lambasting politicians and policies he deems misguided, although he doesn't call them so. President George H.W. Bush is "George of Oz" and President Ronald Reagan is "Ronnie of Lala Land" and "Ronnie the Dim."

"If you think some public official is a horse's ass," Aregood says, "why say that you have certain difficulties with his performance record? You say he's a horse's ass."

And, as any politician who's come under his editorial microscope can testify, that's just what Richard Aregood does.

Tugs at the Curtain, but Wizard's Lips Remain Frozen

THE PHILADELPHIA DAILY NEWS • MARCH 15, 1990

The Wizard is still behind the curtain. He is urging us to read his lips as the blue smoke billows.

What the hell, it works.

George of Oz is even more popular than his predecessor, Ronnie of Lala Land. Many of us seem to believe the federal deficit will disappear somehow — perhaps a house from Kansas will fall on it.

Sen. Daniel Patrick Moynihan gave a tug at the curtain when he said out loud that the Social Security tax is being used to conceal the enormity of the deficit.

It's somehow sadly fitting that the most regressive of our taxes, the one everybody pays, the one the rich pay the least share of, is the one that's used to hide the cost to this nation of Ronnie's virtual exemption of rich people from taxation.

So Moynihan proposed cutting Social Security taxes. *Zut alors!* The tax-cutters ran for the shelters. Who ever heard of cutting taxes for ordinary people? Doesn't he know we have a deficit? Doesn't he know the president is going to help us all by further cutting capital gains taxes?

Why, once the wealthy start unloading assets to take advantage of capital gains cuts, they will certainly start spending their money to rebuild railroad bridges and care for proletarian children. Perhaps some will even take in a few of the homeless.

This is, of course, a large crock of a substance found in all barnyards, which brings us to the current delicate dance in Washington.

House Ways and Means Committee Chairman Dan Rostenkowski is credited with great courage for coming out with a deficit reduction plan of his own. At least, the Wizard hung a medal on his chest for courage.

There are some attractive aspects to it. It would substantially raise the tax on gasoline, alcohol, and tobacco. These taxes are lower here than in most countries. Besides, what better way to pay for the environmental and health damage those products produce?

His idea to tax the neighborhood jillionaire's income at 33 percent is a small step toward progressivity and fairness in taxation, a concept totally abandoned in the reign of Ronnie the Dim.

Besides, in one of the more interesting irrationalities of tax law, mega-incomes are now taxed at 28 percent, while middle- and upper-middle incomes pay 33.

There's a lot more to it, including many bad ideas and some imperfect ones, like putting a number on defense cuts, thereby imposing a de facto cap.

President Bush says he loves it.

He also says he is still unwilling to consider any kind of tax increases, although he doesn't "want to appear totally inflexible."

Presumably, this means he will continue to pass the buck to the states and cities to do the work of the federal government, which will then be free to bail out savings and loans and ship loaded weapons to trouble spots.

Rostenkowski doesn't blink at being described as "the president's favorite Democrat," which may be part of the cautious reaction of some of his fellow Democrats.

You don't have to be a practicing cynic to think that all this compromise talk might simply lead to a decrease in capital gains taxes for the president's rich friends and a further abandonment of the government's job.

And George, lips still frozen, will blame the Democrats for some imaginary outbreak of homelessness among the wealthy, not to mention the added costs to heavy boozers.

Forget that cutting the deficit might lead directly to a trade deal with the Japanese or a lowering of interest rates.

Forget that there's long-term credit to be had for solving the problem.

And forget that we are already in hock up to our B-2s.

Forget it all. This is Oz we're talking about, where the only courage that's visible is the writing on the Cowardly Lion's medal, where the most outrageous lies and misrepresentations pretend to be policy, and where the thing that is most feared is being seen trying to do something.

This is not a place where one points out that people who spend more than they take in tend to end up in hock.

Once the Wicked Witch and the Wizard cut a compromise, that problem will just go away.

Won't it?

⮜ DONNA BRITT ⮞

Donna Britt is a columnist for *The Washington Post*. She started her career in 1979 at the *Detroit Free Press* and worked for *USA Today* before joining the *Post* in 1989. She won the ASNE award for commentary in 1994.

There are journalists who grow up dreaming of having their pictures over a column of type. They will be the Jimmy Breslins, the Mike Roykos, the Ellen Goodmans of their day. But as an African-American child growing up in Gary, Ind., Donna Britt never harbored such dreams.

"In the '60s and '70s, newspapers described lives that had no discernible relation to my own," she says. "The sections that I was most interested in—the women's pages, the comics, then on to news and sports—had almost no black people in them. . . . It was almost as if real life happened to white people, but problems happened to black people and Hispanic people and Asian people."

As a columnist, Britt changes the rules with insightful, unabashedly personal writing that reveals the extraordinary in the ordinary lives of black Americans.

Britt practices the alchemist's art, transforming everyday experiences into golden musings on life, death, love and hate. She can be equally tough-minded in attacking the corrosiveness of white racism and the brutality of "gangsta" rap, along with the violence toward women it glorifies.

Britt writes like an investigative reporter whose assignment is the emotional landscape of modern life. As a wife, mother of three boys, friend, sister, daughter and journalist, Britt recognizes that writing about yourself honestly, even painfully, can make you a better reporter and editor: more empathetic, more skilled, better able to spot the universal truth in the individual story.

The columnist who chooses to mine her own life for material runs a risk. "Sometimes I get taken to task for being so personal, for exploring my life and the lives of people around me for universal meaning," Britt says. "And sometimes I am concerned about that. I don't want this to seem like some egocentric exercise. But it feels like if I'm open and revealing about my fears and hurts and frustrations, it opens the door for my readers to examine theirs."

Even when she's writing about herself, the columnist can never forget about those readers. That's where craft comes in. Britt's columns are drafted in a burst of activity, followed by silence, rereading and the endless questioning of revision. "Can I say this better? Can I be more direct? Can I make this tighter? Can I clarify this point? Is this insensitive? Is it funny? What can I do to make it jump off the page? What's going to make somebody go with me to the end, ride with me the whole way?"

A One-Word Assault on Women

THE WASHINGTON POST • NOVEMBER 30, 1993

A few years ago, I saw a black teenage girl with a delicate necklace clasped around her throat. I've forgotten her features but remember what sparkled in rhinestones around her neck:

"BITCH BITCH BITCH."

My immediate reaction was to weigh how offensive it would be to approach this child with one obvious question:

"Why are you wearing that?"

I never asked. But the necklace proved something I'd doubted: There really are women who want to be identified as female dogs by all who encounter them—which is good news for the rappers, rockers and regular guys who call all women by the epithet.

Frankly, some women refer to each other that way. On a recent *60 Minutes*, a female lawyer mouthed the word to describe a female judge she disliked.

Still, most women hate being called that. One widely publicized proof: the reaction of female journalists last summer to rapper Bushwick Bill's defense of his use of the B-word at a national African American journalists' convention.

Maybe you read about it. One of several hiphoppers on a music panel, Bill—a dwarf who supposedly lost his eye in a gunfight with a girlfriend—was asked by a woman why he and other rappers routinely call women "bitches" and "ho's" (whores) in their music.

Not all women qualify, Bill said. He'd never describe his mother that way, he continued, because he isn't having sex with her. But, he told the woman, "if I was [having sex with] you, you'd be a ho."

Hmmmmmmmm.

I see why dozens of incensed women stalked out, why several columnists deplored Bill's comments. Yet months later—in the midst of a national debate over the violent words and images characteristic of a small segment of rap music known as "gangsta" rap—the whole thing still makes me sad. Why? Because it makes too much sense.

It makes sense that a less-than-handsome young man who lost half his sight tussling with a woman—and who now, if he's like other rich male celebrities, combs groupies out of his hair—would be contemptuous of all women.

It's also undeniable that almost every name-calling rap or rock video is decorated with the bodies of hip-grinding young women. Even the faintest promise of fame remains as much an incentive for girls to strip for the camera as it was 40 years ago, when young starlet Marilyn Monroe posed nude.

Years later, Monroe said she posed only for the money, because "I was hungry."

But what is it that the name-calling male performers are hungering for? While contempt for women isn't new, entertainers' constant, public use of "bitch," aired on radio and TV, is.

Perhaps it's a genuine expression of increased male resentment, or of certain singers' willingness to disrespect women in hopes of stirring controversy—and increasing record sales.

Are young performers reflecting a harsh world's reality? Or is real life—as in innocent kids parroting epithet-laden songs—reflecting the performers' influence?

Some rappers say they're just being honest. They say nice women—those who are neither sluts nor skeezers (women who use men for money)—should take no offense to names that don't apply to them. They're just dissing the women who deserve it.

Cool. So that means these same brothers would make allowances for a white politician who was revealed to routinely call black folks "niggers" if he only explained, "I use that term only in reference to black people who kill others, you know, criminals. The rest of you— take no offense."

The worst thing about the B-word—and the N-word and every denigrating term—is what it assumes. It assumes that everybody— all women, all black men, all members of any group—are alike. The brother who disses all women because of the actions of some is as unenlightened as the racist who denies all black people's humanity because some blacks act inhumanely.

But I keep going back to Bill—who later apologized to the group for "being myself."

It's no accident that the most negative feelings the rapper revealed weren't directed at women, but at himself: Only a man with a twisted self-concept would assume that any woman who'd have sex with him should require payment.

But maybe, like so much else, it all boils down to money. The fellas who make millions singing their contempt for women—and who at the same time pride themselves for slamming racism in their music—are actually in the business of selling racism's most destructive lies. Singers who wave their Glocks, grab their crotches and dis their women—while thousands of us pay to watch and listen—do more than make themselves and record producers rich.

Too often they tell the world—and the young whites who reportedly are gangsta rap's biggest consumers—what morgues overflowing with the bodies of black men suggest: how deeply some African Americans have internalized the racism they deplore.

The messages many are selling to—and about—blacks:

You don't deserve to live. Your women are sluts and animals. You kill without remorse, and copulate without love or responsibility.

Sure that's all a lie. But slap a beat on it, apply a coat of glamour and someone, somewhere will dance to it.

Or clasp it in rhinestones around her neck.

❧ BAILEY THOMSON ❧

Bailey Thomson, one of the South's foremost editorial writers, died in 2003 of a heart attack at the age of 54, a great loss to the state of Alabama. Like so many other fallen Alabama heroes, Thomson left behind a fleeting sense of greatness, but also the agony of disappointment and questions about whether the loss of his leadership would result in yet another failure to reform the state's political institutions. At the time of his passing, Thomson had evolved from editorialist to university professor to leader of the movement to reimagine Alabama's antiquated constitution.

Thomson's best work as a newspaper writer was a series of editorials titled "Dixie's Broken Heart." In 1999, it earned him an ASNE Distinguished Writing Award and consideration for a Pulitzer Prize. The conception and execution of this series for the *Mobile* (Ala.) *Register* is brilliant, beginning with a piece called "The Two Alabamas."

In his lead, Thomson offers two contrasting images of his state: a shining new automobile plant and the run-down elementary school about a mile down the road. Thomson frames these images side by side to capture the bright hope of Alabama, but also the prison of poverty and corruption that has kept this most Southern of states locked in the darker recesses of its past.

In this series, Thomson identified seven social, economic and political problems that were keeping Alabama behind, including a regressive tax structure, poor health care for children and a degraded civic culture. Then he did something extremely rare in the annals of editorial writing: He hopped in his blue pickup truck and spent the summer traveling around the South to discover how Alabama's neighbors had solved similar problems. Rather than deliver his editorials from on high, Thomson, a son of Aliceville, Ala., sought truth and revelation from behind the wheel of a pickup.

He then revealed the paths to the state's redemption in language that Alabama's finest authors might envy: "We have stumbled to the crossroads of century's end, with too little to show for such a long journey. It is not enough, however, to bemoan lost opportunities. We must raise expectations for public life and hold politicians to a high civic standard. Only then can Alabama's democracy aspire to a politics of hope and accomplishment. . . . But we have miles to go before that happens. Miles to go, and a broken heart to mend."

Why, we asked Thomson at the time of his award, is there a tradition of such excellent, powerful editorial writing in the South? Here's what he said:

> Melville once wrote, "To produce a mighty book, you must choose a mighty theme." And here in the South, we've had mighty themes of racial injustice, poverty, popular revolt. So we have a lot of material to work with, and those experiences create a lot of passion in Southern writers.
>
> Sometimes, events have presented themselves in such a way that no reasonable or compassionate writer could turn away. For example, in 1956, Buford Boone was confronted with mobs

running wild in the street here in Tuscaloosa over the attempted integration of the university [of Alabama].

And he courageously faced down the mob through his newspaper and appealed to the common decency of his fellow citizens. He didn't ask for that assignment, but when the great moment of truth came, he was ready.

So was Bailey Thomson.

Dixie's Broken Heart: The Two Alabamas

MOBILE (ALA.) REGISTER • OCTOBER 11, 1998

Along U.S. 11 in Tuscaloosa County, which parallels Interstate 59, you pass the back door of Alabama's new Mercedes-Benz plant. Rising Oz-like in the distance, its white buildings shimmer through the native pines, suggesting the wizardry and wealth of Alabama's high-tech dreams.

Go east for another mile or so, and you'll see what appears to be a down-at-the-heels trailer park. Families sometimes stop there to inquire about renting. What they find, however, is Vance Elementary School. You can't see the original building from the road because 17 portable classrooms surround it.

Crowding at the school may grow worse. A Los Angeles company plans to develop a real mobile home park nearby that will attract 550 households. The prospect frightens local people—and for good reason. The county has no zoning laws to manage such growth. It can't even levy sufficient taxes and fees to pay for schools, roads and other services that newcomers will need. Still, Principal David Thompson says Vance Elementary will find a way to teach these new kids, even if he has to put them in closets.

Naturally, people who promote Alabama's image would rather have visitors approach Mercedes' front door. Five years ago, the state committed more than $250 million to attract the plant, which caused the company's losing suitors to complain that incentives had gotten out of hand. But since then, Mercedes has exceeded even its own expectations. The plant employs 1,600 people, and recently it underwent a $40 million expansion. Another 1,300 people work in satellite factories that supply the assembly line.

Alabamians can be proud because Mercedes reflects a shining moment when leadership propelled our state to the front of the class. Alabama outbid its rivals, and the gamble is paying off. Equally important, Mercedes has brought something we Alabamians rarely demand of our institutions: excellence.

This success, however, has a short reach. Just outside of the plant's fence, in the community around Vance Elementary, many people can't qualify for those high-paying jobs. They lack skills that the German automaker requires. Instead, they drive trucks, clerk in stores, mine coal or find other work they can do.

Along U.S. 11, within a few square miles of Mercedes' gleaming edifice, is a microcosm of Alabama. In one direction, you see the reward for decisive action and vision, as Alabama workers produce some of the world's finest vehicles. In the other direction, you encounter people struggling to get by, with little hope for good jobs. You see a school suffering from neglect and crowding, and a local government unable to manage costly sprawl.

What you see is a story of two Alabamas—one pegged to a promising future, the other trapped in the weary past.

Our Predicament

On the eve of this century's final gubernatorial election, Alabamians deserve the full story of the state's condition. We may prefer to think of Alabama as purring ahead like one of those Mercedes marvels our workers build. But too much of our state sputters along like an old pickup truck, held together with baling wire.

The gubernatorial candidates illustrate our predicament:

Fob James, the Republican incumbent, has no plan for Alabama. Worse, he doesn't see the need for one. He prefers to deal in symbols rather than solutions. He wraps himself in the Ten Commandments, vowing to protect them. But when he was asked by a reporter to summarize those biblical rules, he couldn't do it.

Mr. James brags about the frugality of his administration. Yet during his term, Alabama has borrowed nearly $1 billion, sloshing more red ink onto the account books than during any recent four-year period.

When a study showed that Alabama had the nation's lowest—and probably most regressive—taxes, our governor whooped with satisfaction. But is it a bargain to tax giant timber companies only about $1 an acre, while saddling working people with sales taxes of 8 percent or 9 percent, even on their groceries?

Meanwhile, thousands of children start school hopelessly behind because Alabama under Mr. James squanders some of the best learning years by refusing to help more poor families secure good child care. Many more children leave school poorly prepared because Alabama has not embraced serious education reform. Such failures, when compounded over decades, help explain why our state's prisons bulge at 169 percent of capacity.

So much for the Republican hope. What about the Democratic nominee?

True, Lt. Gov. Don Siegelman occasionally talks and acts as if he might become Alabama's first New South leader. He is even willing to copy other successful governors. Unfortunately, he has picked a questionable idea as his centerpiece.

Mr. Siegelman's pitch is to impose a voluntary tax on our most vulnerable citizens through a state lottery, which would pay for college scholarships. Polls tell him that most Alabamians think a lottery is a good idea, although Baptists, among other religious groups, condemn the practice—at least publicly.

Where was Mr. Siegelman, however, during the last four years, when as the powerful president of the state Senate he could have spoken forcefully about Alabama's condition? Why was he not more vociferous in advocating fairer taxes, dramatic school reform and sound growth management?

The answer, of course, is that Mr. Siegelman wasn't about to sacrifice any of his political capital by acting like a statesman. He exemplifies the politician who works hard to win an office but then can't think of much useful to do with it.

Ideas Beckon

Good ideas are out there. Our politicians just aren't willing yet to seize them, either because they live in the past, as does Mr. James, or they fear the consequences of sounding too bold and visionary, as may be the case with Mr. Siegelman.

These good ideas beckon at a time when the South is "all shook up," according to a new report by a think tank in North Carolina. No longer the nation's problem child, the region is an emerging powerhouse, where one out of three Americans now lives. Immigration from places like Latin America and Asia is changing the face of the South, while expanding industries are closing the wage gap with the rest of the nation.

At the geographic center of this vibrant region lies Alabama, which for a long time has claimed to be the "Heart of Dixie." But our state provides no successful model for this emerging New South. Indeed, this generation of Alabamians has failed even to elect a governor worthy of regional respect.

Rather than the "Heart of Dixie," Alabama represents Dixie's broken heart. Instead of pride and satisfaction, our state flag evokes an overwhelming sadness and regret that we Alabamians have not been the wise stewards of our inheritance. Certainly, we have failed to invest sufficiently in our greatest resource—our people.

Over the next several days, you will read in this space about some of our neighbors' good ideas. This perspective arises from weeks of travel in those states and close observation of their progress. Dozens of interviews and stacks of documents support the conclusion that Alabama has fallen dangerously behind in its thinking, leadership and results.

If our politicians fear to address matters that are critical to our future, then citizens must force the debate themselves. Later in this series, we will look at how Alabama can rejuvenate its civic culture so that democratic deliberation can replace the selfish rule of special interests and the empty posturing of demagogues.

For now, however, our state remains caught between competing versions of itself, a condition so evident along that stretch of U.S. 11 in Tuscaloosa County. Just beyond the trees glimmers the new Alabama that we would like to show the world. It represents our best thinking, our boldest leadership. But around us lies the other Alabama—the one with crumbling schools, unskilled workers, weak local governments and hurting children. It is that Alabama that haunts this election.

We have coaxed our old pickup about as far as it can take us. Bring on the ideas.

⟿ CYNTHIA TUCKER ⟿

Cynthia Tucker holds what has historically been one of the most influential jobs in American journalism, that of editorial page editor of *The Atlanta Constitution*. She walks proudly in the footsteps of her predecessors, such as Ralph McGill and Gene Patterson, editorialists known for their courageous and independent opinions on civil rights. McGill and Patterson were both white men, writing to change the minds of other white Southerners. Tucker is an African-American woman, the embodiment of one expression of racial progress in the South. As her work shows here, she is as tough on Atlanta's black political establishment today as McGill and Patterson were on the white demagogues of the 1950s and 1960s.

In her prizewinning column "Kings Defend Rogue Who Sullied Famed Name," Tucker puts her moral courage and her writing skills on display. Readers will appreciate the toughness of her language and her persuasive use of evidence to build a case that few others would try.

In her capacity as editorial page editor, Tucker guides the development of *The Atlanta Constitution*'s opinions on everything from foreign policy to gun control to local school board races. She also has considerable reporting experience, covering local governments, national politics, crime and education. She has filed dispatches from Africa and Central America.

Tucker graduated from Auburn University in 1976 and was a Nieman Fellow at Harvard University during the 1988–89 academic year. She is a member of the National Association of Black Journalists and the American Society of Newspaper Editors. She is a frequent commentator on CNN and on PBS *NewsHour with Jim Lehrer*.

Born in Monroeville, Ala., a town famous for its writers, Tucker has developed a distinctive editorial voice that allows her to cover a range of issues. That voice includes the ability to be serious and humorous, theoretical and practical, tough and gentle—sometimes in the same piece.

"Sometimes," Tucker said, "I just want to remind my readers that I'm a woman who grew up in a small town in the South. I have many things in common with them, even if our politics are different. And so there are times when I'm searching not just for that subject matter but for that voice that communicates with readers in a slightly different way."

Kings Defend Rogue Who Sullied Famed Name

THE ATLANTA CONSTITUTION • SEPTEMBER 22, 1999

Sometimes the price of loyalty is just too high. Sometimes, when you attempt to pull a worthless friend out of the hole he's dug for himself, you end up covered in mud, too.

Such was the case last week, when Coretta Scott King used her name and prestige in an apparent effort to persuade a jury to go soft on a scoundrel named Ralph David Abernathy III, the son of Martin Luther King Jr.'s close friend, civil rights leader Ralph David Abernathy Sr. For her trouble, Mrs. King and her entourage are now being investigated by the Georgia Bureau of Investigation for alleged jury-tampering.

Abernathy III capped an ignominious career as a state senator with an indictment on charges of stealing $13,000 from his state-funded expense account. Last week, his trial on those charges ended in a hung jury. While jurors say Mrs. King did not influence them, she has nevertheless sullied her name, giving the impression that she supports rogues and miscreants.

The prosecution seemed to have solid evidence on some of the charges, including a taped conversation in which Abernathy admitted to his PR adviser, Zee Bradford, that he forged her name on expense vouchers and never gave her the money he received. He begged and badgered her to lie, telling her, "Let me tell you this, if you don't lie, it will be your reputation."

For those who've followed Abernathy's high-profile flameout, the theft charges came as no great surprise. His previous career low-lights included smuggling marijuana into the country in his underwear on a return trip from Jamaica; wandering into a women's restroom in a state building but failing to wander promptly back out; and insulting police officers who pulled him over for driving 60 mph in a 30 mph school zone.

Even when he wasn't in trouble with the law, Abernathy was less than impressive as a legislator. His six-year tenure was characterized by laziness, absenteeism, headline-grabbing and attempts to get by on his father's good name. His legislative career was finally ended, mercifully, last year, when he bounced the check he submitted to pay a qualifying fee to run for re-election.

Mrs. King has undoubtedly kept up with Abernathy's troubles. Over the years, despite occasional tensions, the Abernathys and Kings have remained friendly. And, when Abernathy was indicted, Mrs. King may have thought of her own two sons and their struggles to come to manhood in the shadow of their father's famous name. Neither Martin Luther King III nor Dexter Scott King has ever been indicted, but both have tainted their father's legacy with their endless profiteering.

So, last Wednesday found Mrs. King in a hallway outside the Fulton County courtroom where Abernathy was being tried, praying with a group that included the defendant's mother, Juanita Abernathy, state Rep. Tyrone Brooks, New York activist Al Sharpton and Mrs. King's two sons. As the jury prepared to leave the courtroom for lunch, a sheriff's deputy asked the King entourage to leave the area. They ignored him, the deputy said.

When a deputy took the jury out through a different exit, the King entourage followed and barged through the group of jurors. While Mrs. Abernathy claimed it was "an accident," it looked like an attempt to impress upon the jurors the fact that Abernathy III had the support of the King family.

Mrs. King should have left Abernathy III—who will probably be retried—to face the consequences of his reprehensible conduct. Instead, she lent him her reputation in an effort to help him salvage his family name. It's unlikely that Abernathy III appreciates her sacrifice, since he clearly cared so little for the family name himself.

～ ANDREW H. MALCOLM ～

Andrew Malcolm brought a lifetime of experience and excellence to the job when John Carroll, editor of the *Los Angeles Times*, hired him "to write whatever you want to write, as long as I would never expect to see it on the editorial pages." A longtime reporter, feature writer and foreign correspondent for *The New York Times* (he estimates his story count there at 12,000), author and press aide to a Montana governor and Laura Bush, Malcolm combines a legendary eye for detail and life's absurdities with a love of language's many delights.

Those passions translate into writing "feature editorials that don't look like editorials," as Malcolm describes the work that won him the 2003 editorial writing award from the American Society of Newspaper

Editors. "One of the great values of growing up," he says, "is that you don't get lectures from Dad anymore." Malcolm's editorials are devoid of the form's pedantic traditions. "I've never wanted to be in the business of telling people what they ought to think. Now I might try to lead them there through the writing, but everyone should feel that they came to the conclusion themselves."

His vehicle for persuasion is the editorial as story instead of sermon, a product developed through interviews as well as reflection and analysis. It often begins with a search for a person whose story can bring an issue or development to life with judicious use of the tiniest details, such as a goateed professor who started out as the son of a West Virginia typewriter repairman, memorialized in the editorial reprinted here. Malcolm's playful language and unconventional approach also move his tribute to the column's subject beyond the realm of the obituary page, making it an exemplar of persuasive writing.

Malcolm lives by what he calls "the lingerie theory" of communication: Less is more. A graduate of Northwestern's Medill School of Journalism, he spent part of his youth at a military academy and brings a cadet's discipline to the editorial's limitations. His words, rarely more than 500 at a time, are chosen carefully, with a focus on those that do the work of two or three. "A Thesaurist Leaves, Exits" displays his penchant for brightening even bad news with a whimsical approach. Journalism has been described as the challenge of squeezing "a beer keg's worth of information into a perfume bottle." Malcolm's ability to do just that here (in just 345 words) may be one of the purest illustrations of Shakespeare's observation, in *Hamlet*, that "brevity is the soul of wit."

A Thesaurist Leaves, Exits

Los Angeles Times • March 3, 2002

Regrettably, unfortunately, lamentably and mournfully, Robert L. Chapman is deceased, demised, departed and dead at 81. The son, boy and male offspring of a West Virginia typewriter mechanic, Chapman once drove trucks, then studied poetry and medieval literature before editing the timeworn, antiquated, irreplaceable Roget's International Thesaurus.

He transformed, altered and caused the transmutation of the stuffy, dull, ill-ventilated compendium of synonyms and antonyms into a hip, cool, with-it collection of words and associations, not only piquing the intellects of language lovers but saving the behinds, fannys and GPAs of countless late-night collegiate essay writers (see also Indolent, Slothful, Procrastinating). With their new shoes, underwear and a Webster's, college-bound juveniles have long packed a Roget's, hoping to sound more educated while getting there.

Before (Slang) cashing in his chips and giving up the ghost, Chapman quietly shaped the way we speak and think of words and idioms as tools to effectively communicate to each other the multi-toned richness of the human experience (see Feeling, Knowledge). You know how people in 19th century photographs posed as if nailed to boards and never smiled? Today's photographers encourage relaxed and open. Same difference for thesaurus editors.

A doctor and Londoner despite his French name, Peter M. Roget produced in 1852 more than a mere alphabetical listing of similar and dissimilar words. He also created categories such as Kindness, Benevolence to suggest enlightening linguistic links likely to be missed by word seekers. The goateed Chapman was engagingly subversive in his academically rooted but pragmatic, populist approach to chronicling and improving how English speakers speak and write. His computers also tracked word usage to update and expand categories and words for new times, inserting AIDS, Scud, hacker, fax, ecosystem, even new dog breeds and slang and modern phobias (i.e. Fear of Flying, not prominent in 1850). Roget's perusers find themselves wandering the distinctive wordways of Chapman's lexicon, encountering new meanings, associations and phrasings through serendipity, an increasingly rare modern commodity and a delicious entry that needs no synonym. As things eventuated, credit goes to Robert Chapman, who has no synonym.

⟿ LEONARD PITTS ⟿

At 18, Leonard Pitts fulfilled his boyhood dream of being a writer when he sold a piece to *Soul* magazine. Pitts, who grew up in Los Angeles, entered the University of Southern California at 15, graduated with honors four years later and spent a decade as a writer and editor for music publications and radio stations, including a gig as a writer for *Casey's Top 40 with Casey Kasem*. In 1991, he became a music critic for *The Miami Herald*, which gave him the opportunity to write outside his beat and ultimately earn his own twice-weekly column.

Pitts' early career was a fitting training ground for the award-winning syndicated column he would eventually write. If there's music to be found in a newspaper, its rhythms and melodies usually resound in the column, a destination for opinion presented with literary grace. Pitts tries to touch readers' hearts as well as their heads. "You need to get them in both places, I think, if you're really going to move them at the most profound level," he says. He does so by blending history, logic and wisdom in columns that rise and fall like a satisfying piece of music or a powerful sermon. A column on South Carolina's decision to keep the Confederate flag flying over the state capitol ends with two phrases that indelibly echo—and reject—the Dixie anthem behind the controversial emblem: "Look away, look away."

Columnists traditionally challenge the acts and beliefs of others. Pitts is not afraid to examine and reassess his own deeply held beliefs to "achieve some sort of moral and logical consistency," as he does in "Second Thoughts Following New York Verdict." Writing about race relations with honesty, he makes it possible for readers, black and white, to look closely at what they believe. He shuns the "voice of Black America" label often foisted upon columnists of color. "I'm just a guy spewing in the newspaper," he says, "trying to figure out what to say twice a week and trying to make sure that he doesn't bore himself in the process."

To achieve that goal, he polishes his prose relentlessly, often reading a column 20 times before hitting the send button. The results are columns that focus not just on race but also on family and social issues. His incisive commentary provokes readers, whatever their own opinions, to rethink those beliefs. In 2004, four years after winning the ASNE award for commentary/column writing, Pitts received the Pulitzer Prize for commentary.

We chose Leonard Pitts' column for this chapter's X-Ray Reading because of the way his honesty, both intellectual and emotional, contributes to its persuasive power. The best writers often draw their greatest strength from acknowledging their ambivalences and then shoring up their arguments with the best evidence they have at their disposal. The result: a frank conversation about conflicting ideas rather than a one-sided debate.

Second Thoughts Following New York Verdict

THE MIAMI HERALD • MARCH 2, 2000

Leading with a quote is unusual but emphasizes and bolsters theme

". . . [A] wallet in the hand of a white man looks like a wallet, but a wallet in the hand of a black man looks like a gun."
—Bill Bradley

Indirect lead requires reader to solve the mystery

I was ready to jump to conclusion. Then four black women got in the way.

Meaning the four who sat on the Albany, N.Y., jury that last week acquitted four white cops in the shooting death of an unarmed African immigrant.

Right to the point: subject is a recent news event

Author acknowledges that readers know the story, yet he still summarizes it

By now, you know the story. How New York City police officers encountered Amadou Diallo standing in front of his apartment building early last year. How he went into his pocket for something. How somebody yelled, "Gun!"

Sentence fragments and concrete details used for economy and speed

How they shot him. And then shot him some more. Forty-one rounds fired over eight seconds, 19 of them finding their mark.

Then the awful discovery: the "gun" was only a wallet.

Echoes quote at top of column

The thing seemed cut and dried to me. Which is why the jury's verdict was . . . impossible. Not guilty of murder, not guilty of manslaughter, not even guilty of criminal negligence? Now New York City is steaming, the kettle of racial acrimony threatening to boil. And I'd be ready to boil right along with them, except . . .

Ellipses signal trailing off

Imagery and metaphor build outrage

Except for the inconvenient fact of those four women.

Author lures readers on

I find myself caught between—not able to believe, not able to dismiss. And I'm forced to confess that they are the only reason I'm willing to cut the justice system even that sliver of slack.

Repetition and alliteration used to reveal conflict

(CONTINUED)

161

Reasoning defended with rhetorical questions

Columnist's freedom: using an unnamed source to strengthen argument

Writer considers the problem: racism in the criminal justice system

Cites evidence using the "rule of three" to support argument and provide symmetry

Author acknowledges hole in his argument

Conditional reasoning: author's conclusion based on an implication

Argument framed as three (again) almost-rhetorical questions

It's a painful admission. It's also an unavoidable one. How many times has an encounter with a white lawman resulted in the unjustifiable injury or death of an innocent African-American woman or man? And how many times has an all-white jury justified it anyway?

So it makes a difference—it shouldn't, but it does—that four of the jurors who vouched for the legal blamelessness of these cops are black. Granted, blackness is no more a character reference than whiteness is a character defect. But you're more willing to listen—a friend says she had to think twice—because of the race of those women.

It's a sad truth that speaks volumes about the reputation cops and courts have earned in minority communities. If trust is the currency of justice, then the justice system is bankrupt in those neighborhoods.

Fact is, black folks know a different system than their white countrymen do. Think Rodney King, smashed to a pulp by Los Angeles police while the nation stood witness. An all-white jury set those officers free. And then there's O.J. Simpson, whose defense team drew laughter with the suggestion that Los Angeles cops might plant evidence or frame suspects. Over 20 L.A. cops have recently been fired or disciplined for planting evidence and framing suspects.

Understand those things and you'll understand why blacks have no trouble believing cops could willfully execute a man in the vestibule of his own building. Or why they would distrust a jury that said otherwise.

Here's the question: If Amadou Diallo was white, would he still be alive? Would some jittery cop have been so quick to see a gun where there was none? Would they have been so filled with fear that they'd fire 41 times—*41 times!*—to bring him down?

We cannot, of course, ever know for sure. And I'm not at all convinced the conclusion I

"Jump" echoes lead

was ready to jump to is not in fact the correct one. Yet at the same time, I'm troubled by the realization that we as African-American people jump by reflex now. That experience has taught us this is the wise thing to do.

I feel sorry for those women, having to bear the weight of expectation. I don't like having to trust more in the fact of blackness than in the promise of justice.

But that's where we stand. And until courts and cops begin to work equally hard at earning the trust of all citizens, it's where we're likely to stay.

Until that moment, these episodes will continue to move with sad predictability.

White cop shoots unarmed black person. Outrage burns like fire. And we jump.

Author circles back to the four women

Contrast drives home dissatisfaction with the choices

Sets up an inevitable and dispiriting scenario

Note the third "jump": Racial conflict affects all sides

Staccato sentences bring column full circle

Chapter 7

THE PROFILE
AND FEATURE STORY

The "human interest" story did not always exist in American news-papers. It was created, in part, to increase circulation, to appeal to readers not so interested in the inner workings of business and government. Many of these stories focused on the bizarre or scandalous, what became known as "yellow journalism." As in our own time, these newspapers were condemned for their sensationalism and for straying from their higher civic purpose.

Some feature writers offer us models of the fading art of the profile. Cynthia Gorney and Saul Pett focus on the famous. Gorney reveals Dr. Seuss in his fully human guise, a creative and quirky genius, the creature of his father's perfectionism. Saul Pett describes New York Mayor Ed Koch as a "mixed metaphor of a politician," as complex and salty as the city he represents.

Other writers demonstrate that the civic and the literary can be reconciled, that public institutions are represented by people with human flaws, that the personal can become political. Mirta Ojito offers a penetrating and personal account of changes in her native Cuba, a powerful example of feature reporting that connects international news with individual lives. Thousands of miles away, Blaine Harden takes us on a journey down an African river to reveal another culture in need of reform and revitalization.

If one goal of the feature writer is to find the human being behind the celebrity, another is to discover what is worth celebrating in the life of uncommonly common men and women. David Finkel tackles a powerful challenge—a portrait of a good man who has fallen from grace, the result of a historic accident that led to a terrible tragedy. Tommy Tomlinson spins a fascinating narrative of a mathematician's drive to solve a seemingly unsolvable problem.

Nothing is more local—or more universal—than an interest in the weather. Ken Fuson, known for writing long features and narratives, turns his craft to the task of writing a weather story. In this selection, he travels around Des Moines, Iowa, on the day winter breaks and captures the energy and joy of a city thawing out. And he does it in a single glorious sentence.

A cynical school of thought would have us believe that journalists are exploiters of their sources, that they ultimately violate their confidence for the sake of an interesting story. The writers here have a different reputation. They are known as hard workers and good listeners. They are curious, persistent, energetic and empathetic. Those virtues gain them access. They honor the privilege of access by rendering the lives of their subjects with fairness, honesty, thoroughness and courtesy.

In the modern era, the line between news and feature writing has broken down. More news stories contain scenes, anecdotes and the voices of newsmakers. And more feature stories and profiles—about AIDS, the care of children, ethics and religion—reflect powerfully upon the issues of the day.

Journalists in the new century will serve their readers best with their versatility—the ability to write long and short, about news and people, about facts and experience, for newspapers and new media. Ultimately, people want to read about people, making the feature story increasingly important whether the context is entertainment, the arts, politics, technology, public health, diversity or the family.

~ CYNTHIA GORNEY ~

Cynthia Gorney was a reporter for *The Washington Post* Style section when she won the ASNE award for feature writing in 1980. She left the paper in 1991 to work on a book, *Articles of Faith: A Frontline History of the Abortion Wars*, published in 1997. Her work also has been featured in *The New Yorker* and *The New York Times Magazine*. She now teaches journalism at the University of California at Berkeley.

Anyone who would like to reclaim the profile as a newspaper art form should read and reread Gorney's character sketch of Dr. Seuss. It is a story grounded in solid research, built on thorough reporting and expressed in a writing voice that echoes the whimsical genius of its subject.

Gorney won the ASNE award at the age of 26 for a collection of stories that was astonishingly diverse for a writer so young. In addition to the Seuss profile, she wrote about frog-jumping contests, political assassins and women suffering from a terrible illness.

Gorney's eye for detail is richly exhibited in the Seuss piece. Readers learn that Seuss had a dog that he might have drawn, that *There's a Wocket in My Pocket* translates to *Ik heb een Gak in Myn Zak* in the Netherlands, that Seuss kept his father's rifle target on the wall as a spur toward perfection.

Detail, observation, telling anecdote, revealing quotation, testimony of friends and family, biography, history, reading and research — these are the building blocks with which Gorney constructs her celebration of Seuss's life and work.

Gorney worked this magic with the help of her editor, a relationship that could serve as a model for all writers and editors. She says, "What makes an editor great is support. I don't know a writer who isn't insecure. An editor has to say, 'We think you're wonderful; we know you can do wonderful work,' even when your work is terrible."

And when a story needed more work, her editor would not seize control of it. Instead, he turned it back to Gorney for revision: "A great editor will make you feel like a real trouper," she says, "a truly talented person for being able to fix a story, for being able to send something in that's flawed and then make it better."

How did such a young writer develop such skill and sensitivity? "You have to read a lot," she says. "And when you find a writer you love, you read everything you can get your hands on by that writer."

And this, for Gorney, is the essence of feature writing: "You have to be passionately interested in everything. You have to want to learn about frogs or cancer or assassins, everything there is to know. You have to know five times as much as you're ever going to use in the story."

Dr. Seuss: Wild Orchestrator of Plausible Nonsense for Kids

THE WASHINGTON POST • MAY 21, 1979

LA JOLLA, CALIF.—One afternoon in 1957, as he bent over the big drawing board in his California studio, Theodor Seuss Geisel found himself drawing a turtle.

He was not sure why.

He drew another turtle and saw that it was underneath the first turtle, holding him up.

He drew another, and another, until he had an enormous pileup of turtles, each standing on the back of the turtle below it and hanging its turtle head, looking pained.

Geisel looked at his turtle pile. He asked himself, not unreasonably, What does this mean? Who is the turtle on top?

Then he understood that the turtle on top was Adolf Hitler.

"I couldn't draw Hitler as a turtle," Geisel says, now hunched over the same drawing board, making pencil scribbles of the original Yertle the Turtle drawings as he remembers them. "So I drew him as King What-ever-his-name-was, King" (scribble) "of the Pond" (scribble). "He wanted to be king as far as he could see. So he kept piling them up. He conquered Central Europe and France, and there it was."

(Scribble.)

"Then I had this great pileup, and I said, 'How do you get rid of this impostor?'

"Believe it or not, I said, 'The voice of the people.' I said, 'Well, I'll just simply have the guy on the bottom burp.'"

Geisel looks up from his drawing board and smiles—just a little, because a man is taking his picture and he has never gotten used to people who want to take his picture.

Dr. Seuss, American institution, wild orchestrator of plausible nonsense, booster of things that matter (like fair play, kindness,

Drum-Tummied Snumms, Hooded Koopfers, and infinite winding spools of birthday hot dogs), detractor of things that don't (like bullying, snobbery, condescension, gravity and walls), is 75 years old this year.

As usual, he is somewhat embarrassed by all the fuss.

"It's getting awful," Geisel says, "because I meet old, old people, who can scarcely walk, and they say, 'I was brought up on your books.' It's an awful shock."

There is probably not a single children's book author in America who has matched the impact, popularity and international fame of the spare, bearded California prodigy who signs his books Dr. Seuss.

Since 1936, when Ted Geisel the advertising illustrator first wrote *And to Think That I Saw It on Mulberry Street,* his books have sold 80 million copies in this country alone.

Mulberry Street was an effort, he explained later, to expel from his brain the maddening rhythm of a ship engine he had heard during the whole of a transatlantic voyage (da da Da da da Da da da Da da da da).

The late Bennett Cerf—at a time when his Random House writers included William Faulkner and John O'Hara—is on record as having called Geisel the only genius of the lot.

The drawings, manuscripts, and half-formed doodles of Dr. Seuss (who did not officially become a doctor until 1956, when Dartmouth College made him an honorary Doctor of Humane Letters), are kept in locked stacks of the Special Collections division of the UCLA library. He won two Academy Awards for his World War II era documentary film and one for the cartoon "Gerald McBoing-Boing," which he created. His books are published in about 45 countries outside the United States, including Brazil, Japan, the entire British Commonwealth and the Netherlands, where *There's a Wocket in My Pocket* translates to *Ik heb een Gak in Myn Zak!*

On his last visit to Australia, his plane was met by reporters, television cameras, person-sized Cats in Hats, small children with "I love you, Dr. Seuss" badges, and a newspaper headline that read "Dr. Seuss Is Here." An official in the Afghan embassy sent him a collection of brilliant blue sculpted animals with mysterious shapes and corkscrew necks, all made according to traditional design in a tiny Afghanistan town whose name Geisel could never pronounce, but which he says has been unofficially renamed Seussville. "Somebody discovered they were stealing my stuff 3,000 years ago," Geisel says, gazing down admiringly at a small sort of yak. "They're pretty good Seuss, though."

Geisel has lived for 30 years in La Jolla, which is a coastal town just north of San Diego that has developed a flowery, almost Caribbean sparkle as the wealthy build homes up the side of the mountain. At the very top of one of the mountains, with the diminishing acres of wild land to the east and to the west the wide blue curve of the Pacific, Geisel and his wife Audrey share an old stucco observatory tower and the elegant, helter-skelter maze of rooms they have built around it. "It just grew," Audrey Geisel said, "Seuss-like."

They have a swimming pool, a small Yorkshire terrier whose front end is indistinguishable from the back at first glance ("I've been accused of having drawn him," Geisel says), and a gray Cadillac Seville with GRINCH license plates — which took them several years to obtain, because when they first applied they learned that an ardent Seuss-lover with four children had already put GRINCH on the license plates and both sides of his RV. He finally moved to Iowa City and released GRINCH back to the Geisels, with a note of apology for having hogged it so long.

San Diego children know Dr. Seuss lives in a white castle on the hill, and on occasion they will pack up peanut butter and jelly sandwiches and set out for the summit, seeking an audience. Mrs. Geisel has come to expect this. "Breathing on the intercom," she calls it. Geisel has no children of his own (Mrs. Geisel, whom he married 12 years ago after the death of his first wife, has two from a previous marriage), and although he is almost always polite to his callers, the sheer numbers of intercom breathers sometimes overwhelm him.

He cannot answer all his letters, either, because they come every month by the hundreds to his home and the Random House offices in New York — love letters, valentines, air letters from India and New Zealand, photographs of cakes decorated with Hippoheimers or Loraxes, various homemade varieties of Oobleck, the nasty green slime that rains on Bartholomew Cubbins; and in one dismaying delivery, Geisel says, a carefully wrapped package of green eggs and ham.

"These days I spend my birthday in Las Vegas," Geisel says, with unconvincing grumpiness. "Nobody will look for a children's book author in Las Vegas."

He is a private, engaging, intensely driven man, with a lean and sharp-nosed look that gives him an air of severity at first. His house is scattered with his own paintings and busts of creatures unlike anything anybody ever saw before, and as he leads visitors through the halls he makes congenial introductions, as though presenting boarders: "This is a green cat in the Uleaborg, Finland subway . . . this is a cat who was born on the wrong side of town . . . this is my religious period. This is Archbishop Katz . . . this is called, 'Good god, do I look as old as all that?' "

He will not wear conventional neckties—only bow ties. He reads paperback books—history, biography, detective novels—so voraciously that his wife makes regular bookstore runs (often to a certain store that saves new books for him in a special Geisel cubbyhole) and then stashes the paperbacks away so she can hand him new ones in the evening, one at a time. He reads for distraction. He needs it. When he is at work, the names, the verse, the story line, the colors, the shapes and sizes of his extraordinary characters all press upon him. He tapes the working drawings to the wall and stares at them, rearranging, reading aloud to himself, feeling the rhythm of the words.

In his new book, a volume of tongue twisters coming out in the fall, Geisel has drawn a green parrot. He has studied all the colors on the Random House art department printing chart—his usual procedure— looking for the printer's ink shade that most closely matches his working drawings in colored pencil. There are 60 different shades of green on the chart, and Geisel cannot find the right one. This one is too yellow, that one too red. He does not explain to the art department why each green is wrong—just not parrotty enough, or something.

They know better than to ask. They will have the printer make up the precise shade of green.

"His color sense," says Grace Clarke, executive art director of the Random House junior books division, "is the most sophisticated I've ever run into." Geisel had to completely relearn color during the last two years, after undergoing an operation for removal of a cataract. The right saw brilliant color, following the operation: "the other eye, which still has a small cataract, sees everything like Whistler's Mother." The second cataract is to be removed next year, after which, says Geisel, deadpanned, "They claim I'll be as good as Picasso."

Geisel does not read children's literature, unless he is editing it, which is part of his job as the founder and head of the special early readers' Random House Division called Beginner Books. Then he is fierce in his judgment, dismissing instantly the noxious breed of children's books that coo and mince and pat little heads.

"Bunny-bunny books," he calls them. "Sugar plums, treacle, whimsy." He once turned down a manuscript from Truman Capote. (Diplomatically, neither Geisel nor the Random House people remember what it was about.) "I try to treat the child as an equal,"

Geisel has said, "and go on the assumption that a child can understand anything that is read to him if the writer takes care to state it clearly and simply enough."

There is a vast difference, of course, between respectful simplicity and invention, and Geisel is as mystified about that as anybody—about what makes one man dull a ship engine's throb with aspirin, or neat whiskey, while another hears the beginnings of an imaginary backstreet elephant-and-giraffe parade. Geisel never set out to be a children's book writer. He was born in Springfield, Mass., the son of a German immigrant who had been, at various times, a brewer, a park superintendent, and a world champion rifle shot. Ted Geisel grew up in Springfield, graduated from Dartmouth, and spent a year at Oxford, during which time he is reported to have proposed (unsuccessfully) a new edition of *Paradise Lost*, which would include such illustrations as the Archangel Uriel sliding down a sunbeam with an oil can to lubricate his trip.

He lived in New York, selling drawings, stories and political cartoons to magazines of the day—*Judge*, *Vanity Fair*, the *Saturday Evening Post*—and for 15 years he worked in advertising for Standard Oil of New Jersey.

He drew insecticide ads, "Quick, Henry! The Flit!" That was Geisel's creation.

He illustrated two volumes of jokes, tried unsuccessfully to sell an alphabet book, and then in 1936 laid out the wonderfully paced mad fantasy of the boy named Marco in *And to Think That I Saw It on Mulberry Street*. Before a publishing friend of Geisel's took the book in at Vanguard Press, 20 publishers turned it down.

He had an easier time with the next one. "I was sitting in a railroad train, going up somewhere in Connecticut," Geisel says. "And there was a fellow sitting ahead of me, who I didn't like. I didn't know who he was. He had a real ridiculous Wall Street broker's hat on, very stuffy, on this commuting train. And I just began playing around with the idea of what his reaction would be if I took his hat off and threw it out the window."

Geisel smiles a small, slightly evil smile.

"And I said, 'He'd probably just grow another one and ignore me.'"

Which gave us *The 500 Hats of Bartholomew Cubbins*. Boy, confronted in castle by snooty royalty, cannot doff his hat because new hats keep appearing to replace it.

"In those days 90 percent of the stuff that was written was literary fairy tales," Geisel says. "I began to think of appurtenances around the castle, and one of them would be a bowman, and then it occurred to me there would also be an executioner. And I said, 'We gotta get a little bastard of a crowned prince in here.' And I would draw and semi-write that sequence up. Then I would put it on the wall and see how they fit. I'm not a consecutive writer."

Once in a while there is an echo of something like anguish in Geisel's accounts of the workings of his own imagination—some constant, furious homage to the 1902 rifle target, its bull's-eye perforated by his father's exacting shots, that Geisel keeps mounted on the wall.

"To remind me of perfection," he says.

He will sometimes work late into the night, or break off into an entirely different project, when some flaw in a book begins to gnaw at him. He spent a full year struggling over the smallish gopher-like creature called the Lorax. "Once he was mechanized. That didn't work. He was big at one point. I did the obvious thing of making him green, shrinking him, growing him."

And then? "I looked at him, and he looked like a Lorax."

But he was equally stumped by the story itself, a dismal tale about the Once-ler, who hacks down all the Truffula Trees to mass-produce Thneeds, thereby driving away the Swomee-Swans, starving out the Brown Bar-ba-loots, and—as the wheezing, outraged Lorax cries—"lumping the pond where the Humming-fish hummed." It was the angriest story Geisel had ever written, and he could not figure out how to make sense of it, how to keep it from turning into a lecture—"a preachment," as Geisel says. Geisel has a horror of preachments. Audrey Geisel, who quite rightly believes that the best way to come unstuck is to stand on your head and try looking at things that way, suggested they go to Africa for a while, which they did.

"I hadn't thought of the Lorax for three weeks," Geisel says. "And a herd of elephants came across the hill—about a half mile away—one of those lucky things, that never happened since. And I picked up a laundry pad and wrote the whole book that afternoon on a laundry pad." The final version of *The Lorax* still begins in its ominous, haunting way:

> *At the far end of town*
> *Where the Grickle-grass grows*
> *And the wind smells*
> *slow-and-sour when it blows.*
> *And no birds ever sing excepting*

> *old crows.*
> *Is the street of the Lifted Lorax.*

But it ends with some hope. One Truffula Tree seed makes it through. And that, for Geisel, redeems the preachment. Happy endings, he has said, are vital: "A child identifies with the hero, and it is a personal tragedy to him when things don't come out all right."

Geisel, in an early fit of misguided inspiration, once wrote a book for adults. "My greatest failure," he says, pulling a rare copy off the bookshelf. "This is a book that nobody bought."

Its thesis is that there were in fact seven Lady Godivas (Gussie, Hedwig, Lulu, Teenie, Mitzi, Arabella, and Doreas J.), each of them engaged to one of the seven Peeping Brothers. In order to avenge the unfortunate death of their father, who was tossed by an arrogant horse en route to the Battle of Hastings, the Ladies Godiva set out to discover Horse Truths (don't look a gift horse in the mouth, and so on) while displaying limited but alluring portions of their anatomies.

"I don't think I drew proper naked ladies," Geisel says sadly. "I think their ankles came out wrong, and things like that." The book was published in 1937, priced steeply during the depression at $2 a copy, and less than a quarter of the 10,000 sold. They now go for $100 to $200. Geisel has a private fantasy about making the Godivas into an animated film, but he is not certain about how to present nudity — the ankles, and things like that.

But the bulk of Geisel's audience will always be children. "Writing for adults doesn't really interest me anymore," he said. "I think I've found the form in writing for kids, with which I can say everything I have to say a little more distinctly than if I had to put it in adult prose."

He pulls from a file some typewritten pages from his new book. "You want to try reading one?" Geisel asks.

His visitor, reading slowly, makes a stab at it:

> *One year we had a Christmas brunch*
> *With Merry Christmas Mush to munch.*
> *But I don't think you'd care for such*
> *We didn't like to munch mush much.*

There is a rather bad moment of tongue-twisting at the end and Geisel looks delighted. "These things are written way over the ability of first-grade kids, and I think it's going to work," he said. "They're stinkers (the tongue-twisters, not the children).

"I think one reason kids are not reading up to their potential is a lack of being urged—you can't urge them with a big stick, but you can urge them with competition."

Well now, demands his visitor, Geisel has to read one.

"Not wearing the right glasses," Geisel says quickly. "I can't."

～ SAUL PETT ～

The late Saul Pett was a special correspondent for the Associated Press when he won the ASNE award for non-deadline writing in 1981. He also won a Pulitzer Prize for feature writing.

One of America's great newspaper writers, Pett never met a good story—especially one told in a saloon—that he didn't love. Pett often talked about taking notes "on a cocktail napkin." He also bragged that, after a satisfying interview, "I never go to the office immediately. My goodness. I stop at a bar and tell myself what a grand interviewer I am."

No reader should be fooled by such generational bravado. Pett, like the New York mayor he describes, was a "mixed metaphor" of a writer, a journalistic oxymoron, a poet who worked for a wire service. When big-shot editors declared a preference for short, straightforward leads, Pett served up long, winding ones. "I once set a course record," he said, "by writing a lead that was 280 words long. It was a long sentence describing all the confusing things that had come up in a single day at a Republican convention. It ended up with the word 'clear?' Of course, it wasn't clear. But then the day's activities weren't clear. The length of sentences and all those mechanical standards are kind of silly."

In that spirit, he begins his profile of Mayor Ed Koch with a 65-word sentence, a lovely catalog of character traits, beginning with subject and verb, that has the nourishing flavor of a delicious bowl of chicken soup. What follows is a three-word fragment: "Clearly, an original." This variation of sentence length and structure characterizes Pett's style and sets the pace and rhythm for the reader.

Among journalists, Pett was a great selector. Gathering in his brain and on the page dozens of metaphors and images, he'd toss aside the so-so ones and leave readers with the gems: "He is seltzer with a lifetime fizz" or "Koch beamed like a kosher pumpkin."

Before accepting praise, Pett would say, "You don't know about the metaphors I threw away. Some of them must have been horrors."

It may be instructive to count and number the anecdotes in the story, selected from dozens more, noticing how each one advances the reader's understanding of Koch's political character. These anecdotes, woven through the profile with Koch's own words drawn from the interview, complete a compelling picture of a mayor and an era.

Koch Grabs Big Apple and Shakes It

ASSOCIATED PRESS • NOVEMBER 30, 1980

NEW YORK—He is the freshest thing to blossom in New York since chopped liver, a mixed metaphor of a politician, the antithesis of the packaged leader, irrepressible, candid, impolitic, spontaneous, funny, feisty, independent, uncowed by voter blocs, unsexy, unhandsome, unfashionable and altogether charismatic, a man oddly at peace with himself in an unpeaceful place, a mayor who presides over the country's largest Babel with unseemly joy.

Clearly, an original. Asked once what he thought his weaknesses were, Ed Koch said that for the life of him he couldn't think of any. "I like myself," he said.

The streets are still dirty. The subways are still unsafe. The specter of bankruptcy is never farther away than next year's loan. But Edward Irving Koch, who runs the place like a solicitous Jewish mother with no fear of the rich relatives, appears to be the most popular mayor of this implausible town since Fiorello LaGuardia more than a generation ago.

He is a Democrat, an excommunicated liberal, a symptom of his time, the leader of a city traditionally in the vanguard of the country's troubles.

Long before the conservative convulsion changed the face of national government this month, Ed Koch offended traditional liberals by being the mayor who says no to a variety of causes, by speaking constantly of the limits of government, by seeking to restore what he calls a balance between the rights and needs of the majority and those of the minorities, the rights of the victim and those of the accused.

But more than programs or policies, it is personality that makes this mayor special. He is seltzer with a lifetime fizz. When other Democrats were prostrated by the Reagan sweep, Ed Koch was genially philosophic.

"If God wanted us to have life tenure," he said, "he would have made all of us federal judges."

Every day of this year's 11-day transit strike, rain or shine, Koch stationed himself near the Manhattan end of the Brooklyn Bridge applauding the commuters on foot. "Thank you for being strong," he sang out. "Thank you for coming to work." The sight was so undoing that some of the reluctant hikers found themselves saying, "Oh, you're welcome. It's our pleasure."

Dedicating a new shopping mall in Brooklyn, Koch was well launched into his theme ("New York is on the way back") when one of the many blacks in the audience yelled, "We want John Lindsay."

Koch paused at this reference to the former mayor, who stood high with the blacks. "Everybody who wants Lindsay back," he said, "raise their hands." Some hands went up. Whereupon, hizzoner leaned forward like a scolding school teacher and roared, "DUMMIES!" The crowd loved it. Koch beamed like a kosher pumpkin.

Other mayors have complained about the burdens of the job, the second most difficult in the country, goes the cliché. Not this mayor. He thrives on the tumult, the contention, the push and pull and what he calls the immediacy of his constituents. No other job brings a leader so close to the people, he says, citing a piquant reason.

"If you want to picket the governor, it costs you $18 to go to Albany. If you want to picket the president, it costs you $60 to go to Washington. But if you want to picket the mayor of New York, it costs you only 60 cents, subway or bus. And believe me, they picket."

But picket legally they must or Koch throws them out. He suffers no guff, regardless of race, creed, or color. He refuses to be a punching bag for pressure groups. His bluntness is ecumenical; at one time or another he has angered whites and blacks, Jews and Gentiles, management and labor.

In 1978, his first year in office, he received a group of black ministers at City Hall. They demanded that all summer federal jobs go to non-whites. Koch said that's illegal, the program is based on poverty and "there are some poor whites, you know."

The ministers said unless Koch yielded to their demand they would sit outside his office, sing and let no one in or out. Koch said they could sing all they wanted outside of City Hall. They wouldn't leave. Koch told the nearest cop to remove them. "What if they re-sist?" asked the cop. "Have you never heard the word ARREST?" said the mayor. The ministers were arrested and Koch never again had trouble with illegal demonstrations within City Hall.

In his third month in office, Koch went to a large meeting of white, middle-class constituents at a Catholic high school in Queens, where his administration was to be put on "trial." Koch asked if he could have two minutes for opening remarks. The presiding priest said he could have one minute. Koch said in that case he was leaving, and left.

"Now, nobody walks out on 1,100 Irish and Italian Catholics in a church setting," the mayor recalled. "Somebody asked me, how can you do this? I said, you don't treat me with respect, I walk out. They've got a kangaroo court in there and I don't happen to be a kangaroo."

In 1978, some 3,000 Chassidic Jews, infuriated by the murder of an elderly member of the sect, stormed a Brooklyn police station and held it for a time. Koch expressed sympathy for the victim but deliv-ered a stern lecture to the effect that no one, but no one, has the right to seize a police station. That earned him enmity among some mem-bers of his own religion.

More recently, the mayor was asked at a discussion group in a synagogue if he could think of any great leaders in the world today. "Anwar Sadat," said Koch. The audience booed. "Oh, stop the boo-ing already, don't be ridiculous," said hizzoner, going on to extol the courage of the Egyptian president.

The mayor has outraged civil libertarians by advocating the death penalty for murder, by berating judges who impose lenient bail (in one case, the accused proved innocent), by calling for a revamping and speeding up of the criminal justice system, which lawyer Koch says, succinctly, "stinks."

His pursuit of the lawless has been known to be personal and re-lentless. In 1971, Koch, then a member of Congress, was braced by a black man in a Manhattan park and threatened with mayhem unless he gave him a quarter. ("He was 6-feet-3, and every time I tell the story he gets bigger.")

Koch refused and threatened the stranger with arrest. The man looked at Koch as if he were crazy and ran off. In the distance, Koch saw him succeed in getting coins from two other people. A block later, Koch found a police car and demanded that the cops find the menacing panhandler. The cops said that would take time. Let's take the time, Koch said, even though he was already late for a banquet of Jewish constituents.

Ultimately, in the ensuing hours, the culprit was nabbed, brought into court (where an assistant district attorney tried vainly to dissuade Koch from pursuing such a small matter), fined $50 for harassment and, claiming he was employed but broke at the moment, was given three weeks to pay.

Three weeks later, still in pursuit, Koch wrote the court clerk asking if the fine had been paid. No answer. Six weeks later, he tried again and was told the defendant had failed to pay the fine, a warrant was out for his arrest but he couldn't be found, having given a false name and address.

"I said you don't know his right name. You don't know where he lives and you issued a warrant for his arrest! Hah, hah, hah. And I realized how screwed up our court system was."

The mayor of New York is 56, a bachelor, tall, fit and quick (last year he wrestled an egg-throwing heckler to the floor before the cops could move.) His face—it must be the most unpoker face in politics today—is framed by a bald pate and wispy sideburns and seems never in repose. His voice, like his face, is never without expression. He talks in sing-song, allegro, andante, fortissimo, pianissimo, and in the crescendos of emphasis he stretches out syllables in capital letters. When he says, ONE BILL-Y-ON-DOLL-ARS, you can see the whole pile, in singles.

Like presidents, governors and other mayors around the country, Koch finds that bureaucracy is a "colossus that sits and sits and you have to push and push. The civil servants know there isn't a thing you can do about getting rid of them; they're all going to be here long after you're gone." So, he pushes.

On Jan. 20, 1978, Koch's 20th day in office, he was awakened at three in the morning by a call from the city's personnel director.

"Mr. Mayor, it's snowing."

Koch thought that was a novel way to get the news.

"So?"

"Do you want me to declare a Snow Day?"

"What does that mean?"

"A Snow Day means that when a city employee comes in to work he gets time-and-a-half. If they don't come in, they get paid anyway."

"Henceforth, in the city of New York, there will be NO more Snow Days."

The snow that day was the heaviest in 10 years. There were two more snowstorms that month. By not declaring them, the mayor's office calculates, the city saved $8.5 million. New York, which struggles along on an annual budget of $13 billion, the third largest in American government, employs 250,000 people.

On one of his walks around town, Koch was handed a note by a constituent: "The volleyball nets in Central Park are six inches too high. They're screwed up."

The mayor passed the note along to the appropriate bureaucrat with orders that, if the nets were as described, "unscrew them." After some days of cost analysis, that underling reported back that the posts holding the volleyball nets would have to be pulled up at high cost. "Why," asked the mayor "do you have to pull up the posts? Just untie the nets and lower them." Eureka! It was done.

Koch thinks Ronald Reagan won big because people are fed up with the heavy hand and the high cost of government. He calls himself a "liberal with sanity" as opposed to traditional liberals who thought they could solve problems by throwing money at them. He now regrets that for nine years in Congress, he was one of the money-throwers.

With others, he voted for a law requiring cities to make mass transit equally accessible to the handicapped.

"Sounds terrific, doesn't it? But do you know what that MEANS? It means that in New York City we would have to spend over a BILL-Y-ON-DOLL-ARS—the federal government doesn't provide dollar one—for elevators and other things so that people in wheelchairs could use the subways. For the number who'd use them, that comes to $50 a ride. We say we'll take them wherever they want to go by limousine. It would be cheaper."

The government also insists that the city provide special classes for emotionally and physically handicapped children. For this, the feds provide $8.5 million.

"So go do it. But the added cost is $300 million. Where is the money going to come from? From the police, the firemen, sanitation, corrections? WHERE?"

The mayor's voice, now at a high screech, descends into quiet reality. "People understand that being told to do good things, when you can't afford them, is not doing good things. There are no free lunches. SOMEBODY pays, and that's what the election was all about."

On matters of race and equality before the law, the mayor says that racism can be a two-way street, that discrimination is not solved by reverse discrimination, that there are "black rednecks as well as white rednecks," that the rights of society must be paramount.

He cites the case of a black man arrested on the complaint of a woman who said he twice shoved her onto the tracks of a subway. Out on the street of a quiet residential area, the man fights and screams as two cops attempt to handcuff him. Windows go up. Somebody yells, "Stop that police brutality!"

That, the mayor says, is symptomatic of the "liberal syndrome." Too many people, he says, have indulged in self-flagellation and guilt over matters of race.

"I am not guilt-ridden. My father was not a slave holder. (Louis Koch, a Polish immigrant to New York, worked in the fur business by day and a hat-check concession at night during the Depression.) We were poor. (Nine people in a two-bedroom walkup.) I want to help poor people, right?

"But you don't help them by pandering or preferential treatment. I'm against racial quotas in employment. I am for affirmative action in which you reach out and say, come, come if you don't have the skills we'll teach you. But when you take the test, you take it EQUALLY with EVERYBODY."

Edward Irving Koch loves his job but says a mayor without a sense of humor would go out of his skull. Thus, this mayor threw up his hands in roaring, laughing futility when told that illegal street peddlers were now using merchandise racks two feet too long for the police vans used to confiscate them.

He goes around town telling people that he intends—he doesn't say hopes—to be mayor for three terms, 12 years. "If you happen to throw me out at the end of four years," he says, in his sing-song way, with the certitude of a man dealing with unassailable reality, "I'll get a better job but you won't get a better mayor."

⌒ MIRTA OJITO ⌒

In 1998, Mirta Ojito returned to Cuba for the first time since she and her family fled their native island 18 years before in the Mariel boatlift that brought more than 125,000 of her compatriots to U.S. shores during a five-month period.

She didn't go there as many Cuban exiles do, as former residents visiting relatives. The teenage girl who arrived in America had become a journalist for *The New York Times* and was part of a team sent to cover the visit of Pope John Paul II. Among her assignments,

Ojito was to visit a neighborhood and describe what life was like in Cuba. To make the best use of limited time, she chose familiar territory, her old neighborhood. On the advice of an editor, she departed from journalistic tradition and wrote about it in first person. *The New York Times* then went another, historic step further: The editors put the account on the front page.

Ojito insists that she "had little to do with" "A Sentimental Journey to *la Casa* of Childhood," one of four stories awarded the ASNE award for covering the world in 1999. "I just sat there and it happened. Then I sent it."

But that modesty masks the reportorial discipline that Ojito developed at *The Miami Herald* and its Spanish-language sister publication, *El Nuevo Herald*, where she spent the first nine years of her career before joining *The New York Times* in 1996. "Remember, there are three things you need to know in journalism," she recalls a *Miami Herald* editor, Bill Rose, drumming into her. "Details, details, details." She's never forgotten it, as the 20 steps she counts in the story's second paragraph attests.

It's been said that the more personal you are, the more universal you become. Notice how Ojito's meticulously recorded visit to Santos Suarez connects with themes that resonate with all of us, no matter where our childhood homes are found. In the lovingly rendered particulars—a chipped floor tile, a set of glasses, the family's old soap holder—Ojito demonstrates journalism's ability to bridge the differences that separate us.

While working at *The New York Times*' Miami bureau, Ojito was part of the team of reporters who won the 2000 Pulitzer Prize for national reporting for their series "How Race Is Lived in America." In 2005, she returned home again in *Finding Mañana: A Memoir of a Cuban Exodus*, a book that, like the story here, combines reporting with first-person writing to provide an intimate look at history.

A Sentimental Journey to la Casa of Childhood

THE NEW YORK TIMES • FEBRUARY 3, 1998

HAVANA—This is the moment when, in my dreams, I begin to cry. And yet, I'm strangely calm as I go up the stairs to the apartment of my childhood in Santos Suarez, the only place that, after all these years, I still refer to as *la casa*, home.

I am holding a pen and a reporter's notebook in my hand and, as I always do when I am working, I count the steps: 20. In my memory, there were only 16. The staircase seems narrower than I remember, the ceiling lower.

Perhaps I have grown taller, perhaps my hips have widened with age and pregnancy. I am buying mental time, distracting my mind from what I am certain will be a shock.

After 17 years and 8 months, I have returned to Cuba as a reporter. I am here to cover the visit of Pope John Paul II, not to cry at the sight of a chipped, old tile on the floor.

The last time I went down these steps I was 16 years old and a police car was waiting for me and my family downstairs. They had come to tell us that my uncle, like thousands of other Cuban exiles who had returned to Cuba to claim their relatives, waited at the port of Mariel to take us to Miami in a leased shrimp boat.

It was May 7, 1980, the first days of what became known as the Mariel boat lift, the period from April to September 1980 when more than 125,000 Cubans left the island for the United States.

That day I left my house in a hurry. The police gave us 10 minutes to get ready and pack the few personal items we were allowed to take: an extra set of clothing, some pictures, toothbrushes. Everything else, from my books to my dolls and my parents' wedding china, remained behind. There were dishes in the sink and food in the refrigerator. My underwear in a drawer and my mother's sewing machine open for work.

Since then, I have often thought about this house, remembering every detail, every curve and tile and squeaky sound. The green walls of the living room, the view from the balcony, the feel of the cold tiles under my bare feet, the sound of my father's key in the keyhole and the muffled noise from the old refrigerator in the kitchen.

A stranger opens the door and I tell her who I am and what I want. "I used to live here," I say. "I'd like to take a look."

Surprisingly, she knows my name. She asks if I am the older or the younger child who used to live in the house. I say I am the older as I look over her head. Straight into my past. My home remains practically as we left it, seemingly frozen in time, like much of Cuba today.

There, to the right of the bedroom's door, is my father's handiwork—two glass shelves he screwed into the wall—and my mother's set of orange and green glasses. Later, I learn that no one ever drinks from those glasses. If they break, the new owner of the house tells me, they cannot be replaced. Under the shelves is my bookcase, painted a fresh coat of dark brown. A carpenter friend of my father's had built it for me when I was a little girl.

My books are gone, though. When the Cuban Government declared a few years ago that it had entered a "special period" of shortages and books all but disappeared, she took my books to the school where she teaches. I am pleased to hear that. It is a much nicer fate than I had imagined.

One book remains, *Captain at 15*, by Jules Verne. I want to take it to New York with me, to show it to my son. But I do not say anything and the yellowing book remains there, inside the bookcase. My mother's pots and pans are in the kitchen. The old wooden ironing board remains where it always was, behind the door to the patio.

The dining set is exactly the way it was, except the table is covered by a plastic tablecloth and I do not feel the coldness of the beige Formica when I sit at the table as I used to. A painting of red, white and yellow hibiscus that always hung over my sofa bed is still in the same spot in the living room. It was painted by one of my mother's cousins, who now lives in Florida.

This is a strange feeling. I knew I would face my childhood by coming here, but I never expected to relive it as I am doing now. I go out to the balcony and then, as if on cue, I hear someone calling out my childhood nickname, "Mirtica! Mirtica!"

For a moment, I do not know who is calling or even if the call is real. It sounds like my mother calling me for dinner. But it is the neighbor from the corner who looked up from her terrace and somehow recognized me. I wave faintly. I want to stay in this apartment for a long time. I want to be left alone. But I cannot. It is no longer my home.

The Jiménez family now lives in the house. He is a truck driver, just as my father was. They have a 15-year-old son who sleeps on a sofa bed in the living room, just as my sister and I did. The Government gave them the apartment a few months after we left. Their own house, nearby, had been badly damaged in a hurricane.

They were shown three apartments, all in the same neighborhood. They settled in ours, they said, because it seemed the nicest. It does not seem so nice anymore. It is rather small, smaller than I remember. The floor tiles are porous and lackluster and chunks of plaster have fallen from the ceiling. There is no light in the living room, because nowadays in Cuba light bulbs are luxury items. But it is home. And, yes, I cry.

Despite their warm welcoming, I am acutely aware of what the Jiménezes may be thinking. For years, one of the propaganda campaigns that the Cuban Government has mastered is that of instilling in ordinary Cubans the fear that exiles in the United States want to return to the country to recover the homes and businesses they lost when they left the country.

There is even a television short that mocks the Helms-Burton Act, a law intended to strengthen the United States embargo against Cuba, that warns Cubans to watch out for people like me, returning exiles.

I have no interest in my former home and whatever furniture still exists there, other than a purely sentimental one. But I do not know what the Jiménezes are thinking. They are, however, extremely generous with their time and space. They serve me coffee. We discuss the good features of the apartment, as if this were a real estate transaction. They tell me they love the old American refrigerator, a white Hotpoint that, miraculously, still stands.

I roam through the house as if it were my own. When, upon leaving, I apologize for the inconvenience, Mr. Jiménez tells me: "Don't mention it. This is your home."

I knew this would be an emotional visit. Before I mustered enough courage to go up to the apartment, I had walked through the neighborhood. As my father asked me to do, I visit *la bodega* and search for Juan, the Spaniard who once owned it and, after it was confiscated by the Government in the early years of the revolution, remained there as an employee of the state.

He is retired now, but I find him helping out at another bodega, and we chat. I take a picture for my father as he stands behind the counter with a pencil balanced behind his ear, as he always did.

I walk the streets and find faces I recognize. I approach some; others approach me because, they tell me, I remind them of my mother. Some even call out her name, which is also mine, from across the street: "Mirta, what are you doing here? You've come back?"

They tell me who died and who left. The son of my sixth-grade teacher lost a leg in a bicycle accident. My next-door neighbor left for Spain with her son, Pepito, to claim an inheritance. The musician from downstairs died of bone cancer; his daughter married an Italian and left.

The downstairs neighbors returned to the province where they were born. For years, she was the president of the watchdog neighborhood committee; he wore a green olive uniform, a military man forged in the mountains of Sierra Maestra with Fidel Castro and later trained in the Soviet Union. Their two children left for the United States.

My old neighbors tell me how they live, how they survive, as one woman put it. They make sweets at home and sell them in the street. They receive money monthly from the United States. They steal from the Government. They save and scrape and work very hard just to put food on the table every day.

The old movie theater is gone, demolished two years ago because it was crumbling with age and disrepair. Another theater has been condemned. The front door is covered with bricks. The hardware store is now a Government office. The glass of the windows broke years ago; crude wooden boards cover the empty shelves. The streets are unpaved and full of potholes. Workers rip them open to fix water or gas pipes and then do not have the materials to finish the work.

In a way, I'm reporting the story of a neighborhood, a typical one in Havana. But I'm also reporting the life I never got to have. Through their stories, I see what my life could have become. I search for parallels. I imagine myself as my neighbors.

What would have become of me? Could I have become a professional like the two girls from the corner who now teach? Would I have left in a raft like my next-door neighbor? Or perhaps I would have gone crazy, like the woman across the street, Regina, who could not recall my name after years of electroshock and pills. Her husband was accused of counterrevolutionary activities in 1979 and executed by a firing squad.

Had I stayed, would I have talked to a returning neighbor the way they talk to me? They tell me about the sadness of their lives, their husbands, their lovers, their misguided children, their ungrateful relatives, their never-ending litany of needs: bread, toilet paper, sanitary napkins, underwear, freedom.

Because I left, and because they know I will leave again, I become a depository of their penury. They are happy I have returned, glad that I remembered. A woman gives me a rose from her garden; another, two lithographs from an old book of paintings and a silver cross that has been in her family for years.

The Jiménezes give me a plastic bird that hangs from its beak from a wooden stand and, more important, our old soap holder, a white enamel piece from Poland that my mother always kept in the patio.

Down the block I find a man I never knew before. He stops me and asks if I am a foreign journalist. I say yes. "I want to ask you something," he says. "Perhaps you know. Why is it that children can no longer eat breakfast in the morning?" He is 70 years old and has lived in the same house for 44 years. His grandson goes to my old school, down the block. It is the man's birthday and, he says, he cannot even buy a bone in the market to make himself a soup. I get a lump in my throat and wish him happy birthday.

I cross the street to the school and ask to see the library. It is here where I became a reader and, therefore, I think, a writer. I hardly recognize the place. The marble columns are there, but the bookcases lean precariously to the side. The books are dusty and yellowing.

I ask for the French literature section, but there is not one anymore. The librarian tells me that last year she received only two books, copies of *La Edad de Oro*, by José Martí. The year before, none. In fact, except for those two books she does not remember the last time she got a shipment. Children now use the library as a classroom.

After a second visit to the apartment, I leave. And I leave exactly the way I left almost 18 years ago, profoundly sad, surrounded by friends and neighbors, people glad that I remembered them, unselfish people who are happy that I left and live better than they do.

Who says that Cubans are divided by politics or even by an ocean? In Enamorados Street, at the foot of a small hill called San Julio, my home and my people remain.

∼ DAVID FINKEL ∼

David Finkel is a writer for *The Washington Post*. He was a reporter for the *St. Petersburg* (Fla.) *Times* when he won the ASNE award for non-deadline writing in 1986. He has been a finalist for the Pulitzer Prize and, in 2000, an ASNE finalist for his deadline reporting from Kosovo.

No one living in the Tampa Bay area at the time will forget that May morning in 1980 when a freak storm drove a huge tanker into the Sunshine Skyway Bridge. More than 1,000 feet of bridge collapsed. Cars and a Greyhound bus fell more than 100 feet off the end of the broken bridge and into the bay, killing 35 people.

The man who steered the *Summit Venture* into the bridge was John Lerro. He quickly became the object of curiosity and investigation. He received threats. He became the butt of jokes. Songs were written about him.

Five years after the event, David Finkel captured the fully tragic nature of Lerro's experience. Finkel's treatment of Lerro reads like a yarn or ballad, a good man struggling like Job against a cruel fate. Lerro's words are chilling: "I spent thousands of hours thinking about that day. Thousands of hours. Trying to figure out, Why me? You know what the answer is? Because. Why me? Because. Why the poor souls who died? Because. In other words, no answers."

Such quotes come only to journalists who practice the unnatural act of listening—and to journalists who spend time with the subject of their stories. "I spent two full days with him without a break," said Finkel. "And it was all necessary. We never went over the same thing twice. As soon as I got there, I could sense what had happened to that man. No matter whether he was at fault or not, there was so much tragedy in what had happened to him since the day he hit that bridge. But I didn't want him to say that to me. I wanted to be able to show it in the things he did, by the way he carried himself, by his posture, by the conditions of his life. He was leery of the press; he had had a lot of bad press. So I hung out for a couple of days until he felt comfortable enough with me to be himself. And tragically he was."

Finkel is a meticulous writer who paces around the newsroom, an act of creative procrastination, until he finds a way into a story. He paced so much at one newsroom that other "busier" reporters complained and his editor asked him to please pace outside. When the sentences come, they come one after another. He simplifies and polishes each one until it feels right. "It's all revision," he says.

Beginning his career at a publication called *Urology News*, Finkel now writes for one of the nation's most important newspapers. His work reflects the most simple and most noble of goals: "The point is just to tell a nice little story."

For Lerro, Skyway Nightmare Never Ends

ST. PETERSBURG (FLA.) TIMES • MAY 5, 1985

NEW YORK—On a gray, miserable April day, a man with a beard is limping toward a boat on the East River. He looks cold. He looks lousy. He has tears in his eyes from the wind and a cast on his left hand from punching a wall. Because of the cast, he can't button his jacket, and it's flapping around in the icy wind.

His name is John Lerro. He doesn't want to be here. He would rather be in bed asleep. Or in sun-blessed Florida. Or in the arms of a beautiful woman. Or even eating breakfast. But it is Tuesday. On Tuesdays he has to be on the water by 8 a.m.

So he has awakened before he wanted to, thrown some bran in a bowl, added some raisins and wheat germ he keeps under his bed, watered the mixture down in the bathroom sink, and stumbled into the unwelcoming arms of a new day.

"I feel terrible," he says. He is limping because of multiple sclerosis, and the wind gusts are playing havoc with his balance. He says, "I look like a drunk."

At the dock, six students from the State University of New York's Maritime College are waiting for him. All of them are glad when he arrives. All of them are anxious. Today's the day they're going to learn how to dock a boat.

And Lerro—John Lerro of the Sunshine Skyway Bridge disaster, the John Lerro—is going to teach them.

Taking his seat in the boat, he has only one piece of advice to offer. He is the voice of experience, and the students are attentive.

He says, "If you misjudge, you've got hell to pay."

"I'm Living Like an Animal"

This Thursday, it will have been five years since Lerro, standing on the bridge of the 608-foot-long freighter *Summit Venture*, felt the sickening sensation of his ship grinding against a support column of the Skyway bridge.

He can still see the bridge collapsing, the cars falling, the Greyhound bus pitching forward and turning upside down. Now he is 42, and there are moments when he doesn't seem eager to make it to 43.

Of the accident, he says, "It screwed up my profession, it screwed up my significance, it screwed up everything."

Of his mental state, he says: "Am I p----- off and frustrated? There aren't words in the dictionary."

Of his life: "I'm living like an animal."

He is living on a ship these days, a ship that, believe it or not, is docked beneath a bridge. He doesn't see any irony in this, or in the fact that he is teaching 18-year-olds how to steer boats. He is teaching, he says, because he needed a job, and he is living on the ship because he can't afford a place of his own.

The ship is called the *Empire State*. Once it was a passenger ship, then it carried troops, now it is the teaching ship for the Maritime Academy. It is just over 500 feet long and has several closet-sized cabins. One of them—No. 18, the one next to a room labeled "Slop Sink Locker"—is Lerro's.

The cabin is five steps long, two steps wide. It has a low ceiling, blue walls, and a porthole that Lerro has covered with a dark blanket. Furnishings include a radio tuned to a classical music station, a wheezer of an old TV that someone loaned him when he broke his hand, and a humidifier that is propped on a box and aimed at his pillow.

The humidifier runs constantly. Unless the air is moist, like in Florida, Lerro gets a sore throat. He can't stand the dry air of the North, but he has to be here because of the multiple sclerosis. The heat, he says, wipes him out.

"I think back to my life in Tampa," he says. "It was beautiful. I died and went to heaven. Now I have filth. I touch things, and I'm filthy."

The ship smells of diesel oil. The halls are narrow, the steps are steep. Even in winter, the showers are cold. And when the radio's off, the sounds are of trucks crossing the Throgs Neck, the bridge across the East River connecting the Bronx to Queens.

Like the Skyway, the Throgs Neck is a huge bridge, breathtaking to see, but it is built differently. For one thing, around each support column are fenders to help stave off ships.

"If I had hit that bridge," Lerro says of the Throgs Neck, "nothing would have happened."

He says this in a New York accent. He was born here in the Bronx. His mother was a teacher. His father worked construction. He wanted to be a ballet dancer.

Instead, in 1960, he ended up as a student at the school where he is now teaching. He studied hard, became a merchant marine, married a woman named Sophie, fathered a son named Charles, and spent the next 20 years on ships.

"If I had life to do over again," he says, "I'd be a flute player."

"Forty Miles of Bad Road"

His career, if not remarkable, was at least well-rounded.

He was a third mate, then second mate, chief mate, and ship's master. He took container ships to Japan, passenger ships to South America, chemical tankers to Europe. Eventually, he became one of the 150 or so pilots qualified to guide a ship through the Panama Canal.

"I had identity," he says. "I had self-assuredness. Forget the bridge. I've done a lot. I've been around the world."

His only problem came on small ships headed directly into the wind. For reasons no one could explain, he would get seasick.

It was a problem easily managed. He began carrying plastic bags with him. "Yes, I felt terrible," he says. "Did I make a mess? Never. And the boatsmen appreciated me for it."

In 1976, he became the first outsider to penetrate the closed world of the Tampa Bay Pilots Association.

For years, the 20 pilots in the association had hand-picked their new members in what Lerro describes as a "good-ole-boy system." Then, in the mid-'70s, the state stepped in, openly advertising a new slot in the trade guild.

Lerro, down in Panama, heard of the job and applied. "I memorized every inch of that channel," he says. "I sat up at night after Panama Canal transits. I took study cards with me." After the Skyway accident, there would be trial testimony that Lerro's bosses in Panama were dissatisfied with his work and were thinking of dismissing him. But Lerro says he wanted the job so he could come back to the United States and settle down.

Starting pay was $500 a month. The job was to guide any ship entering or leaving the Port of Tampa through the curves and turns of the bay's 40-mile-long shipping channel, the one pilots call the toughest in the state.

"Forty miles of bad road," Lerro calls it now.

At first, he felt less than welcome. "I was chosen by the state. I was an outsider. I was an Italian outsider. I was a New York, Italian outsider. I was an ex-Panama Canal, New York, Italian outsider. What I'm saying is they had their reasons."

But the job, he decided, was a dream. "This little man is moving that big thing. You're a very significant person. It was the reason for getting up, the reason to be."

By 1980, Lerro says, he knew the channel as well as any of the other pilots. He was earning $40,000 a year. He had been up and down that channel 800 times. He had piloted 865-foot-long ships, among the longest allowed, and ships carrying a pressurized gas called anhydrous ammonia, which, if spilled, would form a vast, poisonous, explosive cloud.

By majority vote, the pilots decided to promote him from deputy to senior status. It was a big promotion. His salary would instantly increase beyond $100,000. The one hitch was that he had to pay the association the customary initiation fee of $120,000.

In early May, he arranged for a loan, he says, and scheduled the closing for the afternoon of May 9. The only thing he had to do before going to the bank was bring in the *Summit Venture*.

"MAYDAY, MAYDAY, MAYDAY"

Headed to Tampa for a load of phosphate, the freighter sat empty and high at the mouth of the bay. It was nearing daybreak when Lerro approached. As had become his habit, he carried a seasickness bag with him as he jumped from the pilot boat and crimped the rope ladder hanging over the freighter's side.

For all practical purposes, once he reached the pilot house, the *Summit Venture* became his.

The trip to the dock was expected to take about four hours. Monitoring the two-way radio, Lerro knew the bay was dotted with showers, some of them bad. At one point, using his radar, he helped direct an outbound vessel lost in a fierce little squall.

Then his storm hit. It was toward 7:30. He was watching the channel, watching the radar, watching the clouds, when out of nowhere, it seemed, blinding rain and darkness engulfed the *Summit Venture*.

It was an impossible storm to figure, Lerro would say later. At first, the winds were out of the southwest. Then, suddenly, they began to swirl, and the rain came from all directions, slanted almost sideways. The drops hit hard enough to sting.

Trapped in this storm, the ship moved up the channel at about 5 mph, past the final buoys before the bridge, into the final turn.

Then, just as suddenly as it had come on, the storm began to clear, revealing a sight that Lerro has yet to get out of his mind.

"At first I saw nothing. And then, way off the starboard side, I saw a piece of the bridge," he says. "I saw a piece of the bridge that I never should have seen from that angle."

Later, Lerro would be asked why he hadn't stopped when the bad weather was building. Or why he didn't veer off and ground the ship in the spoils. "You think that way afterward," he said, "but not before." There had been other storms in his four years, he noted, some of them blinding, all of them navigable.

But this time, as the weather cleared to the south, the bridge appeared where it shouldn't have been. The ship was off the channel's center line by 800 feet. Right then, Lerro says, he knew.

"It was not clear ahead yet, but because of that I did emergency full astern. I ordered both anchors dropped. And just then it cleared dead ahead, and I saw my bow was dead on. That's when I ordered hard port rudder. She was about a ship's length away. That's 600 feet. That ain't enough time to do s---. The ship started turning to the left. Then the flare of the apron on the bow grazed—just grazed—the side of the bridge. That's all I saw. The ship went under the bridge, and then the whole bridge fell down. Then I saw two cars drive off the edge and disappear. Then I grabbed the radio and called, 'Mayday.' "

"Mayday, Mayday, Mayday," he yelled into the microphone. "Mayday, Mayday, Mayday, Coast Guard.

"This is—all the emergency—all the emergency equipment out to the Skyway Bridge. The Skyway Bridge is down. This is a Mayday. Emergency situation. Stop the traffic on that Skyway Bridge!

"People are in the water."

While he stayed on the ship, divers began bringing up the bodies, 35 in all. Only a few had water in their lungs, signifying drowning. Most of the victims had died when their cars fell 150 feet and smacked against the surface of the water.

"One decision," Lerro says, thinking back. "I was so proud of myself as a pilot. I was so proud of my ability."

"Why Did It Happen?"

After the funerals came the questions.

Was Lerro at fault? Partially, ruled the National Transportation Safety Board.

Should he become a full-fledged pilot, as had been scheduled before the accident? No, Lerro and the other pilots informally agreed.

Should his piloting license be revoked? No, decided a state hearing examiner.

That decision came eight months after the accident. During that period, Lerro retreated from publicity as much as he could. A few days after the accident, driving toward his home north of Tampa, he stopped at a Catholic church, walked inside, and began crying. "He needed to talk, desperately," remembers Father Tom Cummins, who approached him. "He wanted to know, 'Why did it happen?'"

He tried religion. He tried philosophy. He took comfort in people who stopped by his house and told him to keep faith, that he was a victim, too. But for every one of those, there was someone who would call and threaten him, or cuss him out. "My son, 13 years old then, got a phone call. 'How does it feel to be the son of a murderer?' He was devastated."

In March 1981, two months after the state hearing examiner recommended that Lerro be allowed to keep his license, the state Board of Pilot Commissioners agreed, 7-0.

The decision meant Lerro could return to work on Tampa Bay, and on April 9—11 months to the day after the accident—he was piloting once again.

He remembers his first trip. "The captain was wearing a Mickey Mouse shirt. I'll never forget that. By the time we got to the bridge, he knew something was up. He said, 'You're the guy who hit the bridge.' He said, 'Don't worry. I'm a born-again Christian. This was meant to be.' He was very relaxed. He sat there with his Mickey Mouse shirt, and I kept driving."

At the bridge, he says, he remembers looking up only to see reporters watching over the edge and helicopters with camera crews hovering just beyond.

He remembers the second trip. "You won't believe it. You know what it was? An ammonia ship."

He remembers the rest of the trips that followed:

"The captain would be looking through binoculars and say, 'Oh, what happened!' They didn't know it was me. I'd say, 'Ship hit a bridge.'

" 'What'd they do with the pilot?'

" 'He's still piloting.'

" 'Did many people die?'

" 'Yeah. Thirty-five.'

" 'Oh. Very bad.'

" 'Yeah. It was.' "

"If Not for This Job . . ."

Late in 1981, Lerro went to a chiropractor. He was having trouble climbing the rope ladders onto ships. He was staggering a bit. He didn't drink, but people accused him of being drunk.

The chiropractor took a pen and ran it along the bottom of Lerro's left foot. Involuntarily, his toes curled upward. The chiropractor sent him to a neurologist.

The neurologist also ran a pen along his foot. Again his toes curled. The neurologist asked him to track a pen with his eyes. His right eye jumped. "That's right brain damage," the neurologist said.

Another neurologist said the same thing. So did another. Without a doubt, they all agreed Lerro had multiple sclerosis. A chronic nerve condition, it would only get worse.

So on Dec. 24, 1981, a year and a half after the accident, Lerro stopped piloting. He had no choice. He couldn't pass the necessary physicals.

He did find work as a third mate on a container ship. But soon into the voyage he had to fly home because of the multiple sclerosis, which was growing worse because of stress. Sometimes he got dizzy. Especially on hot days he could barely get out of bed.

He sold real estate. He tried to write a book. He spent a lot of time alone. His wife, Sophie, had become a ship's radio operator and was off at sea. They weren't getting along anyway. He began sending out resumes by the dozen.

In response, polite refusals began stacking up.

Then came the letter from the Maritime Academy. Yes, they remembered him from his days as a student. Yes, they were aware of what had happened to him. Yes, they would be happy to hire him as an adjunct professor, to teach a class called Nautical Science 306.

Yes, he could live on the *Empire State.*

In January, he headed north. He was optimistic. "If not for this job, I don't know what I'd do," he joked. "I can't even rob banks because you have to be able to run."

There were a lot of new buildings at his old college, but many things were still the same. The freshmen still were required to move around campus in double time. The picture of him on the rowing team was still hanging. And the Throgs Neck, built while he was still in school, still arched supremely over the campus.

Then, one night, all the frustrations welled up at once, and before he knew it, he had smashed his left fist into a wall. For a moment, it felt good. Then the pain came on.

"In Other Words, No Answers"

Sitting in the boat, surrounded by cadets, he shivers. The wind is strong. The East River is covered with whitecaps.

"If you misjudge," he warns, "you've got hell to pay."

The object is to dock. The first cadet takes the wheel. "These kids are beautiful," Lerro says. He knows they have been checking out the federal report on his accident from the school library, but he doesn't mind. "I love these kids."

The first student overshoots the dock, then tries to back in, realizing too late there's another boat in the way.

Bump.

Another student takes over and tries to drift in with the wind.

Thunk.

For two hours, it goes like this. The wind gets stronger. There are snow flurries. Finally, Lerro takes the wheel and brings the boat toward the dock. He comes in slowly at a 30-degree angle, swings parallel to the dock, cuts the engines.

"Hey, a pretty good docking!" he says.

"Not bad for an old man," one of the students says.

Class over, they scatter. Limping, Lerro heads back to the *Empire State*. He's having a particularly bad day. The wind is hell to walk against.

"I don't get any balance messages from my feet anymore," he says.

At the ship, he rests. Then, gripping the handrail, he makes his way up the gangway.

"I spent thousands of hours thinking about that day. Thousands of hours. Trying to figure out, Why me? You know what the answer is? Because. Why me? Because. Why the poor souls who died? Because. In other words, no answers."

Out of the wind, he feels better. But the steps leading to his cabin are especially tough.

"Yeah, I feel pretty guilty about it," he says. "I don't feel stupid, but I feel guilty. The weather was bad. I didn't rise above it."

Up the stairs, down the hall, past the slop sink. "I failed at being a pilot, but I'm teaching these kids good stuff."

Dragging his leg, he wobbles to his room. He is through the door and past the closet when he begins to teeter. It's his equilibrium. He is falling. He throws out the arm without the cast, pushes off a wall, falls back the other way, ducks his head, collapses onto his bed.

"Anyway," he says, "it's a miserable existence."

~ TOMMY TOMLINSON ~

Tommy Tomlinson usually writes a three-times-a-week column for
The Charlotte (N.C.) *Observer*. Fortunately for the newspaper's readers, his editors don't pigeonhole their columnist, but allow him to
"roam around and try different stuff," as he puts it. In 2003, Tomlinson took two months to pursue a pair of stories more expansive than
the boundaries of a metro column. They earned him the ASNE's first
award for profile writing, among other honors.

Tomlinson's detailed reporting and cinematic style elevate the
profile beyond a superficial "person in the news" report. He creates
layered portraits of individuals who must overcome what appear to
be insurmountable odds—a mathematician in search of a solution, a
badly burned police recruit determined to beat the obstacle course
that stands between him and a badge.

Tomlinson keeps our attention with concrete details, creative ap-
proaches to structure and a narrative sense that anticipates and serves
the reader's interest. He's also sparing with quotes, reflecting his belief that quotations "really have to have some deep insight into the
person I'm talking about or to the subject of the story, or [they have]
to move the story forward in a really compelling way even better and
faster than I could."

"A Beautiful Find" reconstructs the four-year quest of young
mathematician John Swallow to solve a problem that had eluded others for decades. The title plays off *A Beautiful Mind*, the biography
and movie about Nobel Prize-winning mathematician John Nash. To
convey the arcane science of Swallow's world, Tomlinson borrows a
device from the poet's toolbox, relying on metaphors, such as comparing the problem to a "carpet that was too small for the room."

To organize his prizewinning profiles, Tomlinson takes advantage
of structural elements present in the material he is writing about. In
"A Beautiful Find," he mimics an examination's question format to
arrange the themes he wants to explore. During the revision of a
story, Tomlinson's editor, Mike Gordon, aids the process by reading
the story aloud with the writer sitting beside him. The technique provides telltale clues to what's working and what needs work, an experience Tomlinson describes as "excruciating and incredibly powerful
at the same time."

Tomlinson, who was born in Brunswick, Ga., in 1964, the son
of sharecroppers, graduated from the University of Georgia with a

journalism degree. Before starting his column in 1997, he was a bureau reporter and music critic for the *Observer*.

A Beautiful Find

THE CHARLOTTE (N.C.) OBSERVER • NOVEMBER 16, 2003

Question One: You decide you want to solve a math problem that's so hard, no one's come close in 25 years. How do you begin?

John Swallow began four and a half years ago, 6,000 miles from home, staring out the window of a bus.

He's the guy you want next to you on the bus seat. Friendly but quiet. You might not remember him later, unless you glanced over when he'd just thought of something, and you saw his left eyebrow rise over the rim of his glasses.

Swallow started writing computer code when he was 7. He aced college calculus when he was 13. He entered grad school at Yale when he was 19.

But here he was at 28, in Haifa, Israel, with a problem that clogged his mind like kitchen sludge.

Swallow teaches at Davidson College. He went to Israel on a working sabbatical to trade ideas with a professor named Jack Sonn. Swallow and Sonn are two of maybe 100 people in the world who are experts in their particular side street of math.

They study algebra at its highest levels. They work with sets of numbers called Brauer groups, named for a Jewish mathematician who left Germany when Hitler took over. They apply ideas based on Galois theory, named for a 19th-century French mathematician who died in a duel.

The work has practical uses, such as cryptography—the making and breaking of codes. But to Swallow, it combines the things he loves about math: the beautiful patterns in numbers and the challenge of seeing how far his skill and imagination can stretch.

In Israel, Swallow and Sonn spent a semester warming up with some minor theorems. Then one day Sonn suggested a problem that other experts in their field had thought of back in the '70s. Many mathematicians worked on it into the '80s—Sonn among them—but no one ever came up with an answer.

In every branch of math there are problems no one has ever solved. They are numerical shipwrecks. If you dive deep enough you could find treasure. But you might spend years and come out with nothing.

The problem Sonn suggested involves analyzing two Brauer groups—huge algebraic structures, whole fields of numbers—and trying to show that they're the same.

The numbers in Brauer groups aren't just the ones you use to balance the checkbook. They're irrational numbers (like the square root of 2) that can't be reduced to a fraction. They're even imaginary numbers (like the square root of -1) that don't show up on a calculator.

Swallow came to think of his problem as comparing two forests. They look exactly alike. The heights of the trees match. But to prove that they're identical, you have to get down to every needle and every hunk of bark.

He had never worked on a problem that required so many techniques, so many new ideas, so much brainpower.

For months he sat in Sonn's office every afternoon, the two of them staring at the blackboard, sometimes for so long that Sonn would doze off.

At night Swallow rode home on a city bus. The other passengers chatted in Hebrew or Arabic, languages he didn't understand. Swallow thought about all the rest he didn't understand, the equations on the blackboard, the numbers skittering out of reach.

He wondered if he had come this far only to find something he had never run into: a problem that was stronger than his mind.

Question Two: You're struggling to solve a math problem that's so hard, no one's come close in 25 years. You also have a normal life. How do you balance the world inside your head with the one outside?

Cameron Swallow calls it "the math-problem expression." She describes it as "an abstracted gazing into the middle distance."

She first saw it in her husband half their lives ago. They met in choir practice at the University of the South in Tennessee. She was a freshman at 17. He was already a sophomore at 16.

They both loved math and music and English literature. They had long romantic talks about quadratic equations. He had enough credits to graduate early, but he stayed an extra year—partly to finish off a double major, partly to be with her. They got married in 1991, when John was at Yale.

In 1994 they came to Davidson. Soon they had a daughter, Ruth, and then another, Sophie. The talk shifted to whose turn it was to change diapers and when to buy the minivan. John became, as Cameron puts it, the Kitchen Spouse. He makes a mean Reuben sandwich in the Crock-Pot.

In Israel their kids were still small, so John and Cameron had time to talk about the math problem. But he and Sonn weren't getting far. They had spent six months digging and hadn't hit anything solid. And it was time for the Swallows to go back to Davidson.

Swallow resumed his regular life—teaching during the day, spending time with family at night. He worked on the problem in spare hours, between classes and church services and oil changes. He filled sheets of paper with equations next to phone numbers for the DMV.

Sonn had gone on to other projects. Swallow worked by himself for months. But he kept getting stuck. He thought of it like trying to lay carpet that was too small for the room. Every time he got one corner to fit, another would pop loose.

He worried that he had lost his confidence, lost his aggressiveness, lost his faith.

He put down the problem for nearly a year.

He taught, traveled, read to his daughters. He got in touch with a Canadian collaborator. They worked on a smaller problem that they wrapped up in a few months.

When they were done Swallow went back to the folder in his file cabinet, the one marked *"Current" Research.*

It was filled with copied pages from textbooks, scribbles on graph paper, half-finished thoughts on index cards. The Brauer groups, those two huge fields of numbers, ran all over the pages. He was sure they were the same. But he had to prove it.

He read the notes over and dug in again.

He spread out his work on a table at Summit Coffee across from the Davidson campus. He tried out theories in his head as he drove back from family visits, Cameron and the kids asleep in the minivan, a band called String Cheese Incident playing on the stereo.

Sometimes he forgot what he'd already done and repeated the mistakes he and Sonn made in Israel. Sometimes he worked for days and ended up back at the same wrong place.

But then he thought about the smaller problem he'd already finished. He realized that some of that work overlapped.

He still wasn't getting far. He wasn't even doing enough to call his progress slow and steady. Slow and unsteady, maybe.

Still, after two and a half years, the stubborn numbers in Swallow's head began to shift a little.

His eyebrow rose.

Question Three: You've spent countless hours trying to solve a math problem that's so hard, no one's come close in 25 years. What will it take to finally break through?

The speaker was boring. Worse yet, he was boring in French.

By now it was July 2001. Swallow had come to Lille, France, north of Paris, for a math conference. He knows French. But this guy at the front of the lecture hall was talking so fast that Swallow couldn't understand half the words, and didn't care about the rest.

Eventually he gave up. He reached over and pulled out his notes on the problem he and Jack Sonn had been working on.

All of a sudden a fresh thought flashed in his mind.

He grabbed a pen and wrote one word.

Suppose.

He followed that word with a string of equations that set new limits on the number fields.

Maybe if he put just a few restrictions on the problem, narrowed the scope just a bit, it would work. He went back to the idea of trying to lay a carpet that's too small for the room. Maybe the answer was to make the room a little smaller.

For the next couple of days he did calculations in every spare moment. The numbers were lining up, making graceful curves on his worksheets. But there were still places where the numbers strayed.

One morning Swallow skipped the conference and went looking for coffee. He ended up in a shopping center and found a table in a restaurant called Quick—a European version of McDonald's.

He doesn't remember much about the scene around him. The steam coming off the coffee. A woman pushing a baby stroller.

Then, another flash.

All along he had struggled with a few key places where the two number fields could have been different. If they were the same, he could apply an equation to both fields and the two sides would add up to zero. But one side always came up with the wrong result.

This time Swallow tried a new technique, something he'd never thought of before that moment in the fast-food joint in France.

It was as if he had been trying to train a dog for months, and the dog finally came.

Lots of dogs. Whole fields of them.

The numbers lined up and sat still.

Swallow applied an equation to both Brauer groups. Did the calculations.

They added up to zero.

Perfect balance.

He had made it down to the needle and the bark. The forests were the same.

Swallow still had to try his new thoughts on other parts of the problem. He still had to recheck his calculations. He still had to trust himself.

He went back to Davidson. His wife noticed the old "math-problem expression." Swallow ran through the steps of his solution over and over until he felt sure.

In the fall of '01 he sent Jack Sonn a draft of the solution. For the next six months they e-mailed back and forth, challenging each other's ideas, getting stuck and starting over. Swallow had to refine his work, make the path to the answer more clear.

The revisions took more than a year.

In November 2002, Swallow sent Sonn a draft that contained all the changes. Sonn spent two months looking them over.

And then Sonn e-mailed back with the words Swallow had waited to hear for almost exactly four years:

"Looks good."

Question Four: You think you've solved a math problem that's so hard, no one's come close in 25 years. How do you know when you're done?

At the highest levels, every math problem is solved twice: once in private, once in public.

Swallow and Sonn agreed that they'd found the answer. But now the math world would get to check their work.

They typed up a formal version of the proof: "Brauer Groups of Genus Zero Extensions of Number Fields." It ran 22 pages.

Swallow sent copies to several other experts. He and Sonn posted their work on Web sites devoted to new research papers.

Based on the feedback, they made a few small fixes. Then they got the proof ready for the final step—submitting it to one of the academic journals.

The journals are the hockey goalies of math. If they think a paper is worthy, they send it to referees—other mathematicians who go over every detail. The referees are anonymous. If they agree with the proof, most mathematicians consider the problem solved.

Most journals get more submissions than they can publish. One journal decided not to look at Sonn and Swallow's proof. They sent their work to a second journal. It was now February 2003. Swallow thought it might be another year before they heard back.

Swallow picks up his office mail at the college union. In summer he goes by every couple of days. In early August he found a letter. It was from an editor of *Transactions of the American Mathematical Society*.

I am pleased to inform you that your manuscript . . . has been accepted for publication.

One referee suggested two tiny changes. The other didn't suggest any.

It had been four years and seven months since they started. Now they were officially finished.

Swallow sent Jack Sonn an e-mail. He said it was time for a drink.

Bonus Question: You've solved a math problem that was so hard, no one else came close for 25 years. What did you learn?

The first breath of fall is blowing across Main Street in Davidson. The folks behind the counter at Summit Coffee learned long ago what John Swallow wants. Regular latte if it's the morning, decaf latte if it's the afternoon.

They know what he wants to drink, they might know what he does for a living, but they don't know what he has accomplished. Not many people do — his family, a few other faculty members, maybe 50 mathematicians worldwide.

The problem he solved won't win any of the big math prizes or make it into *Newsweek*. It's not even necessarily the kind of thing that would earn him a raise.

But there are rewards.

He'll move up in the eyes of those who study top-level algebra. People will ask him to speak at conferences, publish papers, collaborate on new ideas. He's already got a textbook due in December.

He knows now that figuring out the mysteries of giant number fields isn't that different from working out the problems of everyday life. You break them down into small steps. You leave them alone now and then so you can come back fresh. Mainly, you trust what your instincts tell you.

These days Swallow is in charge of figuring out supper and hustling the kids to the car pool. Cameron has gone back to work; she teaches algebra at Smith Language Academy, a Charlotte-Mecklenburg magnet school. Ruth is 7, and Sophie's 5. They're ahead of their age groups in math.

Swallow is due for another sabbatical in 2005. He's thinking about taking the family to France. He's had good luck in France.

Meanwhile he daydreams about the next big problem, wonders what mental turn he'll have to take to solve it.

"There are lots of good ideas, but at first they are only ideas," he says. "They have this feeling of novelty and newness. But until you sit down and hack it out, look at the details, you're never sure what you've got. The idea can be beautiful. But only the work can make it beautiful."

And his left eyebrow rises up.

∽ BLAINE HARDEN ∽

Blaine Harden was the Africa correspondent for *The Washington Post*, based in Nairobi, Kenya, when he won the ASNE award for non-deadline writing in 1988. He is the author of *Africa: Dispatches from a Fragile Continent* and *A River Lost: The Life and Death of the Columbia*.

Drawing upon literary models such as *Heart of Darkness*, Harden achieves the effect once described by Joseph Conrad in an essay on the art of writing: "My task which I am trying to achieve is, by the power of the written word to make you hear, to make you feel—it is, before all, to make you see. That—and no more, and it is everything. If I succeed, you shall find there according to your deserts: encouragement, consolation, fear, charm—all you demand—and, perhaps, also that glimpse of truth for which you have forgotten to ask."

Harden, who won the ASNE award at the age of 36, acknowledged that "the river trip is sort of a perennial for African correspondents. . . . I wanted to use the narrative, beginning in Kisangani and going to Kinshasa, as a storyline to tell the readers about Zaire, and what kind of country it is, and what kind of leadership it has, and how that leadership has infected the whole country."

Harden depends heavily on two archetypes: the river as a symbol of the flow of life, and the ship as a microcosm for the world. The

Major Mudimbi turns out to be a kind of Noah's Ark in negative, a floating representation of the corruption of the political and economic system of Zaire.

"Part supermarket, part disco, part abattoir, part brothel, the boat is open 24 hours a day for river business: the brisk exchange of smoked eels and frilly panties, crocodiles and condoms, giant forest hogs and Dear Heart Complete Skin Lightening Treatment."

Abattoir means "slaughterhouse." Yet the use of such big words does not cloud over the mountain of detail, for, in some ways, Harden's story is a bag of lists. Together, these lists become an emblem for the steaming, teeming universe of the ship. They also allow the writer to fill the story without creating a sense of compression.

In the end, Harden's own voice rings through, the result of the grinding work of revision. "I spent a tremendous amount of time writing the first 25 to 30 paragraphs of the story," he said. "I rewrote it maybe 35 or 40 times. And I just kept working at it and pulling up words and testing them out, and I wanted to have elegant language there, and I just kept working at it, and I wanted to have some echoes of Conrad there, but I also wanted to have my own writing."

Life, Death, and Corruption on an African Mainstream

THE WASHINGTON POST • NOVEMBER 8, 1987

ON THE ZAIRE RIVER—The captain, dressed in crisply pressed white pajamas, stalked back and forth on the bridge. As his boat growled downriver through a green-black rain forest, he shouted and whistled and pointed to the deck below.

There, the beasts that had arrived in the night were being auctioned. Glaring white morning light poured over heaps of mottled fur and squirming legs. It was hot and some of the carcasses were ripening.

The night's harvest was mostly monkeys—hundreds of them, some smoked, some rotting, some freshly trapped and twitching. They were tied together by their long tails in easy-carrying bundles. There also were antelope, bushbuck, and a couple of giant forest hogs. A well-muscled sailor with a sharp knife and bloodstained sneakers was methodically cutting throats.

From the bridge, the captain exercised his prerogative as big man on the river. He had first dibs on the game and he bought cheap. His crew hauled the meat upstairs to his private freezer. It would be resold at a 300 percent profit when the boat docked in the capital.

In *Heart of Darkness*, Joseph Conrad used this river, then called the Congo, as a metaphorical highway to the black reaches of the human soul. His short story was rooted in a journey he made on the Congo nearly 100 years ago.

"Going up that river," Conrad wrote, "was like traveling back to the earliest beginnings of the world, when vegetation rioted on the earth and the big trees were kings."

The description still holds—"an empty stream, a great silence, an impenetrable forest." And there is still, at least to Western eyes, an unnerving atavism associated with travel on the river. Where else are sailors' sneakers stained with monkey blood?

But a century of commerce on the river has tamed much of its menace and burned off the Conradian gloom. Monkey trappers carry their simian bundles around the riverboat with the grim workaday manner of tax lawyers toting briefcases.

The "abominable terrors, abominable satisfactions" that chilled Conrad have been supplanted by the more quotidian mercantile intrigues of modern Africa. Once a week for decades, the "heart of an immense darkness" has been penetrated by riverboats such as this one.

Part supermarket, part disco, part abattoir, part brothel, the boat is open 24 hours a day for river business: the brisk exchange of smoked eels and frilly panties, crocodiles and condoms, giant forest hogs and Dear Heart Complete Skin Lightening Treatment.

The *Major Mudimbi*—an ungainly vessel made up of five rusted barges lashed together with cables and pushed downstream by a four-decked, diesel-powered tugboat—is an immense, stinking, noisy, overheated, overcrowded African market.

It is choked with about 3,000 people. There are twice that many animals: a menagerie of farm, forest, and river creatures, alive and dead, stuffed under benches, hanging from roofs, tied to guardrails. They all will be sold in the capital—if they don't die, rot, or fall overboard.

Each year, a quarter of a million passengers and a million tons of freight travel on the river. In Zaire, an ill-governed, impoverished country with one of Africa's worst systems of roads, river transport is a key to keeping the anemic economy alive. The future of this mineral-rich nation, nearly the size of the United States east of the Mississippi, depends on the great river.

Yet no one, except for a few journalists, masochistic tourists, and other refugees from reality, travels on riverboats such as the *Major Mudimbi* for fun. Its decks are slippery with animal and human waste. Passengers occasionally slip off the boat and drown.

The food is bad and often deadly. In August, according to an on-board security officer, the second- and third-class kitchens served up a bean supper that killed several hundred people. Third-class passengers sleep with their creatures and keep a lookout for slop tossed from an upper deck. Cholera is common.

Besides being unpleasant, it is slow. The 1,000-mile journey downriver from Kisangani to the Zairian capital, Kinshasa, takes eight days if things go well. If things don't go well, it can take two to three weeks.

Zairians who travel on the river fall into two categories:

1. Those who are poor and cannot afford any other means of transport. In an almost roadless country of 35 million people where the average income is about $170 a year, this is a very large group. Third-class barges, where a ticket costs $17, are always sold out.

2. Those who want to buy goods and/or make money. At the top of this group is the captain, the man with the white pajamas, the private freezer, and the power to dictate his own prices. At the bottom are river people who briefly board the *Major Mudimbi* to trade, hopefully not with the captain. In between are the petty *commerçants* who reserve second-class compartments and sell their wares to river people at inflated prices.

Besides essentials such as soap and fishing hooks, the riverboat sells good times. For fishermen and hunters of the interior, the boat is a movable feast: warm beer, loud music, and fancy city women. Bright lights on a dark, dark river.

* * *

Lurching along the equator through a forest that for Conrad contained the "stillness of an implacable force brooding over an inscrutable intention," the riverboat is a money-grubbing interloper from the late 20th century, a garrulous whore passing through a gloomy church. It is a paradigm of how modern Africa degrades, delights, and rips off rural people.

The end of the line for riverboats traveling east from the capital is Kisangani. Just beyond the town is a series of impassable rapids.

When Conrad signed on as a riverboat captain on the Congo in 1890, his journey ended at Kisangani. It was the Inner Station, the heart of darkness.

It was carved out of the bush at the end of a network of river trading stations. The network was run by Belgian agents who were in the employ of a colonial creation unlike any other in Africa. The Congo Free State belonged to one man, King Leopold of Belgium. His agents presided over the collection and export of ivory and rubber, and Leopold pocketed the profits.

It was a savage operation. Quota systems were established for production of rubber and ivory. Those who failed to meet the quotas were beaten, raped, or killed by soldiers of the Free State. To prove they had been enforcing the quota, soldiers cut off the hands of those they punished. Smoked hands became a kind of currency. Conrad called it "the vilest scramble for loot that ever disfigured the history of human conscience."

Under pressure from world opinion, the Belgian government took Leopold's grotesque kingdom away from him in 1908. The Congo slid into a half-century of paternalistic Belgian rule. Then, along with the rest of colonial Africa, the Congolese people demanded independence. The new republic—a seemingly ungovernable amalgam of 200 tribes, no single one of which was more than 4 percent of the total—stumbled through five years of anarchy. In the mid-1960s, one man again seized control.

In the Congo Free State, as Conrad wrote, it was impossible to travel the river without feeling the rapacity of Leopold. In modern Zaire, as passage on the *Major Mudimbi* demonstrates, it is impossible to travel the river without being enveloped in the power of the man who reinvented the country and created the mentality by which it still is run.

He renamed the country. He renamed the capital. He renamed the river. He renamed himself.

Christened Joseph Desire Mobutu, he became Mobutu Sese Seko Kuku wa za Banga, which translates as "the all-conquering warrior, who goes from triumph to triumph."

His photograph, with a leopard-skin cap on his head, presides over every office and many homes in Zaire, including the first-class dining room of the *Major Mudimbi*. Tens of thousands of Zairians, including hundreds of passengers on the boat, wear clothing made of material that bears his image. Government-controlled media call him the Guide, the Chief, the Helmsman, even the Messiah.

Mobutu, 57, the son of a cook and a hotel maid, is what African scholars call a patrimonial leader, which means the unity of Zaire is embodied in him. Those who know him say "charm drips off the man." In the capital, diplomats become weak-kneed talking about his "formidable charisma." Without Mobutu, they say, Zaire could easily dissolve into tribal chaos.

*   *   *

African scholars also have come up with a name for the type of governmental system that Mobutu, after 22 years in power, has devised: a kleptocracy. From the top down, the system is greased with graft.

In testimony before Congress six years ago, his former prime minister said that between 1977 and 1981, Mobutu illegally transferred more than $200 million of government funds to his personal account abroad. He, his wife, and his immediate family have vast holdings in the country's mining, diamond, and agricultural industries. He owns estates in Belgium, Switzerland, France, and the Ivory Coast. Estimates of Mobutu's personal fortune are as high as $5 billion.

"There was and is yet a single major obstacle which annihilates all perspective of [economic] improvement [in Zaire]: the corruption of the ruling group."

So wrote Erwin Blumenthal, a West German banker, who came to Zaire in 1978. As a representative of the International Monetary Fund, he came to try to clean up the country's finances. He left a year later in disgust.

Since Blumenthal wrote his report, the World Bank has committed $602 million to Zaire. The IMF has lent even more. In return, Zaire's government has devalued its money, cut its deficits, and streamlined its administration. But current representatives of multilateral lending organizations say it is "naive" to believe that much of this money is not siphoned off at the top. Said one: "The little guy on the street gets none of this."

The ethic of corruption persists in Zaire, according to bankers, diplomats, students, and businessmen. It is a trickle-down system. Ministers demand payoffs for construction projects, teachers demand payoffs from their students, policemen stop motorists to give them a choice between a payoff and arrest.

"It's like termites nibbling away at the structure of a society," said one long-term observer.

The termites began nibbling before the *Major Mudimbi* left the quay at Kisangani. The official who checked my international certificate of vaccination noted that the cholera shot, good for six months, had expired. He was sorry, but travel would be impossible.

But wait, he said, opening a drawer and pulling out an *Officier de Quarantaine* rubber stamp. For 300 zaires ($2.40) and without using a needle, he made me legally immune from cholera.

A rather larger nibble in river service was taken this year by Mobutu himself. The Guide likes to entertain foreign dignitaries and visiting businessmen by taking them on river cruises. With his private riverboat in dry dock undergoing renovation, Mobutu this spring confiscated one of the three functioning riverboats that haul passengers from Kisangani to Kinshasa. The boats are the property of a state bureaucracy called ONATRA. Since the spring, the *Major Mudimbi* has been more overcrowded than usual.

The boat inched away from the dock at 1 p.m. on a Monday, nine hours behind schedule. Several hundred people had come down to the quay to see it off. As they waved goodbye, a mobile crane hoisted stacks of loose lumber over their heads. The mood was festive. No one was hit by falling wood.

On board, the captain, not yet wearing the pajamas that were to be his command outfit, strode the first-class deck, shaking hands with passengers. They included a portly major in the gendarmerie, who was traveling downriver to take up a post in the town of Mbandaka. He was traveling with his two wives, 12 children, and a dog. He wore a Mobutu shirt and sat amiably in a wicker chair in front of his compartment. The major was one of about 10 police and security men on board. They made their presence known as the days passed.

Other first-class passengers included students going to the university in the capital, Asian and Zairian businessmen, and some scruffy British and American tourists. Ten of the Americans were on a four-month trek called Encounter Overland and were bound for London by way of Central Africa and the Sahara. They normally traveled in the back of a truck and cooked their own food. On the boat, they had third-class tickets but had paid bribes to sleep on the roofs of first-class cabins. They traveled hard and dirty and looked it.

Like many of the trekkers, Julie Gunn of Brighton, Mass., was an escapee from her profession. She said she was an intensive care nurse in Boston, where she had seen too many affluent teenagers overdose on cocaine and recover with the help of $20,000 of their parents' insurance money. She also said she worked in fear of AIDS-tainted blood. Traveling in Africa, the 32-year-old nurse said, was a way to forget the hospital: "It is like living *National Geographic*."

On the second-class barge, passengers had come not to forget their professions, but to pursue them. River merchants had booked all the second-class compartments. As soon as the boat got under way, they unpacked their wares and set up displays in the narrow passageways—clothing, soap, nails, fishing line, cosmetics, plastic buckets, and lots of drugs (penicillin, tetracycline, antimalarials, antidiarrheals, all-purpose tonics). Nearly everyone sold hypodermic needles. Many drugs were "for intramuscular injections only." The merchants said river people believe in the curative power of needles.

When they had finished unpacking, the merchants sat on benches and waited for the river to serve up some business. One shirt salesman sat quietly, squinting out at the river, which was silvery white in the midafternoon sun. He shared a cigarette with a chimpanzee that sat beside him in a cage. A goat, tied up under his seat, timidly chewed on the cuff of his trousers.

Soon after the colonial ruins of riverfront Kisangani had slipped out of sight, the forest asserted itself—60-foot-high walls of vegetation sprang up from both sides of the river. From beneath the bush, scores of dugout canoes materialized, racing to intercept the riverboat. Customers!

The docking of the dugouts, accomplished while the boat sailed at full steam (about 10 miles an hour), proved the major entertainment of the journey. It is an athletic event somewhat akin to rodeo steer wrestling.

The dugouts, fashioned by hand from giant trees, were about 40 feet long, 3 feet wide, and wobbly. They were paddled into position downstream from the riverboat. When the angle was right, the canoeists (usually two lean young men) paddled frantically to intercept the boat. The man in the bow then had about two seconds in which to throw down his paddle, spring onto the riverboat, brace himself, and reach back for a rope to secure the dugout.

It was a high-stakes game. Once every 20 or so dockings, something went wrong. A month's work embodied in crates of smoked monkeys, bundles of handwoven mats, buckets of edible maggots— tipped over in the river. The canoeists swam home.

If they made it aboard, the river people were suddenly hostages to the professional buyers and sellers who had been waiting for them. As a rule of thumb, merchants said, they buy game, fish, and agricultural produce for as little as one-fifth the price they expect to sell it for in Kinshasa. They gave a trapper $2.10 for a fresh monkey and planned to sell it for as much as $11. Merchants said the standard markup on goods they sell to the dugout people was 200 percent higher than retail in the capital.

Monkey trappers, especially, argued about the low prices, sometimes screaming in rage and refusing to sell. But they had no choice. The riverboat is the only store in the forest and merchants on board collude over prices. Gouging by middlemen is a time-honored tradition in Mobutu's Zaire. The longer the trappers dickered, the farther they had to paddle upstream to get back home.

Late Monday afternoon, one of six live crocodiles that had been tied up down in the engine room was brought up for slaughter. Seven feet long and trussed to a thick wooden pole, it had been loaded on board at Kisangani. It was bound for the captain's freezer.

On the open deck where the sailor with the sharp knife cut throats, the crocodile was gutted. The spectacle attracted the cameras of rucksack tourists and of the photographer who was traveling with me. The captain, stalking the bridge above, did not like it. Film would be confiscated, he bellowed in French, if anyone took pictures of a *situation bizarre*. The evisceration of any beast headed for the captain's freezer, it seemed, was a *situation bizarre*.

That evening, a sergeant in charge of security on board the *Major Mudimbi* paid a visit to the cabin I shared with the photographer and another journalist. He said the captain's prohibition on photographs would be no problem. He would handle the captain. He would protect us. He would be our friend.

All we had to do was feed him and buy him beer for the next seven days.

⁓ KEN FUSON ⁓

Ken Fuson is a feature writer for *The Des Moines* (Iowa) *Register*. He was a reporter for *The Sun* in Baltimore when he won the ASNE award for non-deadline writing in 1998. He prefers writing long, but proves in this weather story that he can go short.

In the 14th century, Geoffrey Chaucer began *The Canterbury Tales* with a weather report. He reminded his audience of what happens in England when the long cold winter ends with the first burst of spring. The April rains arrive along with sweet winds, helping flowers and crops to grow. Little birds sing and frolic day and night. People burst out of their houses, filled with new life and energy. Instead of

Walt Disney World, they make a pilgrimage to Canterbury to renew their spirit. The father of English poetry accomplishes this feat in 18 glorious lines. Not a bad lead.

Maybe Ken Fuson is the next Geoffrey Chaucer. He takes an assignment made of straw and mud and spins it into gold. OK, so maybe he's Rumpelstiltskin. The assignment from his editor at *The Des Moines Register* was to cover the dramatic change of weather in Iowa as winter thawed into spring. Now Fuson, in spite of his many writing awards, is not famous for writing short — or on deadline. He is known for long narrative projects, such as his ASNE award winner — a series on a high school production of *West Side Story*.

Fuson himself played Charlie Brown in a high school musical and still looks the part. He is self-effacing about his own abilities, but his modesty and good humor barely mask a deep artistic sensibility.

So he accepted his weather assignment and created something unusual, a single luxurious sentence winding from the simple introduction: "Here's how Iowa celebrates a 70-degree day in the middle of March." What follows is an inventory of the senses, a catalog of joyous rejuvenation, a garden of earthly delights. He finally wrote a truly short story, he told his editors. Now, he said, if he could only work on those long sentences.

Fuson writes his "weather sentence" within a great tradition of newspaper writing. The "bright," or "brite," as it was commonly spelled, is a favorite genre for readers, the offbeat or whimsical story that offers up a tasty "slice of life." The headline, the photo caption (or cutline), the news brief — all these forms of short writing, when mastered, can be little gifts for readers, reminders of the daily surprises that make an average newspaper good and a good newspaper great.

Finally, Fuson reminds us that the most common of stories — a weather report — can reflect a deeply human experience, the revival of the spirit, and requires a writer who is up to the task. We have chosen this gem of a story for X-Ray Reading because a close look reveals that just as a small jewel can have many facets, so a single brilliant sentence can offer the reader untold surprises and insights.

Ah, What a Day!

THE DES MOINES (IOWA) REGISTER •
MARCH 16, 1995

*Main idea:
foundation for
one long, long
sentence*

*Wordplay
throughout, like
these "oo" words*

*Repeating "by"
creates parallels*

*Includes realities
that exist but
cannot be seen*

*Exclamations
inject even more
energy*

*Author turns
humor on
himself*

Here's how Iowa celebrates a 70-degree day in the middle of March: By washing the car and scooping the loop and taking a walk; by daydreaming in school and playing hooky at work and shutting off the furnace at home; by skateboarding and flying kites and digging through closets for baseball gloves; by riding that new bike you got for Christmas and drawing hopscotch boxes in chalk on the sidewalk and not caring if the kids lost their mittens again; by looking for robins and noticing swimsuits on department store mannequins and shooting hoops in the park; by sticking the ice scraper in the trunk and the antifreeze in the garage and leaving the car parked outside overnight; by cleaning the barbecue and stuffing the parka in storage and just standing outside and letting that friendly sun kiss your face; by wondering where you're going to go on summer vacation and getting reacquainted with neighbors on the front porch and telling the boys that—yes! yes!—they can run outside and play without a jacket; by holding hands with a lover and jogging in shorts and picking up the extra branches in the yard; by eating an ice cream cone outside and (if you're a farmer or gardener) feeling that first twinge that says it's time to plant and (if you're a high school senior) feeling that first twinge that says it's time to leave; by wondering if in all of history there has ever been a day so glorious and concluding that there hasn't and being afraid to even stop and take a breath (or begin a new paragraph) for fear that winter would return, leaving Wednesday in our memory as nothing more than a sweet and too-short dream.

*Semicolons
break the
sentence into
manageable
parts*

*Evokes
American
archetypes*

*Reflects
regional
experience and
sensibilities*

*Evokes
Ecclesiastes: "a
time for every
purpose under
heaven"*

*Perfect note to
end on*

Chapter 8

TERRORISM, WAR
AND DISASTERS

The news events since September 11, 2001, including the war in Iraq and Hurricane Katrina and its aftermath, have inspired us to include prizewinning stories on the topics of terrorism, war and disasters in this edition of *America's Best Newspaper Writing*. These types of stories can be traced back to the earliest examples of eyewitness reporting, such as accounts of the eruption of Mount Vesuvius in the year A.D. 79. When Richard Zahler of *The Seattle Times* wrote of the destruction of Mount St. Helens in 1980, he was writing in a tradition forged by Roman historians almost 2,000 years ago.

On 9/11, the United States was taken by surprise. After a time of relative peace and prosperity following the end of the Cold War, the country had to face an important new set of national and international challenges. The same could be said for American newsrooms. In the immediate aftermath of 9/11, news organizations—which had been focusing mostly on local coverage—again began to look at broader national and international events. This expanded focus has continued through coverage of the U.S.'s ongoing involvement in Iraq and the massive mobilization following Katrina in 2005.

Terrorism, war and disasters all breed fear, which is why people turn to the news for information, consolation and relief. "Only honest and reliable news media could instruct the world in its vulnerability, summon Americans to heroic acts of rescue, and ignite the global search for meaning and response," argued Max Frankel, former editor of *The New York Times.* "Only trusted news teams could discern the nation's anxiety, spread words of hope and therapy, and help to move us from numbing fear toward recovery."

Frankel could easily have had in mind the coverage of 9/11 represented here. Galvanized by a devastating attack blocks from their own newsroom, the reporters of *The Wall Street Journal* fed Bryan Gruley the stunning details he was able to turn into an unforgettable narrative, "a first, rough draft of history." Columnist Steve Lopez of the *Los Angeles Times* found his voice using a classic reporting technique: He experienced the destruction in New York City through the eyes and tears of a cabdriver who taxied him through a vision of hell and hope. And Jim Dwyer of *The New York Times* mined this monumental story for the tiny objects that brought it to life: a window washer's squeegee, a cup of water given in charity, a lost photo.

After these acts of terrorism on American soil, the United States launched wars against Afghanistan and Iraq. Hundreds of journalists, embedded with U.S. troops or working independently, have risked their lives to bring the stories of war home. The riveting accounts of Anthony Shadid, told with unflinching courage for *The Washington Post*, reveal the costs of war for soldiers and civilians alike.

Finally, Mark Fritz of the Associated Press shows us that war rages throughout the world and does not always involve the United States. His report on the genocidal tribal warfare in Rwanda reminds us what can happen when the world does not pay attention to regional disasters. "Look," all these reporters are saying, "do not avert your eyes."

⚊ BRYAN GRULEY ⚊

On September 11, 2001, when terrorist-hijacked planes crashed into the World Trade Center, the Pentagon and a field in rural Pennsylvania, Bryan Gruley was a senior editor in the Washington Bureau of *The Wall Street Journal*. His assignment that historic day is known as "rewrite," a time-honored and high-pressure journalistic role that requires one writer to funnel the reports of many colleagues into a coherent story on deadline.

For Gruley, that meant synthesizing information from more than 50 reporters and editors, many of whom had to evacuate their damaged newsroom opposite the World Trade Center, into a gripping Page One narrative. The story delivers a detailed, painfully vivid and exceptionally lucid account of the chaos that enveloped New York, Washington and the rest of the country that day. In about three hours, Gruley transformed nearly 30,000 words of e-mailed notes into a 4,000-word story, using the clock as his principal aid. "It was really just a matter of falling back on what always works, particularly when you have a story that unfolds in chronological order, as this did," says Gruley, who joined *The Wall Street Journal* in 1995 after 11 years of covering business for *The Detroit News*. "Just fall back on the chronology."

"People and small details illuminate stories, and so they are the essence of good reporting," says Jon Hilsenrath, an economics reporter, one of several *Journal* staffers who risked their lives to report from the World Trade Center site. Those anecdotes and unforgettable quotes mined in the field bring the timeline to life with a painful procession of details that remain etched in the nation's consciousness. "As always, writing is almost 90 percent reporting," Gruley says modestly. "If you have the stuff, it's a lot easier to write than if you don't. And I certainly had it."

"Nation Stands in Disbelief and Horror" is the lead story in a package of reportage and analysis that won the ASNE's Jesse Laventhol Prize for Deadline News Reporting by a Team, as well as the Pulitzer Prize for breaking news reporting. Gruley moved to Chicago in 2005 to head the paper's bureau there.

"Five months after the terrorist attacks, the riveting detail in this outstanding report still puts the reader at Ground Zero," the ASNE judges commented. "The *Journal* and its staff rose above the particular challenges they faced on September 11 to produce an account that is worthy of the biggest news story of our professional lives."

Nation Stands in Disbelief
and Horror

THE WALL STREET JOURNAL • SEPTEMBER 12, 2001

They were like scenes from a catastrophe movie. Or a Tom Clancy novel. Or a CNN broadcast from a distant foreign nation.

But they were real yesterday. And they were very much in the U.S.

James Cutler, a 31-year-old insurance broker, was in the Akbar restaurant on the ground floor of the World Trade Center when he heard "boom, boom, boom," he recalls. In seconds, the kitchen doors blew open, smoke and ash poured into the restaurant and the ceiling collapsed. Mr. Cutler didn't know what had happened yet, but he found himself standing among bodies strewn across the floor. "It was mayhem," he says.

Around the same time, Nestor Zwyhun, the 38-year-old chief technology officer of Tradecard, an international trading firm, had just stepped off the New Jersey commuter ferry and was walking toward the World Trade Center when he heard a sound "like a jet engine at full throttle," he says, then a huge explosion. Smoke billowed in the sky and sheets of glass were falling everywhere. "I stood there for two seconds, then ran," Mr. Zwyhun said.

More than 100 floors above him at the trade center offices of Cantor Fitzgerald, someone put a call from the company's Los Angeles office on the speaker phone. What was happening there? The Los Angeles people heard someone say, "I think a plane just hit us." For more than five minutes, the Los Angeles people listened in horror as the sounds of chaos came through the speaker phone, people screaming, "Somebody's got to help us. . . . We can't get out. . . . The place is filling with smoke." Then the phone went dead.

Three hundred miles to the south, in Washington, D.C., a jet swooped in from the west and burrowed into the side of the Pentagon building, exploding in a tower of flame and smoke. Mark Thaggard, an office manager in the building, was there when the plane hit. People started running this way and that, trying to get out. "It was chaotic," Mr. Thaggard says. "It was unbelievable. We could not believe this was happening."

The nation stood in shock and horror yesterday after three apparently hijacked jetliners, in less than an hour's time, made kamikaze-like crashes into both towers of the World Trade Center and the

Pentagon, killing hundreds, maybe thousands, of people and leaving countless others maimed and burned.

The streets of downtown Manhattan were strewn with body parts, clothing, shoes and mangled flesh, including a severed head with long, dark hair and a severed arm resting along a highway about 300 yards from the crash site. People fleeing the attacks stampeded through downtown and streamed across the Brooklyn Bridge while looking over their shoulders at the astonishing sight of the World Trade Center collapsing in a pile of smoke and ash.

Andrew Lenney, 37 years old, a financial analyst for the New York City Council, was walking to work a few blocks from the trade center when, he said, "I saw the plane out of the corner of my eye. You're accustomed to a plane taking up a certain amount of space in the sky. This plane was huge. I just froze and watched the plane.

"It was coming down the Hudson. It was banking toward me. I saw the tops of both wings," he said. "It was turning to make sure it hit the intended target. It plowed in about 20 stories down dead center into the north face of the building. I thought it was a movie," Mr. Lenney said. "I couldn't believe it. It was such a perfect pyrotechnic display. It was symmetrical."

Outside the Pentagon, hundreds of workers who felt the building shake on impact poured outside amid spewing smoke. Inside, lights had switched off and alarms were blaring. "We heard a loud blast, and I felt a gust of wind," said a civilian Pentagon worker who asked not to be identified. "I heard a loud explosion, and somebody said, 'Run, let's get out of here.' And I ran."

The president learned of the initial plane crash in New York before joining a class of schoolchildren in Sarasota, Fla. At 9:04 a.m., Chief of Staff Andrew Card whispered word of the second attack into his ear as Mr. Bush was reading to the children. About a half hour later, he appeared on television to inform the nation that terrorists were behind the tragedy. He said he had ordered a full-scale investigation to "hunt down and to find those folks who committed this act."

Shortly before 9 a.m., American Airlines Flight 11 from Boston, hijacked by suspects with knives, slammed into one trade center tower. Eighteen minutes later — as millions watched the first tower burn on live national television — a second hijacked jet crashed into the other tower. By midmorning, the south tower had exploded and collapsed, raining debris and sending choking dust and smoke across lower Manhattan. Within half an hour, the second tower caved in.

As that scene unfolded, a third hijacked jet crashed into the Pentagon. The side of the building caved in, with secondary explosions bursting in the aftermath and huge billows of smoke rising over the Potomac River, where they could be seen all the way to the White House.

A fourth plane, also hijacked, crashed about 80 miles south of Pittsburgh. United Airlines said it was a Boeing 757 en route from Newark, N.J., to San Francisco. It crashed in a remote field, killing all 45 on board. Virginia Rep. James Moran, a Democrat, told reporters after a military briefing yesterday that the rogue plane could have been headed to the Camp David presidential retreat in the mountains of Maryland.

The FBI, with 20 agents at the site, said that it was treating the crash as a crime scene. Early reports indicate that there were no ground fatalities.

In Pennsylvania, Daniel Stevens, spokesman for the Westmoreland County public-safety department, confirmed that its 911-call center received a call from a man aboard United Flight 93 over Pittsburgh at 9:58 a.m. The caller, claiming he was locked in a bathroom, said "the plane is being hijacked," and repeatedly stressed that his call was "not a hoax." Mr. Stevens said he thinks the call was bona fide. On the same flight, a flight attendant from Fort Myers, Fla., called her husband on a cellphone shortly before the plane crashed.

A federal official said a crew member on one of the American flights called the company's operations center and reported that several crew members had been stabbed and relayed the seat number of one of the attackers.

The crashes shattered a placid, clear morning in New York and Washington. By early afternoon, fighter jets were patrolling Manhattan, and downtown New York hospitals were turning away people offering to give blood because of long lines. With cellphones not working, people swarmed pay phones and huddled around radios. And the trade center towers had disappeared from the skyline.

Vincent Fiori was on the 71st floor of the first tower that was hit. "I'm sitting at my computer and I heard a rumble and my chair spun around," he said. Most people weren't sure what had happened. On the street, people gazed up at the gaping, smoking hole in the building, some holding handkerchiefs over their mouths, more curious than frightened.

The mood changed quickly when the second plane hovered into view and swerved into the other tower. Mr. Zwyhun, the Tradecard executive, was on the upper deck of a ferry, returning to New Jersey, when he saw the second crash and realized "this wasn't an accident."

Panic ensued, as stock traders, secretaries, construction workers and store clerks ran for cover. But there was bizarre calm, too, as some businesspeople rescheduled meetings on cellphones. Police showed up in numbers, ordering everyone to move uptown as fast as possible.

The top floors of the buildings were engulfed in smoke, and people began leaping from windows, one at a time, hitting the ground, shrubbery, and awnings. On the Brooklyn Bridge, dust-covered New Yorkers trooping homeward jammed the pedestrian walkway. A man in shorts and a T-shirt, running toward Manhattan with a radio to his ear, shouted "The Pentagon is burning, the Pentagon is burning!" and a young woman talking on her cellphone shouted, "My mother works there. I don't know where she is. What is happening? What is happening?"

Pedestrians streaming off the Williamsburg Bridge were met by local workers who had dismantled office water coolers, stacked mountains of plastic cups and hauled cases of water to the foot of the bridge. Tom Ryan, a burly ironworker who was handing out cups of water, said, "Our lives are never going to be the same. Now we're going to go through the same things as other countries."

Ferries, police boats and pleasure craft cruised up to the side of the promenade near the towers to whisk people away—children and the injured first.

Paul and Lee Manton, who moved to New York only a month ago from Australia, were holding their two children, ages 3 and 5, and frantically trying to find out where to go. The family lives near the towers, and after the planes hit, Mr. Manton stared out his window at the flaming buildings. "I said, 'These are going to go down,' and just as I said it the building started falling." Fifteen minutes later, he and his wife rushed their children outside in search of escape.

For more than 45 minutes after the second plane smashed into the second World Trade Center tower, the skyscrapers still stood—burning but apparently solid. Workers in the nearby buildings flooded out, and the promenade along the Hudson River was where many of them went. When the tower started to cave, it began with a low rumble. Slowly, amid a dark cloud of smoke, the debris rained down. "My God, it's falling," someone shouted. Mesmerized, no one moved.

A firefighters union official said he feared an estimated 200 firefighters had died in rescue efforts at the trade center—where

50,000 people worked—and dozens of police officers were believed missing.

Father John Doherty, a Roman Catholic priest, was on the street not far from the Marriott Hotel adjacent to the World Trade Center. "I was buried and dug my way out," he said, speaking on a stretcher in Battery Park City a few blocks south of the ruins. He paused to spit, and out came a wet, gray wad of ash. In the pitch dark of the smoke, he said, he made it to safety only by following a guard rail that runs along the riverside. "It's only the finger of God that saved me," he said.

Timothy Snyder and two other employees of Thermo Electron were in their 85th floor office in the North Tower of the World Trade Center when the plane hit three floors above them. They didn't know it was a plane; Mr. Snyder believed it was a bomb.

"We were just working," he says. "All of a sudden, we heard this slamming sound that was so loud. The debris started falling outside the windows, and the door to the office blew open. The building started swaying, and it was hard to say if the building would remain standing. I was in my chair, and I just grabbed onto my desk.

"After five or 10 seconds, the building stopped moving, and we knew we had to leave. We all grabbed our bags and headed out." They walked down to the 78th floor where they were guided to another stairwell, crossing a lobby with a bank of elevators. The marble walls of the lobby were buckled.

As they walked down, the stairwells were crowded but calm. "There was air you could breathe," he says. "We didn't feel we were being suffocated." They were guided through the mall under the World Trade Center. Just as they came out, World Trade Center Two collapsed. "Being in the cloud of smoke was like being in this very dense, unbreathable air that was so black no sun was getting through." He ran for safety and made it.

"We feel, since the plane hit only three floors above us, amazingly thankful we're all alive. But there were emergency workers going up those steps while we were going down. They were trying to save others and they didn't make it."

In New York, officials set up a triage center in Jersey City, N.J., in front of the Datek Online Holdings building on the Hudson River. At Chelsea Piers, a recreational complex along the Hudson River, emergency officials set up a makeshift trauma center in a cavernous room that appears to be used as a set for TV shows and films. "Trauma" was spray-painted in orange letters over one entryway, and inside there were more than 50 beds—many converted from fold-out tables and lit with the aid of television studio lights. Some 150 surgeons, in town for a medical conference, reported to the trauma center and were prepared to take patients. Emergency workers prepared several dozen volunteers who were to be assigned one-on-one to accompany patients as they came in for treatment.

But as of 4:30 p.m., more than seven hours after the first plane struck one of the World Trade Center towers, there weren't many patients—only a handful of emergency personnel had come in for treatment of minor injuries. One emergency official, communicating through a bullhorn, told the waiting doctors, nurses and emergency medical technicians that the New York Fire Department at the scene wasn't permitting rescue workers to head into the rubble. "It's still too hot," the official said. And the city's hospitals still had vacant beds.

Mike Athemas, a 46-year-old volunteer fireman, headed downtown [after the attacks] and didn't leave until midafternoon. "Everywhere you turned, there was someone taking bodies out of the rubble," he said. Making matters worse, documents that had been blown from the building were catching fire and igniting vehicles outside the World Trade Center. "There were 20 cars and trucks—police cars and emergency vehicles—on fire," said Mr. Athemas. One New York city firefighter sobbed aloud, "My company is dead. They're all dead."

After the first plane hit the World Trade Center, New York City firefighter Craig Gutkes was part of a ladder company in Brooklyn that was called in to Manhattan. When he was still on the Brooklyn side, his company saw the second plane roar over their heads. "It sounded like a freight train," he said. They watched that plane plow into Tower No. 2. When he arrived on Liberty Street, "It was like a war zone when we got there. There were body parts all over the street."

In midtown, in front of St. Bartholomew's Church, an Episcopal church, assistant rector Andrea Maier stood in the street in white vestments, handing out a specially printed prayer for peace to the dazed throngs walking uptown. Dozens of people prayed inside the church. Special services for peace were being held every hour to accommodate people walking in off the street to pray. "We'll just do this all night if we have to," said the church rector, the Rev. William Tully.

Amir Chaudhary, a 24-year-old taxi driver, watched the second tower collapse from across the Hudson River in Jersey City. "In a blink of my eye the twin towers were gone. There was no boom even. Didn't hear anything. Guys were on their knees crying, begging me to give them a ride away. I feel like maybe it's a bad dream: If I wake up, I could get the twin towers back."

Although the White House was not damaged, its people were not untouched by the tragedy. Barbara Olson, wife of U.S. Solicitor General Theodore Olson, was on board the Los Angeles-bound airplane that took off from Dulles Airport and crashed into the Pentagon. Ms. Olson, a frequent political commentator, used a cellphone to call her husband just moments before she died. Late in the day, President Bush took time from his security briefing to call Mr. Olson and offer his condolences.

Before sending his aides home, Sen. John Warner of Virginia recalled to them, "I was in Washington when I heard about the Japanese attack on Pearl Harbor. This is another Pearl Harbor, and now your generation will have to meet the challenge."

By yesterday evening, military vehicles were patrolling the city, and police had cordoned off a three-square-block area near the White House.

In Arlington, Va., abutting Washington, fishermen plunking for catfish at a marina near the Pentagon said they could feel the heat from the explosion. The White House, the Capitol, and the Treasury and State departments were evacuated shortly after the crash at the Pentagon. "Get out! Get out!" police yelled as they swept through federal buildings. As legislators streamed out of the Capitol, the memorial chimes across the street played "God Bless America."

∼ STEVE LOPEZ ∼

Steve Lopez won the 2001 ASNE award for commentary, for a provocative and poignant string of columns he wrote during his first six months at the *Los Angeles Times*. But Lopez, who has worked at seven newspapers, six of them in his native California, is no stranger to the art and craft of persuasive writing, or to receiving awards for his work. In 12 years as a *Philadelphia Inquirer* columnist, he won the H.L. Mencken Writing Award, the Ernie Pyle Award for human interest writing and a National Headliner Award for column writing. He then spent four years writing for *Time, Sports Illustrated, Life* and *Entertainment Weekly* as an editor-at-large before joining the *Los Angeles Times* in May 2001 to write a local column, "Points West."

Lopez writes novels as well as newspaper columns, but at heart he's a street reporter who believes that "the biggest mistake columnists make is to think that they have something important to say, and they forget the thing that sustains most columns, which is reporting."

"Amid the Ruins, a Separate Peace" features a staple of newspaper columns—an eminently quotable taxi driver. Unlike the stock figure of news narrative, cabby Vincent Bury has a name that was eerily symbolic on the rainy late night four days after 9/11 and a featured role as a symbol of the grieving city.

Lopez admits that he hesitated before writing the column. "The cheapest trick in the book is to interview the cabby," he says. "Every journalist will say, 'Oh, yeah, nice work. Hail a cab and write a column. That's really difficult.' "

But then Lopez reminded himself, "Readers are going to read it, not journalists, and that's who I'm writing for."

Lopez judges his own columns with a litmus test that every reporter might consider while working on a story: "Would I read this thing? Is this idea big enough? Am I advancing a story people already know about? Am I giving them something new and different to think about? Am I going to entertain them? Am I going to inform them?"

It's that reader-centric philosophy that separates Lopez and his work from the rest of the pack.

Amid the Ruins, a Separate Peace

LOS ANGELES TIMES • SEPTEMBER 15, 2001

NEW YORK—Midnight came and went, and Manhattan couldn't sleep.

"Look at this. Just look at this," Vincent Bury said as he aimed his yellow cab toward the smoke. "That used to be a beautiful view of the towers, but I'm going to tell you something. You see all these people out here? Everybody helping out in whatever way they can? They tried to break us up, but this city's never been more unified."

Vincent Bury drove slower than any cabby has ever driven in New York, loving his wounded city. The heavens thundered with an advancing storm, and flashes of lightning illuminated American flags that hung from fire escapes.

A few poor souls wandered the streets like ghosts, photos of missing loved ones taped to shirts or strung around their necks. They were consoled by people they did not know and would never see again.

"Look at this," Vincent Bury said again, his heart full.

He turned a corner at 15th Street and 11th Avenue to find a group of teenagers cheering. "Thank you Thank you Thank you," said the signs they held. They were spending the night at the intersection to greet rescue workers who came up for air after digging with their hands for hours. Digging for miracles. Ambulances lined the streets, waiting for a call.

On a normal night, Vincent Bury would have been driven off the road by angry motorists leaning on horns. But they passed politely, letting him mourn in his own time. He calls himself the last white native New York cabby, and he is different in another way too. Instead of ramming fenders and bumpers, like you're supposed to do to let off steam, he meditates.

"The inner self never dies," he said, and he was sure something good was going to come of this tragedy.

"Where to now?" he asked.

"A Hundredth and Riverside. The fireman's memorial."

Bury parked on Riverside and got out of the car with a camera. He said that in his 49 years, he had never seen the fireman's memorial and its twin statues of Courage and Duty. He wanted to take the memory home to Brooklyn with him.

A little earlier in the evening, an advertising man named John Avery had left his Upper West Side apartment to walk his poodle Gracie. Avery had been in a state of shock over the attack on New York, but the shock was becoming sadness and anger. A co-worker lost her husband in one of the towers, and it was hitting Avery in a way it hadn't until then.

He was thinking, too, about the estimated 300 firefighters believed to have died under the rubble of what used to be an American symbol.

Three hundred.

Avery walked two blocks to the memorial that has stood since 1913. Firefighters never hesitate, he was thinking as Gracie tugged on the leash. They take chances with their own lives to save others, and there is a striking gallantry about them. The bravery, the bond, the cut of the uniform.

On this night, candles had been left at the memorial, and they flickered in the breeze of the coming storm. Bouquets were laid about, and some well-wishers had written anonymous notes of thanks and sympathy.

"The whole world is a very narrow bridge," said one. "Words can not express our sorrow," said another.

Avery's eyes filled, and anger floated just beneath the sadness. President Bush and the rest of America have to have the guts to root out terrorists wherever they are, he said, his voice deepening.

"We must go after the terrorists and anyone who harbors or finances them. It's not about revenge; it's about protection. If we don't do it, this can happen again. But if it's about revenge, we've sunk to the morality of the terrorists."

The storm had moved across the Hudson, bringing with it a drenching rain that sent John Avery and Gracie the poodle home.

Vincent Bury took a picture of the memorial, which has the following inscription:

"To the men of the fire department of the city of New York, who died at the call of duty. Soldiers in a war that never ends."

Vincent Bury drove away at funeral speed, in touch with both the living and the dead. It rained like everyone was crying all at once, and it seemed to me that New York had never been more beautiful.

⤳ MARK FRITZ ⤳

Mark Fritz is a national writer for the *Los Angeles Times*. His coverage of the Rwandan massacres in 1994 won the first Jesse Laventhol Prize for Deadline News Reporting from the American Society of Newspaper Editors and the Pulitzer Prize for international reporting. He is the author of *Lost on Earth: Nomads of the New World*.

Foreign correspondence is often a confusing blend of alien names and even stranger situations, comprehensible perhaps to the reporter on the scene but a puzzle to the average reader. Mark Fritz's chilling series of dispatches for the Associated Press are powerful because they help us begin to understand the incomprehensible—the mass slaughter of hundreds of thousands of men, women and children at the hands, clubs and axes of their neighbors.

His method was to steer clear of the journalistic pack and find the stories that could communicate the reality of the horror. His goal:

to make average Americans care about news they think has no impact on their lives. His tools: thorough reporting backed by research and critical and creative thinking that enabled him to produce deadline storytelling under harrowing conditions.

Behind Fritz's virtuoso performance under great time pressure were years of practice at a job that demands speed and accuracy. Fritz acquired mastery of what he calls the "little tricks" that are the essence of the reporting and writing craft: "writing in your head, jotting a transition," hunting for "precision detail," putting away your notes to "think about what your story is about and what example you have that most compellingly explains your story."

Drawing on those work habits, Fritz wrote a lead that departs from the traditional Five W's to home in on the central meaning of what he had witnessed in Karubamba. "Nobody lives here any more" is a five-word declarative sentence that commands readers' attention.

The next four paragraphs explain the mystery behind that sentence, in gruesome detail, taking readers along on Fritz's own journey.

Fritz then backs up to provide the background American readers need to understand the context. What makes his stories exceptional, beyond the enterprise and raw courage they demanded, was the homework—reading, researching, scouring databases, interviewing experts—that preceded his field reporting.

Even while he is describing the complex power struggles behind warring tribes, Fritz never loses sight of the people whose individual stories allow readers to bridge the gap between their own experiences and those on another continent. Reporting and writing under harrowing conditions and brutal time constraints, Fritz used the reporter's tools—curiosity, observation and empathy—and the writer's techniques—analogy, metaphor and unforgettable imagery—to convey the human consequences of an unfathomable horror.

Only Human Wreckage Is Left in Karubamba

ASSOCIATED PRESS • MAY 12, 1994

KARUBAMBA, RWANDA—Nobody lives here any more.

Not the expectant mothers huddled outside the maternity clinic, not the families squeezed into the church, not the man who lies rotting in a schoolroom beneath a chalkboard map of Africa.

Everybody here is dead. Karubamba is a vision from hell, a flesh-and-bone junkyard of human wreckage, an obscene slaughterhouse that has fallen silent save for the roaring buzz of flies the size of honeybees.

With silent shrieks of agony locked on decaying faces, hundreds of bodies line the streets and fill the tidy brick buildings of this village, most of them in the sprawling Roman Catholic complex of classrooms and clinics at Karubamba's stilled heart.

Karubamba is just one breathtakingly awful example of the mayhem that has made beautiful little Rwanda the world's most ghastly killing ground.

Karubamba, 30 miles northeast of Kigali, the capital, died April 11, six days after Rwandan President Juvenal Habyarimana, a member of the Hutu tribe, was killed in a plane crash whose cause is still undetermined.

The paranoia and suspicion surrounding the crash blew the lid off decades of complex ethnic, social and political hatreds.

It ignited a murderous spree by extremists from the majority Hutus against rival Tutsis and those Hutus who had opposed the government.

This awesome wave of remorseless mayhem has claimed 100,000 to 200,000 lives, say U.N. and other relief groups. Many were cut down while cowering in places traditionally thought safe havens: churches, schools, relief agencies.

One stroll past the bleached skulls, ripped limbs and sun-baked sinews on the blood-streaked streets of Karubamba gives weight to those estimates.

Almost every peek through a broken window or splintered door reveals incomprehensible horror. A schoolboy killed amid tumbling desks and benches. A couple splattered against a wall beneath a portrait of a serene, haloed Jesus Christ.

Peer into the woods every few hundred feet along the red-clay road to Karubamba and see piles of bodies heaped in decaying clumps.

News from Rwanda has been dominated by accounts of the carnage in Kigali or of millions of refugees living in mud and filth in vast encampments just outside the border. But what happened in Karubamba has happened—and is still happening—in villages across this fertile green nation of velvety, terraced hills.

Survivors from Karubamba say when early word came of the Hutu rampage, people from surrounding towns fled to the seemingly safe haven of the Rukara Parish complex here.

On the night of April 11, the killers swarmed among the neat rows of buildings and began systematically executing the predominantly Tutsi population with machetes, spears, clubs and guns.

"They said, 'You are Tutsi, therefore we have to kill you,' " said Agnes Kantengwa, 34, who was among dozens holed up inside the yellow brick church.

"We thought we were safe in church. We thought it was a holy place."

It wasn't.

Her husband and four children were butchered amid the overturned pews. Bodies stretched to the ornately carved hardwood altar beneath a large crucifix.

Somewhere amid the stinking human rubble is the Rev. Faustin Kagimbura, "who tried to protect us," Kantengwa said.

Down the road, outside the maternity clinic next to the hospital, about 25 bodies lie beneath a cluster of shade trees; most appear to be women, but it is difficult now to be sure.

"They were women waiting to have babies," Kantengwa said. "The killers made them go outside and kneel down, then cut them in the head with machetes and spears. They said, 'You are Tutsi.' "

Mrs. Kantengwa, her 6-year-old son and 6-month-old daughter survived with a mosaic of machete wounds. They share one hospital bed in nearby Gahini, a larger town that breathes bustling life as easily as Karubamba exudes the suffocating stench of month-old death.

At the primary school midway between the maternity clinic and the church, a man lies prone beneath a meticulously drawn blackboard sketch of Africa, the capitals of each nation listed alongside.

Serena Mukagasana, 16, said the man was teacher Matthias Kanamugire.

The girl also was in the church when the slaughter began. By the time it was over, she was an orphan.

"All my family was killed," she said. She fled outside during the slaughter and watched from the bushes.

"They just killed and killed," she said.

The Tutsi-dominated Rwandan Patriotic Front that has been battling the government since 1991 has made huge gains in the countryside since the rampage began.

Their secured areas are relatively stable and well-policed, though scores of villages remain empty and thousands of people line the roads looking for safe places to stop. More than 1.3 million people in this nation of 8 million are displaced.

The rebels took Gahini and set up a base just days after the massacre at Karubamba. It is one of the staging areas for what is believed to be an imminent rebel assault on Kigali, where guerrillas are battling government troops backed by Hutu militias.

Capt. Diogene Mugenge, the rebel commander in Gahini, said an estimated 1,500 to 2,000 people died in the carnage at Karubamba. The only sign of human life in the area is a lone sentry posted roughly where the fresh air begins.

When asked about the massacre, and the fact that mutilated, battered bodies remain frozen in the moment of agonizing death just a few miles from his base, Mugenge shrugs.

"It's happening everywhere," he said.

⌁ ANTHONY SHADID ⌁

Anthony Shadid of *The Washington Post* arrived in Iraq about two weeks before war broke out in March 2003. One of his first challenges was to convince his editors back home to let him stay after the bombs began to fall. Their approval enabled Shadid to carry out a dangerous but essential journalistic mission. In Baghdad, Shadid operated as a "unilateral," unfettered by the constraints of "embedded" reporters traveling with the U.S. military. Whereas most journalists focused on combat, Shadid used the war as the backdrop for his stories about ordinary life in a capital under siege.

Shadid is an Arab-American. His Lebanese grandfather immigrated to Oklahoma City, where Shadid grew up. He studied Arabic at the University of Wisconsin and the American University in Cairo, Egypt. He began his career with the Associated Press in Cairo, where he reported from the region's hot spots from 1995 to 1999. He then spent two years as a Washington-based reporter for *The Boston Globe*. On temporary assignment in the Middle East in March 2002, Shadid was shot in the shoulder while walking on a street in the West Bank city of Ramallah.

Shadid avoided the media pack in Baghdad as much as possible, preferring to find stories by driving around the city. That was how he stumbled across the funeral of 14-year-old Arkan Daif, killed in an explosion along with two cousins as they dug a trench to shelter their families during day-and-night bombing attacks.

Amid the war's carnage, the death of "a boy who . . . was 'like a flower' " in a "dirt-poor, Shiite Muslim neighborhood" would probably have gone unnoticed. Shadid says that he saw an opportunity to humanize the impact of war by focusing on the universal "ritual of death" to make the lives of ordinary Iraqi civilians understandable to *The Washington Post*'s readers. From the ritual washing of the body in the mosque to the coffin's departure for the cemetery, Shadid watched and listened. Knowing that "a lot of times . . . the color's more important than the quote," he stepped back like a photographer to "capture the scene." But he also needed to do the painful yet essential work of eliciting details from grieving relatives. A notebook brimming with details isn't enough, though. Even on deadline, Shadid recognizes the power of planning, often spending "as much time outlining my stories as writing them."

Under conditions both terrifying and exhausting (Shadid filed 24 front-page stories) he provided eyewitness testimony of the costs of war, enabling his newspaper to "have eyes and ears everywhere, not only with the troops, but in Baghdad and anywhere it's possible." In addition to the ASNE's Jesse Laventhol Prize for Deadline News Reporting, Shadid won the Pulitzer Prize for international reporting for his stories from Baghdad.

A Boy Who Was "Like a Flower"

THE WASHINGTON POST • MARCH 31, 2003

BAGHDAD, Iraq—On a cold, concrete slab, a mosque caretaker washed the body of 14-year-old Arkan Daif for the last time.

With a cotton swab dipped in water, he ran his hand across Daif's olive corpse, dead for three hours but still glowing with life. He blotted the rose-red shrapnel wounds on the soft skin of Daif's right arm and right ankle with the poise of practice. Then he scrubbed his face scabbed with blood, left by a cavity torn in the back of Daif's skull.

The men in the Imam Ali mosque stood somberly waiting to bury a boy who, in the words of his father, was "like a flower." Haider Kathim, the caretaker, asked: "What's the sin of the children? What have they done?"

In the rituals of burial, the men and their families tried, futilely, to escape the questions that have enveloped so many lives here in fear and uncertainty. Beyond some neighbors, family, and a visitor, there were no witnesses; the funeral went unnoticed by a government that has eagerly escorted journalists to other wartime tragedies. Instead, Daif and two cousins were buried in the solitude of a dirt-poor, Shiite Muslim neighborhood near the city limits.

The boys were killed at 11 a.m. today when, as another relative recalled, "the sky exploded." Daif had been digging a trench in front of the family's concrete shack that could serve as a shelter during the bombing campaign that continues day and night. He had been working with Sabah Hassan, 16, and Jalal Talib, 14. The white-hot shrapnel cut down all three. Seven other boys were wounded.

The explosion left no crater, and residents of the Rahmaniya neighborhood struggled to pinpoint the source of the destruction. Many insisted they saw an airplane. Some suggested Iraqi antiaircraft fire had detonated a cruise missile in the air. Others suggested rounds from antiaircraft guns had fallen back to earth and onto their homes.

Whoever caused the explosion, the residents assigned blame to the United States, insisting that without a war, they would be safe. "Who else could be responsible except the Americans?" asked Mohsin Hattab, a 32-year-old uncle of Daif.

"This war is evil. It's an unjust war," said Imad Hussein, a driver and uncle of Hassan. "They have no right to make war against us. Until now, we were sitting in our homes, comfortable and safe."

As he spoke, the wails of mourners pouring forth from homes drowned out his words. He winced, turning his head to the side. Then he continued. "God will save us," he said softly.

At the mosque, hours after the blast, Kadhim and another caretaker prepared Daif's body for burial — before sundown, as is Islamic custom.

Bathed in the soft colors of turquoise tiles, the room was hushed, as the caretakers finished the washing. They wrapped his head, his gaze fixed, with red and yellow plastic. They rolled the corpse in plastic sheeting, fastening it with four pieces of white gauze—one at each end, one around his knees and one around his chest.

Kadhim worked delicately, his gestures an attempt to bring dignity to the corpse. He turned Daif's body to the side and wrapped it in a white sheet, secured with four more pieces of gauze. Under their breaths, men muttered prayers, breaking the suffocating silence that had descended. They then moved toward the concrete slab and hoisted the limp body into a wood coffin.

"It's very difficult," said Kadhim, as the men closed the coffin.

On Friday, he had gone to another mosque, Imam Moussa Kadhim, to help bury dozens killed when a blast ripped through a teeming market in the nearby neighborhood of Shuala. The memories haunted him. He remembered the severed hands and heads that arrived at the Shiite mosque. He recalled bodies, even that of an infant, with gaping holes.

"It was awful and ugly," he said. "This is the first time I've ever seen anything like this."

In an open-air courtyard, the men set the coffin down on the stone floor of a mosque still under construction. In two rows, they lined up behind it, their shoes removed before them. Their lips moved in prayers practiced thousands of times.

"God is greatest," they repeated, their palms facing upward in supplication.

In the background, men discussed the war. In the repression and isolation that reigns in Iraq, rumors often serve as news, and the talk today was of carnage unleashed on a convoy taking the body of an 80-year-old woman to be buried in the southern city of Najaf, where U.S. forces are confronting Iraqi irregulars and soldiers.

For Shiite Muslims, Najaf is among their most sacred cities, housing the tomb of Ali, the son-in-law of the prophet Muhammad, whom Shiites regard as his rightful heir. Tradition has it that the dying Ali asked his followers to place his body on a camel and bury him wherever it first knelt; Najaf was the site. Millions of pilgrims visit each year, and devout Shiites will spend their life's savings for the blessings of being buried in the vast cemeteries that gird the city.

The woman from Rahmaniya never made it. Residents said U.S. forces attacked three cars, one carrying her body. It was another ignominy visited on the city, the men agreed. They insisted that infidels would never enter the city by force of arms. The U.S. siege of the city—its severity accentuated as rumors circulated—was an act of humiliation.

"It's a disgrace," said Hattab, one of Daif's uncles.

Hussein, another relative, echoed the words of others. "They didn't come to liberate Iraq," he said, "they came to occupy it."

In his words was a fear that strikes deep into the Iraqi psyche. Many worry that the U.S. invasion is a threat to their culture and traditions. They wonder if an occupation would obliterate what they hold dear, imposing an alien culture by force on a society that, in large part, remains deeply conservative and insulated.

"We don't want the Americans or British here. Our food is better than their food, our water is better than their water," he said.

With the prayers over, the men hoisted Daif's coffin over their heads. They left through the mosque's gray, steel gates and ventured into the desolate, dirt streets awash in trash. Some were barefoot and others wore sandals.

"There is no god but God," one man chanted. "There is no god but God," the pallbearers answered. Bombing on the horizon provided a refrain. The men crossed the street, past concrete and brick hovels, the Shiite flags of solid black, green, red and white flying overhead.

As they approached Daif's house, its door emblazoned with the names Muhammad and Ali, they were greeted with wails of women covered by black chadors. They screamed, waving their hands and shaking their heads. The cries drowned out the chants, as the coffin disappeared indoors. The despair poured out of the home, its windows shattered by the blast that killed Daif.

"My son! My son!" his mother, Zeineb Hussein, cried out. "Where are you now? I want to see your face!"

The men in Daif's family embraced each other, sobbing uncontrollably on their shoulders. Others cried into their hands. From within the house came the sounds of women methodically beating their chests in grief.

In the houses along the street, neighbors and relatives spoke of injustice — a resonant theme in the lives of Shiite Muslims, whose saints and centuries of theology are infused with examples of suffering and martyrdom.

"We're poor. We can't go anywhere else. What is the fault of the families here? Where's the humanity?" asked Abu Ahmed, a 53-year-old neighbor sitting in a home with three pictures of Ali and a painting of his son, Hussein. "I swear to God, we're scared."

Their talk was angry, and they were baffled.

If the Americans are intent on liberation, why are innocent people dying? If they want to attack the government, why do bombs fall on civilians? How can they have such formidable technology and make such tragic mistakes?

In Hussein's Iraq, with a 30-year political culture built on brutality, some were convinced the Americans were intent on vengeance for the setbacks they believed their forces were delivered in Basra and other southern Iraqi cities. Others, in moments of striking candor, pleaded for the United States and Britain to wage war against their government, but spare the people.

"If they want to liberate people, they can kick out the government, not kill innocent civilians," one relative said. "The innocent civilians are not in business with the government. We're living in our houses."

Before dusk, Daif's coffin was carried from his house. It was set on the back of a white pickup truck headed for the cemetery. As it drove away, kicking up clouds of dirt, some of the neighbors and relatives shouted, "God be with you." Other men waved, a gesture so casual that it suggested the strength of their faith, that they would eventually be reunited with Daif.

Hattab, the uncle, looked on at the departing coffin. His eyes were red, and his face was drawn.

"He has returned to God," he said. "It's God's wish."

◂ RICHARD ZAHLER ▸

Richard Zahler began working at *The Seattle Times* in 1973 after writing for newspapers in Walla Walla and Spokane and for the Associated Press. Since then, Zahler has held countless reporting and editing jobs at *The Seattle Times*, including city hall reporter, copy editor, assigning editor and special projects editor, a job that has both writing and editing responsibilities. A skillful coach and teacher, Zahler helped lead *The Seattle Times* writing group, an effort to improve the quality of writing at the newspaper.

In 1980, Zahler attended one of the first writing seminars conducted by The Poynter Institute, a school for journalists in St. Petersburg, Fla. As chance would have it, the final day of the seminar, a stormy Friday morning, brought a disaster to Tampa Bay. The storm drove a giant oil tanker into the huge Sunshine Skyway Bridge, destroying more than 1,000 feet of the span and sending 35 people to their deaths. (For more on this, see "For Lerro, Skyway Nightmare

Never Ends" by David Finkel on page 186.) As Zahler flew back to
Seattle, pondering these events, he promised himself that he would be
ready to cover the next big disaster. Days later, back in Washington
State, Mount St. Helens exploded. Zahler was ready.

What follows is Zahler's brief introduction to his long narrative
reconstruction of the explosion and its aftermath. This smooth reconciliation of factual reporting and vivid storytelling shows Zahler's
innovative thawing of the frozen structure of the Five W's: He has
created story forms in which "Who becomes Character; What becomes Plot; Where becomes Setting; When becomes Chronology;
Why becomes Motivation."

1,200 Feet of St. Helens Tossed
to the Wind

The Seattle Times • May 18, 1980

Eruption.

At 8:32 yesterday morning, Mount St. Helens ended seven weeks
of nervous convulsions with an explosion brewed deep in the earth's
primeval cauldron.

At least nine people were killed.

When the top of the volcano blew, upwards of 1,200 feet of
mountaintop were pulverized. Instantly, the unimaginable tons of
rock became tiny pebbles that fell as far away as Mount Rainier. The
rock became gray sand in the streets of Yakima. It became a fine dust
drifting like storm clouds in the sky above Spokane, then over Western Montana. Highways and airports were closed across the state.

The hot rock and ash also settled on the slopes of the mountain.
A winter's mantle of ice and snow, already dingy from St. Helen's
warm-up eruptions, melted into flowing death and destruction.

Within minutes of the eruption, snow, hot ash and superheated
gases churned into mudflows dozens of feet thick. The mud started
slowly down the mountain's broad flanks, gathered speed, then
roared through timber and into the thin river valleys that normally
carry burbling spring runoff.

The runoff yesterday was 12 feet high, a wall of water that
gouged earth and timber from banks, spilling a mile-long logjam toward the Cowlitz and Columbia Rivers.

The water was so hot into the Toutle River that fish leaped from it to the banks, trying to escape.

The mud cascaded into Spirit Lake. The waters literally boiled, and the lake apparently was given a new shape. One pilot said it seemed virtually to have ceased to exist.

On the mountain's south slope, the mud rolled in the Swift Reservoir, the uppermost of the three reservoirs on the Lewis River. There was enough of it that the broad reservoir's level rose 6 feet in 15 minutes.

Ahead of the crushing water and earth, minutes after the mountain's explosion, local police went door-to-door in Toutle, telling residents to leave or move to higher ground.

Most did. Some people in the area, apparently sight-seeing or hiking closer to the volcano, didn't get the word.

Five bodies were found at Camp Baker, a logging camp about 15 miles west of the mountain. Later, 1½ miles closer to the mountain, the bodies of a man and a woman were found in their car. Officials said they may have died from the heat of mud and gas churning by. The bodies of two campers were found nearer the mountain.

As volcanos have shaped the Northwest, so yesterday did Mount St. Helens leave its mark on the region: A black or gray cloud that hid the sun for thousands of square miles.

The ash filled the sky, and then it settled toward earth.

At noon in Yakima, it might as well have been midnight—"as dark as the darkest night you've ever seen," said a deputy sheriff.

Traffic stopped. Streetlights and neon signs flickered on.

The volcano began putting people into hospital emergency rooms a hundred miles away, with respiratory problems, with injuries suffered in accidents. Headlights could barely penetrate the black fog, and tires found little purchase on the slippery strata of ash on the highways.

There may be more from St. Helens. "It seems right now that the activity will go on for quite a while," a Geological Survey scientist said last night. "It could be hours or days."

~ JIM DWYER ~

Jim Dwyer is a native New Yorker who writes about New York for *The New York Times*. His career, values and style are so grounded in the city that he has earned those three references to New York in that first sentence. For Dwyer, the standard "New York, New York" (the city so great they named it twice) seems one short of the mark.

In the face of New York City's greatest catastrophe, the September 11, 2001, terrorist attacks on the World Trade Center, Dwyer focused his writing on the small, everyday objects that had stories hiding inside them: a window washer's squeegee, a photograph recovered from the rubble, a plastic cup for water. "Now memories orbit around small things," he wrote as the lead for his first piece in the occasional series. After 9/11, Dwyer's work captured the attention of the nation, as well as his second ASNE award, in 2002. (He won his first in 1991 for his *Newsday* columns.)

Having crafted hundreds of columns over the past two decades, Dwyer has perfected the art of the short newspaper story, the category for which he earned the 2002 prize. Dwyer tells the story of how he got so "fed up" with his early columns that he wrote down a list of rules on writing he could follow. He kept the list in his wallet—which, alas, he lost to a pickpocket. But he remembers these:

1. Save something good for the end.
2. Never put numbers in the lead.
3. Always cut a hundred words.

Dwyer is the son of Irish immigrants. He was born in Manhattan, grew up in a working-class environment and attended the city's parochial schools. He decided to major in science at Fordham University, with hopes of becoming a doctor, but came under the benevolent influence of the Jesuit priest and writer Ray Schroth. At Columbia University Graduate School of Journalism, Dwyer studied under teachers who, like Schroth, mentored him in both the craft and the moral dimensions of journalism.

The young Dwyer honed his reporting skills at the *Hudson Dispatch*, the *Elizabeth Daily Journal*, and *The Record* of Hackensack, all in New Jersey. He then moved on to *Newsday*, the *New York Daily News* and, finally, *The New York Times*. In addition to his ASNE awards, he has won a Pulitzer Prize and the Mike Berger

Award—Meyer "Mike" Berger being *The New York Times* writer whose work Dwyer's most closely resembles. (To read a piece by Mike Berger, turn to "About New York" on page 281.) He is the author of a book on the New York subways and co-author of books on the first World Trade Center bombing and on the causes of wrongful convictions within the criminal justice system.

One of the most talked-about feature stories after 9/11 was Dwyer's "squeegee man" story. We have chosen it for this chapter's X-Ray Reading because of its brevity, power and attention to detail.

X-RAY READING

Fighting for Life 50 Floors Up, With One Tool and Ingenuity

THE NEW YORK TIMES • OCTOBER 9, 2001

A thematic lead

Now memories orbit around small things. None of the other window washers liked his old green bucket, but Jan Demczur, who worked inside 1 World Trade Center, found its rectangular mouth perfect for dipping and wetting his squeegee in one motion. So on the morning of the 11th, as he waited at the 44th-floor Sky Lobby to connect with elevators for higher floors, bucket and squeegee dangled from the end of his arm.

Detail with color so readers can see

A great, funny word in a serious story

An extension of his body

Beginning of "tick-tock," dramatic passage of time

The time was 8:47 a.m. With five other men—Shivam Iyer, John Paczkowski, George Phoenix, Colin Richardson and another man whose identity could not be learned—Mr. Demczur (pronounced DEM-sir) boarded Car 69-A, an express elevator that stopped on floors 67 through 74.

Detail lends authenticity

The car rose, but before it reached its first landing, "We felt a muted thud," Mr. Iyer said. "The building shook. The elevator swang from side to side, like a pendulum."

Quote that also advances the action

(CONTINUED)

First of several dramatic short sentences

Then it plunged. In the car, someone punched an emergency stop button. At that moment—8:48 a.m.—1 World Trade Center had entered the final 100 minutes of its existence. No one knew the clock was running, least of all the men trapped inside Car 69-A; they were as cut off 500 feet in the sky as if they had been trapped 500 feet underwater.

Now passage of time has life-or-death meaning; reminiscent of adventure movies

They did not know their lives would depend on a simple tool.

Reminder of original theme

After 10 minutes, a live voice delivered a blunt message over the intercom. There had been an explosion. Then the intercom went silent. Smoke seeped into the elevator cabin. One man cursed skyscrapers. Mr. Phoenix, the tallest, a Port Authority engineer, poked for a ceiling hatch. Others pried apart the car doors, propping them open with the long wooden handle of Mr. Demczur's squeegee.

Series of short sentences builds suspense

A wonderful, significant name

There was no exit.

Dramatic one-sentence paragraph ups the ante

They faced a wall, stenciled with the number "50." That particular elevator bank did not serve the 50th floor, so there was no need for an opening. To escape, they would have to make one themselves.

Mr. Demczur felt the wall. Sheetrock. Having worked in construction in his early days as a Polish immigrant, he knew that it could be cut with a sharp knife.

No one had a knife.

Echoes earlier short sentence

From his bucket, Mr. Demczur drew his squeegee. He slid its metal edge against the wall, back and forth, over and over. He was spelled by the other men. Against the smoke, they breathed through handkerchiefs dampened in a container of milk Mr. Phoenix had just bought.

Sheetrock comes in panels about one inch thick, Mr. Demczur recalled. They cut an inch, then two inches. Mr. Demczur's hand ached. As he carved into the third panel, his hand shook, he fumbled the squeegee and it dropped down the shaft.

Another plot complication— ante upped again

Tools running out, time running out

He had one tool left: a short metal squeegee handle. They carried on, with fists, feet and handle, cutting an irregular rectangle about 12 by 18 inches. Finally, they hit a layer of white tiles. A bathroom. They broke the tiles.

Short sentences continue

One by one, the men squirmed through the opening, headfirst, sideways, popping onto the floor near a sink. Mr. Demczur turned back. "I said, 'Pass my bucket out,'" he recalled.

Piece of dialogue that shows this guy really likes this bucket

By then, about 9:30, the 50th floor was already deserted, except for firefighters, astonished to see the six men emerge. "I think it was Engine Company 5," Mr. Iyer said. "They hustled us to the staircase."

On the excruciating single-file descent through the smoke, someone teased Mr. Demczur about bringing his bucket. "The company might not order me another one," he replied. At the 15th floor, Mr. Iyer said:

Another quote that advances the action

"We heard a thunderous, metallic roar. I thought our lives had surely ended then." The south tower was collapsing. It was 9:59. Mr. Demczur dropped his bucket. The firefighters shouted to hurry.

Now things are really serious

At 23 minutes past 10, they burst onto the street, ran for phones, sipped oxygen and, five minutes later, fled as the north tower collapsed. Their escape had taken 95 of the 100 minutes. "It took up to one and a half minutes to clear each floor, longer at the lower levels," said Mr. Iyer, an engineer with the Port Authority. "If the elevator had stopped at the 60th floor, instead of the 50th, we would have been five minutes too late.

The atom bomb stops ticking at ".007"

"And that man with the squeegee. He was like our guardian angel."

Since that day, Mr. Demczur has stayed home with his wife and children. He has pieced together the faces of the missing with the men and women he knew in the stations of his old life: the security guard at the Japanese bank on the 93rd floor, who used to let him in at 6:30; the people at Carr Futures on 92; the head of the Port Authority. Their faces keep him awake at night, he says.

Three examples encompass all the lost

(CONTINUED)

Powerful word at the end; the "absence" is not just in his hands but also includes the dead and missing

His hands, the one that held the squeegee and the other that carried the bucket, shake with absence.

Chapter 9

THE
CLASSICS

The American Society of Newspaper Editors inaugurated its Distinguished Writing Awards in 1977 thanks to the leadership of the society's president, Gene Patterson, editor of the *St. Petersburg* (Fla.) *Times.* Patterson was a great stylist himself, the author of columns and editorials on civil rights that earned him a Pulitzer Prize.

Like most great stylists, Patterson learned his craft by reading the work of the fine writers who came before him, reporters whose voices were so powerful they echoed beyond a generation. In that spirit, we offer ten "classic" pieces of journalism. Think of them as the kinds of stories that would have won ASNE recognition if the awards had been instituted in 1900.

Back in 1917, Harold A. Littledale demonstrated that muckraking reporting and other vivid writing could be joined in the quest for social reform. Each paragraph of his exposé of the New Jersey state prison system sounds like the hammer of justice nailing the indictment.

William Allen White was one of the most influential small-town editors in American history. His editorials on politics earned him national and international fame and influence. But of all his essays, the one that endures is "Mary White," a tribute to his young daughter killed in a horseback-riding accident in 1921.

Another classic from the 1920s comes from the pen of Lorena Hickock, one of the most enterprising women in the annals of American journalism. Dissatisfied with the constraints placed on women reporters, Hickock worked her way up from society columns to national news. This account of a small community coming to view the funeral train of a dead president exemplifies her work.

Richard Wright, one of the great figures in modern American literature, writes what looks like a sports column for a communist publication. It is astonishing in its candor about race relations, written in a voice intolerable for the mainstream press of his time (1935), but one that resonates in the early 21st century.

So, too, Dorothy Thompson looks beyond her era and anticipates our own. Peering over the front edge of the television age, her 1938 commentary reveals the potential dangers to democracy posed by a corrupt mass media propagandizing an uncritical and gullible public.

It would be difficult to find, in any era, as beloved a journalist as Ernie Pyle, the chronicler of the lives of everyday soldiers during World War II. Pyle was there the day the dead body of a respected Army captain was carried down from the Italian hills. The reactions of the soldiers still move readers more than a half century after the event.

Marvel Cooke wrote a remarkable series of stories in 1950 about the exploitation of black day workers. Rather than reporting objectively from the outside, Cooke assumed the perspective of the participant-observer. The writing is rich with the details of direct experience.

Red Smith writes about one of the great sporting events of the century. It is fun to watch this wordsmith struggle to find the words to capture the monumental sense of victory and loss expressed in a single amazing moment in 1951.

Of all the writers in this anthology, Meyer Berger, known as "Mike" to his colleagues at *The New York Times,* is near the top of our list of favorites. He could write news, investigations and features. He could write beautifully under the most oppressive deadlines. And he knew how to take his time. He had an old-fashioned nose for news, an ear for the music of the language and an eye for the perfect detail. By the testimony of his peers, he was a warm and witty friend and colleague. Who could ask for more than that?

Finally, we include Gene Patterson's most powerful column, written during one of the darkest days in American history, when four black girls were murdered in a Birmingham, Ala., church bombing in 1963. This column is evidence enough of Patterson's passion for his craft, the same passion that led him in 1977 to establish the ASNE writing awards.

❦ HAROLD A. LITTLEDALE ❧

At a time when the United States is trying to solve its crime and social problems by jailing more and more prisoners, it's instructive to revisit the classic reportage of Harold A. Littledale, writing for the *New York Evening Post*.

In 1917, conditions inside state prison systems were horrific, and Littledale pulls no punches in his lead: "Bad prisons breed crime, and the New Jersey State Prison at Trenton is among the worst in the country." At first that reads like an editorial, but by the end of a story filled with damning evidence, it becomes an inescapable conclusion.

The body of the story is a 44-paragraph indictment of the system, each paragraph beginning with the phrase *"It is a fact."* While this formal repetition seems overdrawn by modern standards, the drumbeat rhythm builds a relentless authority in the piece.

Such authority, the work of dogged reporting, created a political furor in the state of New Jersey. Three weeks after the story appeared, a commission appointed by the governor offered recommendations for reforming the prisons. For his efforts, Littledale won the 1918 Pulitzer Prize for reporting.

Prisoners With Midnight in Their Hearts

NEW YORK EVENING POST • JANUARY 12, 1917

Bad prisons breed crime, and the New Jersey State Prison at Trenton is among the worst in the country. It is bad in its structure, bad in its influence, and bad in its management. By comparison Sing Sing is a cozy corner, for Trenton is monstrous, medieval, unhealthy, and overcrowded.

It is hard to believe that in the twentieth century, one hundred years after Elizabeth Fry visited Newgate and the English convict ships, man's inhumanity to man should express itself as it does express itself at Trenton. It is hard to believe that for infractions of the rules men are placed face to the wall for punishment and deprived of their meals. It is hard to believe that their labor is farmed out to private contractors for a pittance while their families are in want. It is hard to believe that the state's wards are cast into dungeons. It is hard to believe that women are placed with men. It is hard to believe that the insane mingle with the sane, the consumptive with the healthy, the pervert with the pure. But this, and much more, obtains at Trenton; this and much more exists and is sanctioned and is permitted to be.

Here is the indictment:

It is a fact that two, three, and even four men are confined together in the same cell in violation of the law.

It is a fact that dungeons exist and that men are incarcerated therein and given only bread and water twice a day.

It is a fact that men have been chained to the walls of underground dungeons.

It is a fact that every day a man serves in a dungeon is added to his minimum sentence.

It is a fact that women convicts are confined with men, and that cell 55, wing 4, is kept apart for that purpose.

It is a fact that women prisoners eat, sleep, and live in their cells and work on sewing machines in the corridor outside their cells.

It is a fact that there is no dining hall and that men are fed in their cells or in the corridor.

It is a fact that the cries of convicts protesting against their food have been heard by those who passed through the streets outside.

It is a fact that these wards of the state save the scraps of one meal to eat at the next.

It is a fact that the men have only half an hour's recreation a week and that the recreation yard for fourteen women convicts is larger than the recreation yard for 1200 men.

It is a fact that many cells are dark and ill-ventilated.

It is a fact that in the newest wing seventy cells are so damp that they cannot be used, and that on occasions the corridor is so wet that the keepers have to wear rubbers.

It is a fact that a cell building erected in 1835 is in use today.

It is a fact that the state's wards were confined up to last Monday in an old wing that the State Board of Health had condemned as unfit for human habitation.

It is a fact that consumptives circulate with the well, exposing them to contagion.

It is a fact that the degenerate, the pervert, and the homosexual are placed with other convicts, with what result can well be imagined.

It is a fact that the first offender is thrown with the habitual criminal.

It is a fact that a youth was released in December who came to the prison a boy of thirteen years, wearing short trousers.

It is a fact that men are punished by being put face to the wall and that sometimes they are kept there all day without food.

It is a fact that convicts may not receive fruit.

It is a fact that a commodious bathhouse, with hot- and cold-water supply, is used only two months in the year.

It is a fact that for ten months in the year the convicts are given only a bucket of water once a week in which to bathe, that after bathing they must wash their clothes in this water and then wash out their cells.

It is a fact that the lights in the cells are extinguished at 8:30 p.m., and that on Sunday evenings there is no light at all.

It is a fact that the hospital is too small and its equipment inadequate.

It is a fact that the management of the prison is vested in a Board of Inspectors who meet only once a month, and whose members are from scattered parts of the state.

It is a fact that the Board of Inspectors of six members appointed six committees, a chairmanship for each member, creating so much more interference.

It is a fact that paroles can be granted by two independent bodies—the Board of Inspectors and the Court of Pardons.

It is a fact that a salaried schoolteacher is employed, but that there is no schoolroom or furniture, in violation of the law.

It is a fact that three chaplains are employed, but that the chapel seats only 350 persons, while the prison population is usually in excess of 1300.

It is a fact that the salaried moral instructor is the Reverend Thomas R. Taylor, father of Leon R. Taylor, ex-Speaker of the Assembly, and that he was appointed by his son while Acting Governor of the state.

It is a fact that contract labor exists, if not in violation of the law, certainly against the spirit of it.

It is a fact that some of the shops where convicts are employed by private contractors are ill-ventilated and dark.

It is a fact that one contract shop is in the cellar.

It is a fact that more than one hundred men are employed on a contract in violation of the law.

It is a fact that much space is given over to these private contractors for use as storerooms.

It is a fact that the Board of Inspectors turns the convicts over for work on the public roads at the rate of $1.25 a day, which is paid by the taxpayers, but that the board turns the convicts over to private contractors at thirty-five cents a day.

It is a fact that free light, heat, and power are furnished to the contractors.

It is a fact that goods made in the prison for private contractors are not marked "Manufactured in New Jersey State Prison," and that this is a violation of the law.

It is a fact that while the contract shops are put in operation daily, the shop, equipped at a cost of more than $12,000 to make socks and underwear for inmates of state institutions, is idle and has been idle for some months, and that the salaried instructor has nothing to do.

It is a fact that the graded and meriting system was recommended in 1911 and that nothing was done.

It is a fact that the employment of a dietarian was recommended in 1911 by the State Commissioner of Charities and Corrections and that nothing was done.

It is a fact that the keepers are underpaid and overworked.

It is a fact that the powers of the Principal Keeper (Warden) are little more then those of janitor.

It is a fact that convicts are supposed to be paid 2½ cents a day for their work in prison and that they do not get it.

That, then, is the New Jersey State Prison at Trenton, where 1300 men are confined at a net cost in 1915 (the last available report) of more than $253,000. That is how the state's wards are kept. That is how they are punished. That is how they are "reformed." That is how society is "protected." That is the state of affairs in this year of grace, 1917. Is it really one hundred years since Elizabeth Fry found men and women shut together, found them in rags, found them dirty, and inveighed so against the malice and all uncharitableness that the English conscience was stirred and the era of reform begun? In the state of New Jersey today is there no Elizabeth Fry who will come forward and fight this thing? Or is it "mollycoddling" convicts to permit them to see the sun in the day, to give them better food, to give them light in their cells at night that they may read or study as they would, to provide them with dining halls where they might eat like human beings instead of having their food thrust into their cages as if they were wild and dangerous beasts, to end forever the vicious system of contract labor as Chapter 372 of the Laws of 1911 intended it should be ended, to permit them to receive fruit from their friends who wish to bring them fruit, to try to bring out the good that is in each and every one of them, for good there is in all of them, and it is like pure gold. If this is "mollycoddling" convicts it is best to leave them as they are with midnight in their hearts.

A 1921 OBITUARIES AND FUNERALS CLASSIC

～ WILLIAM ALLEN WHITE ～

By the time of his death in 1943, William Allen White was the most famous and influential small-town newspaper publisher in America. As owner of *The Emporia* (Kan.) *Gazette*, White had risen from a boy without a college degree to one of the leading editorialists in the nation and a key figure in Republican politics.

The story goes that in 1896 he found himself in a heated exchange with a political rival, someone who favored the Populist over the Republican position. The encounter left him "boiling mad" and inspired him to write a biting editorial, "What's the Matter with Kansas?" Republican political bosses distributed it across the country, and White was suddenly famous and influential.

His political zeal led him to one unsuccessful run for office. It came in 1924 when the Ku Klux Klan endorsed two other candidates for governor of Kansas. White had attacked the Klan as "un-American and cowardly," and although he lost the race, he helped weaken the influence of the Klan in the state.

In spite of his high profile in national politics, White's most famous newspaper story was the result of a family tragedy. In 1921, his 16-year-old daughter, Mary, was knocked off a horse by a low limb of a tree and died. A short piece ran in the newspaper, followed days later by White's timeless essay. There are too few moments when the newspaper editorialist writes from the heart. This was surely one of them. Her young body might be dead, wrote the father, "but the soul of her, the glowing, gorgeous, fervent soul of her, surely was flaming in eager joy upon some other dawn."

For decades, this column was passed around by journalists who believed that newspaper writing could at times transcend the concerns of daily life to strike a universal chord. This is not to say that White's political values were absent from this intensely personal expression of grief. White describes his daughter as a young champion of racial justice.

Mary White

THE EMPORIA (KAN.) GAZETTE • MAY 17, 1921

The Associated Press reports carrying the news of Mary White's death declared that it came as the result of a fall from a horse. How she would have hooted at that! She never fell from a horse in her life. Horses have fallen on her and with her — "I'm always trying to hold 'em in my lap," she used to say. But she was proud of few things, and one was that she could ride anything that had four legs and hair. Her death resulted not from a fall, but from a blow on the head which fractured her skull, and the blow came from the limb of an overhanging tree on the parking [the grassy strip between side walk and street].

The last hour of her life was typical of its happiness. She came home from a day's work at school, topped off by a hard grind with the copy on the High School Annual, and felt that a ride would refresh her. She climbed into her khakis, chattering to her mother about the work she was doing, and hurried to get her horse and be out on the dirt roads for the country air and the radiant green fields of the spring. As she rode through the town on an easy gallop she kept waving at passers-by. She knew everyone in town. For a decade the little figure with the long pig-tail and the red hair ribbon has been familiar on the streets of Emporia, and she got in the way [habit] of speaking to those who nodded at her. She passed the Kerrs, walking the horse, in front of the Normal Library, and waved at them; passed another friend a few hundred feet further on, and waved at her. The horse was walking and, as she turned into North Merchant Street she took off her cowboy hat, and the horse swung into a lope. She passed the Tripletts and waved her cowboy hat at them, still moving gaily north on Merchant Street. A *Gazette* carrier passed — a High School boy friend — and she waved at him, but with her bridle hand; the horse veered quickly, plunged into the parking where the low-hanging limb faced her, and, while she still looked back waving, the blow came. But she did not fall from the horse; she slipped off, dazed a bit, staggered and fell in a faint. She never quite recovered consciousness.

But she did not fall from the horse, neither was she riding fast. A year or so ago she used to go like the wind. But that habit was broken, and she used the horse to get into the open to get fresh, hard exercise, and to work off a certain surplus energy that welled up in her and needed a physical outlet. That need has been in her heart for years. It was back of the impulse that kept the dauntless, little brown-clad figure on the streets and country roads of this community and built into a strong, muscular body what had been a frail and sickly frame during the first years of her life. But the riding gave her more than a body. It released a gay and hardy soul. She was the happiest thing in the world. And she was happy because she was enlarging her horizon. She came to know all sorts and conditions of men; Charley O'Brien, the traffic cop, was one of her best friends. W.L. Holtz, the Latin teacher, was another. Tom O'Connor, farmer-politician, and Rev. J.H.J. Rice, preacher and police judge, and Frank Beach, music master, were her special friends, and all the girls, black and white, above the track and below the track, in Pepville and Stringtown, were among her acquaintances. And she brought home riotous stories of her adventures. She loved to rollick; persiflage was her natural expression at home. Her humor was a continual bubble of joy. She seemed to think in hyperbole and metaphor. She was mischievous without malice, as full of faults as an old shoe. No angel was Mary White, but an easy girl to live with, for she never nursed a grouch five minutes in her life.

With all her eagerness for the out of doors, she loved books. On her table when she left her room were a book by Conrad, one by Galsworthy, "Creative Chemistry" by E.E. Slosson, and a Kipling book. She read Mark Twain, Dickens and Kipling before she was ten—all of their writings. Wells and Arnold Bennett particularly amused and diverted her. She was entered as a student in Wellesley in 1922; was assistant editor of the High School Annual this year, and in line for election to the editorship of the Annual next year. She was a member of the executive committee of the High School Y.W.C.A.

Within the last two years she had begun to be moved by an ambition to draw. She began as most children do by scribbling in her school books, funny pictures. She bought cartoon magazines and took a course—rather casually, naturally, for she was, after all, a child with no strong purposes—and this year she tasted the first fruits of success by having her pictures accepted by the High School Annual. But the thrill of delight she got when Mr. Ecord, of the Normal

Annual, asked her to do the cartooning for that book this spring, was too beautiful for words. She fell to her work with all her enthusiastic heart. Her drawings were accepted, and her pride — always repressed by a lively sense of the ridiculousness of the figure she was cutting — was a really gorgeous thing to see. No successful artist ever drank a deeper draught of satisfaction than she took from the little fame her work was getting among her schoolfellows. In her glory, she almost forgot her horse — but never her car.

For she used the car as a jitney bus. It was her social life. She never had a "party" in all her nearly seventeen years — wouldn't have one; but she never drove a block in the car in her life that she didn't begin to fill the car with pick-ups! Everybody rode with Mary White — white and black, old and young, rich and poor, men and women. She liked nothing better than to fill the car full of long-legged High School boys and an occasional girl, and parade the town. She never had a "date," nor went to a dance, except once with her brother, Bill, and the "boy proposition" didn't interest her — yet. But young people — great spring-breaking, varnish-cracking, fender-bending, door-sagging carloads of "kids" gave her great pleasure. Her zests were keen. But the most fun she ever had in her life was acting as chairman of the committee that got up the big turkey dinner for the poor folks at the county home; scores of pies, gallons of slaw; jam, cakes, preserves, oranges and a wilderness of turkey were loaded in the car and taken to the county home. And, being of a practical turn of mind, she risked her own Christmas dinner by staying to see that the poor folks actually got it all. Not that she was a cynic; she just disliked to tempt folks. While there she found a blind colored uncle, very old, who could do nothing but make rag rugs, and she rustled up from her school friends rags enough to keep him busy for a season. The last engagement she tried to make was to take the guests at the county home out for a car ride. And the last endeavor of her life was to try to get a rest room for colored girls in the High School. She found one girl reading in the toilet, because there was no better place for a colored girl to loaf, and it inflamed her sense of injustice and she became a nagging harpie to those who, she thought, could remedy the evil. The poor she had always with her, and was glad of it. She hungered and thirsted for righteousness; and was the most impious creature in the world. She joined the Congregational Church without consulting her parents; not particularly for her soul's good. She never had a thrill of piety in her life, and would have hooted at a "testimony." But even as a little child she felt the church was an agency for helping people to more of life's abundance, and she wanted to help. She never wanted help for herself. Clothes meant little to her. It was a fight to get a new rig on her; but eventually a harder fight to get it off. She never wore a jewel and had no ring but her High School class ring, and never asked for anything but a wrist watch. She refused to have her hair up; though she was nearly seventeen. "Mother," she protested, "you don't know how much I get by with, in my braided pigtails, that I could not with my hair up." Above every other passion of her life was her passion not to grow up, to be a child. The tom-boy in her, which was big, seemed to loathe to be put away forever in skirts. She was a Peter Pan, who refused to grow up.

Her funeral yesterday at the Congregational Church was as she would have wished it; no singing, no flowers save the big bunch of red roses from her Brother Bill's Harvard classmen — Heavens, how proud that would have made her! and the red roses from the *Gazette* force — in vases at her head and feet. A short prayer, Paul's beautiful essay on "Love" from the Thirteenth Chapter of First Corinthians, some remarks about her democratic spirit by her friend, John H.J. Rice, pastor and police judge, which she would have deprecated if she could, a prayer sent down for her by her friend, Carl Nau, and opening the service the slow, poignant movement from Beethoven's Moonlight Sonata, which she loved, and closing the service a cutting from the joyously melancholy first movement of Tschaikowski's Pathetic Symphony, which she liked to hear in certain moods on the phonograph; then the Lord's Prayer by her friends in the High School.

That was all.

For her pall-bearers only her friends were chosen; her Latin teacher — W.L. Holtz; her High School principal, Rice Brown; her doctor, Frank Foncannon; her friend, W.W. Finney; her pal at the *Gazette* office, Walter Hughes; and her brother Bill. It would have made her smile to know that her friend, Charley O'Brien, the traffic cop, had been transferred from Sixth and Commercial to the corner near the church to direct her friends who came to bid her good-by.

A rift in the clouds in a gray day threw a shaft of sunlight upon her coffin as her nervous, energetic little body sank to its last sleep. But the soul of her, the glowing, gorgeous, fervent soul of her, surely was flaming in eager joy upon some other dawn.

∼ LORENA A. HICKOK ∼

Late one night in August 1923, Lorena A. Hickok, a reporter for the *Minneapolis Tribune*, stationed herself by the tracks in the tiny Iowa village of Honey Creek to join the townspeople gathered to catch a glimpse of the speeding train that carried the body of President Warren G. Harding.

When Hickok began her career a decade earlier, society news and human interest stories were the only assignments available to women. The daughter of an itinerant butter maker and a dressmaker, Hickok was born in East Troy, Wisc. She started out in journalism covering train arrivals and departures for the *Evening News* in Battle Creek, Mich., for $7 a week. With only a high school degree—she started and dropped out of college more than once—she moved up to society editor at the *Milwaukee Sentinel*. Bored by the women's beat, she persuaded her editor to let her switch to the city desk, where her interviewing skills quickly stood out. In 1917, she joined the *Minneapolis Tribune*, where her editor assigned her political and sports stories, usually reserved for men, including the last train ride of President Harding.

Although Honey Creek's citizenry caught just a fleeting glimpse of the funeral train, Hickok made sure her readers got a detailed picture of an isolated Midwestern community determined to witness this historic event. It's hard to imagine that a news story written today would wait nearly 30 paragraphs before it mentioned the President's name, but Hickok's reporting and style would easily pass muster.

Writing coach William E. Blundell identifies six building blocks for news writers: scope, history, impact, reasons, gathering and action of contrary forces, and the future. In 1,300 words, Hickok covers most of these bases. Her textured and colloquial portrait of the village and its 76 inhabitants, from H.L. Ham, "station agent, postmaster and notary public," to H. French, president of a shuttered bank, contains a larger story, a snapshot of a nation framed by two tragedies, the First World War and the Depression looming on the horizon. Notice how Hickok uses dialogue—the excited chatter along the tracks—and a chronological structure, which follows the summary lead, to convey the event's excitement.

In 1927, Hickok joined the Associated Press, specializing in political reporting and high-profile stories such as the Lindbergh baby kidnapping. When Franklin Delano Roosevelt ran for president in 1932, Hickok was assigned to cover his campaign, soon convincing her editors that Roosevelt's wife, Eleanor, also deserved coverage. She got that beat. The assignment led to a close friendship with Mrs. Roosevelt, but one that Hickok decided made it impossible to perform her duties as a reporter.

Hickok left the AP in 1933 and joined the Roosevelt administration. Crisscrossing 32 states, she provided firsthand reports of the Depression's toll on the same kind of ordinary Americans who had watched history flashing by in a passing train. She never returned to daily journalism but was the author of several books, including a biography of Eleanor Roosevelt. Lorena Hickok died in 1968.

Iowa Village Waits All Night for Glimpse at Fleeting Train

MINNEAPOLIS TRIBUNE • AUGUST 7, 1923

HONEY CREEK, Iowa—Hurling itself into the dawn at 50 miles an hour, the President's funeral train roared past Honey Creek at 4 a.m. today.

A blurred, agonizing glimpse into the dimly lighted observation car heaped to the ceiling with wreaths and flowers was all that Honey Creek got—and for this her 76 inhabitants had shivered on the dreary station platform for hours.

But in the words of H.L. Ham, station agent, postmaster and notary public, as he stared dazedly after the red tail lights dwindling away in the shadows, "Well, it was worth it, wasn't it?"

It was worth it. The long moaning whistle around the bend—the blinding shaft of light down the glittering rails—the roar and wind and trembling of the earth—the breathless wait for the rear car—the flashing vision of wreaths and flags and rigid figures in khaki—the red tail lights vanishing like pin points in the dark—yes, it was worth waiting for.

There was no pomp or ceremony in Honey Creek's tribute to the nation's dead leader. No lines of veterans in uniform, no flowers, no spoken prayers. Honey Creek is not given to fluency and high-sounding phrases.

People went down to see that train for two reasons—to show their respect for the President of the United States and to take their children. In Honey Creek it was deemed highly important that the children should see that train, so that they might tell their children and their children's children.

And so it was that fathers, who had served in the nation's armies during the world war, held their little babies high over their shoulders as the train leaped past Honey Creek this morning. And small boys in overalls gazed in wonder from the top of the fence adjoining the station. The chief concern of the adults was in seeing to it that the children got a good view of the train.

Honey Creek, Iowa, used to be on the Lincoln highway until they moved the highway. Until a year or two ago, it was known from coast to coast among automobile tourists as "the place where you strike that awful hill." Finally, to get away from the hill, they moved the highway out of Honey Creek—and now Honey Creek is slowly dying.

"It used to have a population of 90 when the highway went through here," Fremont Hansen, the garage owner, said last night. "But now—I guess it's not much over 75.

"Before they moved the highway we had two stores and a bank and a Commercial club. But one of the stores burned down, and the bank went out of business, and the Commercial club busted up. So Honey Creek isn't much of a town any more."

It is a straggling village, Honey Creek is—houses scattered about at the bases of the wide sweeping hills that mark the boundaries of the Missouri valley. A garage, a filling station, one store—most of the people are farmers. There isn't any mayor, or council.

"Oh, we manage to worry along without much government," one of the inhabitants remarked last night.

Wherefore Honey Creek's reception of the President's funeral train was bound to be informal. At dusk last night, the town's telephone operator called everybody up and passed out the information that the train would pass Honey Creek at 3 o'clock in the morning. That was all the preparation that preceded Honey Creek's demonstration.

Sitting on their porches, the residents talked it over, porch to porch.

"Well, a thing like this won't happen to Honey Creek again in 100 years," said H. French, who was president of the bank that went out of business.

"It will be something for our children to tell their grandchildren about, all right."

"Sure, I'm going down," announced Mace Hansen, who operated the filling station and who served overseas in the world war. "The President of the United States has got coming to him all the respect I can pay him, hasn't he?"

Alarm clocks were set for 1:45 a.m. One woman announced she would ring her dinner bell to wake up the neighborhood. Dr. J.W. Frazier, physician, farmer and justice of the peace, who lives across the road from the station, said he guessed he would sit up and read. "Might as well," he said. "For I don't think I'd get much sleep anyhow."

I stayed at the home of Mr. French, the former banker. It was agreed that we were to get up at 1:45 a.m. At 1:15 a.m. Mr. and Mrs. French and their two small boys and I were en route to the station.

"Did you sleep?" was the query with which each newcomer was greeted.

"Not much," was the answer over and over. "Every time I heard a train I'd jump out of bed."

Incidentally, Honey Creek is on the main line of the Chicago & North Western railway across Iowa, and 60 trains a day pass through there—most of them, it would seem, in the night.

By 2:30 a.m. the whole population of Honey Creek apparently was out on that station platform, or sitting in cars parked below. There was a great play of pocket flashlights, much tramping up and down and hunting for seats. In low, queerly hushed voices, the people discussed the time, crops, the time, their children, the time again, the probable size of the crowd in Omaha, and again the time.

The song of the crickets from Dr. Frazier's cornfield, on the other side of the tracks, made a sort of orchestral background for the conversation.

At 3 a.m. Mr. Ham came out of the ticket office and announced that the train was an hour late. There had been an accident somewhere over in Nebraska—an accident by which the train would certainly have gone in the ditch had it been traveling rapidly.

"Oh, what a mess that would be—with Pershing and Hoover and all those big fellows aboard," groaned Mace Hansen.

The talk drifted to Mrs. Harding. "They say she's left pretty well fixed," some one remarked. "The paper said he left near a million dollars." "I know," Mrs. French interrupted. "But think how lonely she'll be, how she'd rather have him back than a hundred million dollars."

"If only she had some sons or daughters to be with her," another woman sighed, running her fingers through her little boy's shock of yellow hair.

At 3:45 a light came around the bend—the pilot train, a locomotive, day coach and observation car—plunged past the crowd and on into the darkness.

Honey Creek climbed out of its Fords and got in line on the station platform. Two fathers with babies were given places in the front rank. The small boys hopped up on top of the fence. Miss Agnes Young, gray-haired spinster and owner of a large farm at Honey Creek, climbed up on her stepladder which she had carried half a mile to the station, slipping and sliding over muddy roads on foot in the dark.

A light shining up behind the trees around the bend, a mile away. That long, moaning whistle—

"Here she comes!" shrieked a small boy from his post on the signal tower.

The blinding shaft of light down the glittering rails—

"Don't look at it, Ward—it'll blind you!"

Again the whistle, imperious now, deafening—

"Now—watch for the last car, Junior—that lighted one—way back."

Roar and wind and trembling earth. A breathless, agonizing wait for that last car—

There it is! Yes, but dimly lighted. Now, look—quick—wreaths, flowers, a huge American flag. Swift realization that the casket must lie beneath that flag. A frenzied search for the guards. Red tail lights half a mile down the track—

"Well, it was worth it, wasn't it?"

"It was."

~ RICHARD WRIGHT ~

Several famous American authors began as journalists, but the ones most remembered are white, such as Ernest Hemingway or Theodore Dreiser. This classic revives the first piece of journalism by Richard Wright, author of *Native Son* and *Black Boy*, two influential works of African American literature.

What Richard Wright had to say about race in America in 1935 could not appear in mainstream newspapers or magazines, so he found a platform in *New Masses*, a communist publication. The occasion for this remarkable column was a victory by heavyweight boxer Joe Louis over Max Baer. Louis was black and became one of the most popular American champions of all time. Baer was white, and in the words of Malcolm X, "The ring was the only place a Negro could whip a white man and not be lynched."

The piece opens brilliantly, with the sounds of the count out inspiring a rush of humanity onto the streets of Chicago: "Negroes poured out of beer taverns, pool rooms, barber shops, rooming houses, and dingy flats and flooded the streets." The essay teems with life and energy, from the joyful "snake-lines" in the streets, to the commandeering of streetcars, to the acts of petty theft and vandalism, to the fearful retreat of white shopkeepers, to the counterattack by black police officers. Wright puts us on the scene in what must have felt like a righteous uprising of body and spirit.

Then he gives us more. Fearlessly, he goes beneath the actual events to explore their meaning. We learn that "the blacks began to remember all the little slights, and discriminations and insults they had suffered; and their hunger too and their misery. And the whites began to search their souls to see if they had been guilty of something, some time, somewhere, against which this wave of feeling was rising."

Other subtle insights follow, including how black officers, rather than white ones, were sent in to keep the peace, and how the cops, in spite of their bluster, refrained from violence against the crowd. They acted as a dam to hold back the black river from overflowing. While peace is restored, even the police, even the white folks knew that something had happened: "Here's the real dynamite that Joe Louis uncovered!"

This piece should remind us how many untold stories and how many stifled voices existed in America—and still exist. The great writer struggles out of the cocoon of self-censorship and self-doubt to fly to a place where difficult truths can be examined, expressed and exposed to the light of day.

Joe Louis Uncovers Dynamite

NEW MASSES • OCTOBER 8, 1935

"WUN - TUH - THREEE - FOOO - FIIVE - SEEX - SEVEN - EIGHT - NIINE - THUNN!"

Then:

"JOE LOUIS — THE WINNAH!"

On Chicago's South Side five minutes after these words were yelled and Joe Louis' hand was hoisted as victor in his four-round go with Max Baer, Negroes poured out of beer taverns, pool rooms, barber shops, rooming houses, and dingy flats and flooded the streets.

"LOUIS! LOUIS! LOUIS!" they yelled and threw their hats away. They snatched newspapers from the stands of astonished Greeks and tore them up, flinging the bits into the air. They wagged their heads. Lawd, they'd never seen or heard the like of it before. They shook the hands of strangers. They clapped one another on the back. It was like a revival. Really, there was a religious feeling in the air. Well, it wasn't exactly a religious feeling, but it was the *thing*, and you could feel it. It was a feeling of unity, of oneness.

Two hours after the fight the area between South Parkway and Prairie Avenue on 47th Street was jammed with no less than twenty-five thousand Negroes, joy-mad and moving so they didn't know where. Clasping hands they formed long writhing snake-lines and wove in and out of traffic. They seeped out of doorways, oozed from alleys, trickled out of tenements, and flowed down the street, a fluid mass of joy. White storekeepers hastily closed their doors against the tidal wave and stood peeping through plate glass with blanched faces.

Something had happened, all right. And it had happened so confoundingly sudden that the whites in the neighborhood were dumb with fear. They felt—you could see it in their faces—that *something* had ripped loose, exploded. Something which they had long feared and thought was dead. Or if not dead at least so safely buried under the pretense of good-will that they no longer had need to fear it. Where in the world did it come from? And what was worst of all, how far would it go? Say, what's got into these Negroes?

And the whites and the blacks began to *feel* themselves. The blacks began to remember all the little slights, and discriminations and insults they had suffered; and their hunger too and their misery. And the whites began to search their souls to see if they had been guilty of something, some time, somewhere, against which this wave of feeling was rising.

As the celebration wore on, the younger Negroes began to grow bold. They jumped on the running boards of automobiles going east or west on 47th Street and demanded of the occupants:

"Who yuh fer—Baer or Louis?"

In the stress of the moment it seemed that the answer to the question marked out friend and foe.

A hesitating reply brought waves of scornful laughter. Baer, huh? That was funny. Now, hadn't Joe Louis just whipped Max Baer? Didn't think we had it in us, did you? Thought Joe Louis was scared, didn't you? Scared because Max talked loud and made boasts. We ain't scared either. We'll fight too when the time comes. We'll win, too.

A taxicab driver had his cab wrecked when he tried to put up a show of bravado.

Then they began stopping street cars. Like a cyclone sweeping through a forest, they went through them, shouting, stamping. Conductors gave up and backed away like children. Everybody had to join this celebration. Some of the people ran out of the cars and stood, pale and trembling, in the crowd. They felt it, too.

In the crush a pocketbook snapped open and money spilled on the street for eager black fingers.

"They stole it from us, anyhow," they said as they picked it up.

When an elderly Negro admonished them, a fist was shaken in his face. Uncle Toming, huh?

"What in hell yuh gotta do wid it?" they wanted to know.

Something had popped loose, all right. And it had come from deep down. Out of the darkness it had leaped from its coil. And nobody could have said just what it was, and nobody wanted to say. Blacks and whites were afraid. But it was a sweet fear, at least for the blacks. It was a mingling of fear and fulfillment. Something dreaded and yet wanted. A something had popped out of a dark hole, something with a hydra-like head, and it was darting forth its tongue.

You stand on the border-line, wondering what's beyond. Then you take one step and you feel a strange, sweet tingling. You take two steps and the feeling becomes keener. You want to feel some more. You break into a run. You know it's dangerous, but you're propelled in spite of yourself.

Four centuries of oppression, of frustrated hopes, of black bitterness, felt even in the bones of the bewildered young, were rising to the surface. Yes, unconsciously they had imputed to the brawny image of Joe Louis all the balked dreams of revenge, all the secretly visualized moments of retaliation. AND HE HAD WON! Good Gawd Almighty! Yes, Jesus, it could be done! Didn't Joe do it? You see, Joe was the consciously-felt symbol. He was the concentrated essence of black triumph over white. And it comes so seldom, so seldom. And what could be sweeter than long nourished hate vicariously gratified? From the symbol of Joe's strength they took strength, and in that moment all fear, all obstacles were wiped out, drowned. They stepped out of the mire of hesitation and irresolution and were free! Invincible! A merciless victor over a fallen foe! Yes, they had felt all that— for a moment. . . .

And then the cops came.

Not the carefully picked white cops who were used to batter the skulls of white workers and intellectuals who came to the South Side to march with the black workers to show their solidarity in the struggle against Mussolini's impending invasion of Ethiopia; oh, no, black cops, but trusted black cops and plenty tough. Cops who knew their business, how to handle delicate situations. They piled out of patrols, swinging clubs.

"Git back! Gawddammit, git back!"

But they were very careful, very careful. They didn't hit anybody. They, too, sensed *something*. And they didn't want to trifle with it. And there's no doubt but that they had been instructed not to. Better go easy here. No telling what might happen. They swung clubs, but pushed the crowd back with their hands.

Finally, the street cars moved again. The taxis and automobiles could go through. The whites breathed easier. The blood came back to their cheeks.

The Negroes stood on the sidewalks, talking, wondering, looking, breathing hard. They had felt something, and it had been sweet—that feeling. They wanted some more of it, but they were afraid now. The spell was broken.

And about midnight down the street that feeling ebbed, seeping home—flowing back to the beer tavern, the pool room, the cafe, the barber shop, the dingy flat. Like a sullen river it ran back to its muddy channel, carrying a confused and sentimental memory on its surface, like water-soaked driftwood.

Say, Comrade, here's the wild river that's got to be harnessed and directed. Here's that *something*, that pent-up folk consciousness. Here's a fleeting glimpse of the heart of the Negro, the heart that beats and suffers and hopes—for freedom. Here's that fluid something that's like iron. Here's the real dynamite that Joe Louis uncovered!

A 1938 OPINION AND PERSUASION CLASSIC
～ DOROTHY THOMPSON ～

There is something both bold and prescient in Dorothy Thompson's scathing column on media and mass delusion. Inspired by Orson Welles' 1938 radio broadcast of *The War of the Worlds*, a dramatic narration of an invasion of Earth by Martian monsters, Thompson calls the event "the story of the century."

She means that statement in two ways, in the conventional sense in which we might say that a criminal trial is the "trial of the century." In other words, it's "big, big news." Thompson's commentary suggests a second, deeper meaning: Embodied in this event is an important story *about* the century, a century in which media, politics, culture and celebrity mix in a dangerous, sometimes poisonous, brew.

Journalists and investigative reporters love lists, and this column is organized around two powerful lists in which the public is indicted for its gullibility. The first list begins with "They have," referring to the producers of the radio show and the kinds of social problems they have inadvertently exposed, such as the failure of education, the thin veneer of civilization, "the incredible stupidity, lack of nerve and ignorance of thousands."

The second list is numbered and contains Thompson's sense of the moral lessons to be drawn from this event, including "no political body must ever, under any circumstances, obtain a monopoly of radio." Within a decade, the nation would be introduced to the even more powerful force of television, just as we in our own time have witnessed the political and cultural effects of new media such as the Internet.

This essay stands as a seminal effort in the development of the journalist's role as social and media critic. Thompson seems to be arguing a position similar to one articulated by the Brazilian educator Paolo Freire, that the role of education and journalism is to nurture in citizens a critical literacy, which will keep them free, empowered and protected from the forces of tyranny and corruption.

Born in 1894, Dorothy Thompson became one of the most influential journalists of the first half of the 20th century. After World War I, she served as a foreign correspondent from places such as Vienna and Berlin. From 1936 to 1941, she wrote a column for the *New York Herald Tribune* called "On the Record." Recognizing the power of electronic media, she read commentary on the radio, usually focusing on international affairs. She died in 1961.

Mr. Welles and Mass Delusion

NEW YORK HERALD TRIBUNE • NOVEMBER 2, 1938

All unwittingly Mr. Orson Welles and the Mercury Theater on the Air have made one of the most fascinating and important demonstrations of all time. They have proved that a few effective voices, accompanied by sound effects, can so convince masses of people of a totally unreasonable, completely fantastic proposition as to create nation-wide panic.

They have demonstrated more potently than any argument, demonstrated beyond question of a doubt, the appalling dangers and enormous effectiveness of popular and theatrical demagoguery.

They have cast a brilliant and cruel light upon the failure of popular education.

They have shown up the incredible stupidity, lack of nerve and ignorance of thousands.

They have proved how easy it is to start a mass delusion.

They have uncovered the primeval fears lying under the thinnest surface of the so-called civilized man.

They have shown that man, when the victim of his own gullibility, turns to the government to protect him against his own errors of judgment.

The newspapers are correct in playing up this story over every other news event in the world. It is the story of the century.

And far from blaming Mr. Orson Welles, he ought to be given a Congressional medal and a national prize for having made the most amazing and important contribution to the social sciences. For Mr. Orson Welles and his theater have made a greater contribution to an understanding of Hitlerism, Mussolinism, Stalinism, anti-Semitism and all the other terrorisms of our times than all the words about them that have been written by reasonable men. They have made the reductio ad absurdum of mass manias. They have thrown more light on recent events in Europe leading to the Munich pact than everything that has been said on the subject by all the journalists and commentators.

Hitler managed to scare all Europe to its knees a month ago, but he at least had an army and an air force to back up his shrieking words.

But Mr. Welles scared thousands into demoralization with nothing at all.

That historic hour on the air was an act of unconscious genius, performed by the very innocence of intelligence.

Nothing whatever about the dramatization of the "War of the Worlds" was in the least credible, no matter at what point the hearer might have tuned in. The entire verisimilitude was in the names of a few specific places. Monsters were depicted of a type that nobody has ever seen, equipped with "rays" entirely fantastic; they were described as "straddling the Pulaski Skyway" and throughout the broadcast they were referred to as Martians, men from another planet.

A twist of the dial would have established for anybody that the national catastrophe was not being noted on any other station. A second of logic would have dispelled any terror. A notice that the broadcast came from a non-existent agency would have awakened skepticism.

A reference to the radio program would have established that the "War of the Worlds" was announced in advance.

The time element was obviously lunatic.

Listeners were told that "within two hours three million people have moved out of New York" — an obvious impossibility for the most disciplined army moving exactly as planned, and a double fallacy because only a few minutes before, the news of the arrival of the monster had been announced.

And of course it was not even a planned hoax. Nobody was more surprised at the result than Mr. Welles. The public was told at the beginning, at the end and during the course of the drama that it *was* a drama.

But eyewitnesses presented themselves; the report became second hand, third hand, fourth hand, and became more and more credible, so that nurses and doctors and National Guardsmen rushed to defense.

When the truth became known the reaction was also significant. The deceived were furious and of course demanded that the state protect them, demonstrating that they were incapable of relying on their own judgment.

Again there was a complete failure of logic. For if the deceived had thought about it they would realize that the greatest organizers of mass hysterias and mass delusions today are states using the radio to excite terrors, incite hatreds, inflame masses, win mass support for policies, create idolatries, abolish reason and maintain themselves in power.

The immediate moral is apparent if the whole incident is viewed in reason: no political body must ever, under any circumstances, obtain a monopoly of radio.

The second moral is that our popular and universal education is failing to train reason and logic, even in the educated.

The third is that the popularization of science has led to gullibility and new superstitions, rather than to skepticism and the really scientific attitude of mind.

The fourth is that the power of mass suggestion is the most potent force today and that the political demagogue is more powerful than all the economic forces.

For, mind you, Mr. Welles was managing an obscure program, competing with one of the most popular entertainments on the air!

The conclusion is that the radio must not be used to create mass prejudices and mass divisions and schisms, either by private individuals or by government or its agencies, or its officials, or its opponents.

If people can be frightened out of their wits by mythical men from Mars, they can be frightened into fanaticism by the fear of Reds, or convinced that America is in the hands of sixty families, or aroused to revenge against any minority, or terrorized into subservience to leadership because of any imaginable menace.

The technique of modern mass politics calling itself democracy is to create a fear—a fear of economic royalists, or of Reds, or of Jews, or of starvation, or of an outside enemy—and exploit that fear into obtaining subservience in return for protection.

I wrote in this column a short time ago that the new warfare was waged by propaganda, the outcome depending on which side could first frighten the other to death.

The British people were frightened into obedience to a policy a few weeks ago by a radio speech and by digging a few trenches in Hyde Park, and afterward led to hysterical jubilation over a catastrophic defeat for their democracy.

But Mr. Welles went all the politicians one better. He made the scare to end scares, the menace to end menaces, the unreason to end unreason, the perfect demonstration that the danger is not from Mars but from the theatrical demagogue.

A 1944 OBITUARIES AND FUNERALS CLASSIC

⟞ ERNIE PYLE ⟝

Almost any veteran of World War II can tell you about Ernie Pyle, who became a national hero for his Scripps Howard newspaper dispatches about common, everyday soldiers. Given the antagonism between the press and the military in the post-Vietnam era, it's hard to imagine that any journalist could become beloved by the soldiers he covered. But so it was with Ernie Pyle, and none of his work more exemplifies the qualities that made him great than "The Death of Captain Henry Waskow."

Pay careful attention to the author's use of "I" and then "we." The voice suggests that he feels connected to the community that he covers—he is not a detached observer but bears a special affection for simple acts of courage, friendship, loyalty and duty. Along the way, he also shows exactly where he is positioned, what he can see and what is beyond his understanding: "I stood close by and I could hear."

It is interesting to consider what makes this story stand apart from Pyle's other work. Perhaps it is his sense, expressed in the lead, that Capt. Henry T. Waskow, of Belton, Texas, was truly beloved. Perhaps it is the dramatic setting, a moonlit mountain trail, with pack mules bearing the burden of the dead, and the eerie shadowy wall against which the bodies are laid. Perhaps it is the honest array of raw emotion expressed by the soldiers, one by one, as they come to understand that Waskow is dead, and pay their respects in their own distinctive ways, from bursts of profanity, to respectful silence, to acts of gentle courtesy.

Consider what is left unsaid: the exact age of the captain, the nature of the battle that killed him, a detailed description of his injuries. Instead we get the surreal image of the dead soldiers lying "belly-down across the wooden pack-saddles, their heads hanging down on one side, their stiffened legs sticking out awkwardly from the other, bobbing up and down as the mules walked."

Ernie Pyle died in the line of duty, killed by machine gun fire as he was covering the final days of the war in the Pacific. American soldiers erected a monument to him at the spot he was killed, which told the world they had "lost a buddy."

The Death of Captain Henry Waskow

Scripps Howard Newspaper Alliance • January 10, 1944

In this war I have known a lot of officers who were loved and respected by the soldiers under them. But never have I crossed the trail of any man as beloved as Captain Henry T. Waskow, of Belton, Texas.

Captain Waskow was a company commander in the Thirty-sixth Division. He had led his company since long before it left the States. He was very young, only in his middle twenties, but he carried in him a sincerity and a gentleness that made people want to be guided by him.

"After my father, he came next," a soldier said. "He'd go to bat for us every time."

"I've never known him to do anything unfair," another said.

I was at the foot of a mule trail the night they brought Captain Waskow down. The moon was nearly full, and you could see far up the trail, and even part way across the valley below.

Dead men had been coming down the mountain all evening, lashed onto the backs of mules. They came lying belly-down across the wooden pack-saddles, their heads hanging down on one side, their stiffened legs sticking out awkwardly from the other, bobbing up and down as the mules walked.

The Italian mule skinners were afraid to walk beside the dead men; so Americans had to lead the mules down at night.

Even the Americans were reluctant to unlash and lift off the bodies when they got to the bottom; so an officer had to do it himself and ask others to help.

I didn't know who that first one was. You feel small in the presence of dead men, and you don't ask silly questions. They slid him down from the mule and stood him on his feet for a moment. In the halflight he might have been merely a sick man standing there leaning on others. Then they laid him on the ground in the shadow of the low stone wall beside the road. We left him there beside the road, that first one, and we all went back into the cowshed and sat on water cans or lay on the straw, waiting for the next batch of mules.

Somebody said the dead soldier had been dead for four days, and then nobody said anything more about it. We talked soldier talk for an hour or more; the dead man lay all alone, outside in the shadow of the wall.

Then a soldier came into the cowshed and said there were some more bodies outside. We went out into the road. Four mules stood there in the moonlight, in the road where the trail came down off the mountain. The soldiers who led them stood there waiting.

"This one is Captain Waskow," one of them said quietly.

Two men unlashed his body from the mule and lifted it off and laid it in the shadow beside the stone wall. Other men took the other bodies off. Finally, there were five lying end to end in a long row. You don't cover up dead men in the combat zones. They just lie there in the shadows until someone comes after them.

The unburdened mules moved off to their olive grove. The men in the road seemed reluctant to leave. They stood around, and gradually I could sense them moving, one by one, close to Captain Waskow's body. Not so much to look, I think, as to say something in finality to him, and to themselves. I stood close by and I could hear.

One soldier came and looked down, and he said out loud, "God damn it." That's all he said, and then he walked away.

Another one came, and said, "God damn it, to hell, anyway!" He looked down for a few last moments and then turned and left.

Another man came. I think he was an officer. It was hard to tell officers from men in the dim light, for everybody was bearded and grimy. The man looked down into the dead captain's face and then he spoke directly to him, as though he were alive, "I'm sorry, old man."

Then a soldier came and stood beside the officer, and bent over, and he too spoke to his dead captain, not in a whisper but awfully tenderly, and he said, "I sure am sorry, sir."

Then the first man squatted down, and he reached down and took the dead hand, and he sat there for a full five minutes holding the dead hand in his own and looking intently in the dead face. And he never uttered a sound all the time he sat there.

Finally he put the hand down. He reached over and gently straightened the points of the captain's shirt collar, and then he sort of rearranged the tattered edges of his uniform around the wound, and then he got up and walked away down the road in the moonlight, all alone.

The rest of us went back into the cowshed, leaving the five dead men lying in a line, end to end, in the shadow of the low stone wall. We lay down on the straw in the cowshed, and pretty soon we were all asleep.

A 1950 BUSINESS REPORTING AND EXPLANATORY JOURNALISM CLASSIC

~ MARVEL COOKE ~

There is a long tradition in investigative reporting of journalists going undercover so they can observe or experience the abuses they wish to expose. A classic use of this technique can be found in "The Bronx Slave Market" by Marvel Cooke.

Writing for a short-lived New York City newspaper called *The Daily Compass*, Cooke, the only black person and only woman on the staff, posed as a day worker. With her work clothes in a paper bag, she was hired and exploited by white women looking for cheap domestic labor. As part of the "paper bag brigade," Cooke performed hard physical labor for menial wages, degrading work described in graphic detail in what was originally a five-part series.

Notice the powerful, and unconventional, shift from description to opinion.

> But I was not at peace. Hundreds of years of history weighed upon me.
>
> I was the slave traded for two truck horses on a Memphis street corner in 1849.
>
> I was the slave trading my brawn for a pittance on a Bronx street corner in 1949.

Cooke was born in 1903 and came under the early influence of W.E.B. DuBois, one of the most important African American authors and thinkers of the 20th century. She spent her professional life as a writer and left-wing social activist. At the age of 100, she died in Harlem, her longtime home.

The condensed version of her series is the work of Ben Yagoda. It first appeared in *The Art of Fact*, which Yagoda edited with Kevin Kerrane.

From "The Bronx Slave Market"

THE DAILY COMPASS • 1950

I took up my stand in front of Woolworth's in the early chill of a December morning. Other women began to gather shortly afterwards. Backs pressed to the store window, paper bags clutched in their hands, they stared bleakly, blankly into the street. I lost my identity entirely. I was a member of the "paper bag brigade."

Local housewives stalked the line we had unconsciously formed, picked out the most likely "slaves," bargained with them and led them off down the street. Finally I was alone. I was about to give up, when a short, stout, elderly woman approached. She looked me over carefully before asking if I wanted a day's work. I said I did.

"How much do you want?"

"A dollar." (I knew that $1 an hour is the rate the Domestic Workers Union, the New York State Employment Service and other bona fide agencies ask for work by the hour.)

"A dollar an hour!" she exclaimed. "That's too much. I pay seventy cents."

The bargaining began. We finally compromised on eighty cents. I wanted the job.

"This way." My "madam" pointed up Townsend Ave. Silently we trudged up the street. My mind was filled with questions, but I kept my mouth shut. At 171st St., she spoke one of my unasked questions.

"You wash windows?"

I wasn't keen on washing windows. Noting my hesitation, she said: "It isn't dangerous. I live on the ground floor."

I didn't think I'd be likely to die from a fall out a first-floor window, so I continued on with her.

She watched me while I changed into my work clothes in the kitchen of her dark three-room, ground-floor apartment. Then she handed me a pail of water and a bottle of ammonia and ordered me to follow her into the bedroom.

"First you are to wash this window," she ordered.

Each half of the window had six panes. I sat on the window ledge, pulled the top section down to my lap and began washing. The old woman glanced into the room several times during the 20 minutes it took me to finish the job. The window was shining.

I carried my work paraphernalia into the living room, where I was ordered to wash the two windows and the venetian blinds.

As I set about my work again, I saw my employer go into the bedroom. She came back into the living room, picked up a rag and disappeared again. When she returned a few moments later, I pulled up the window and asked if everything was all right.

"You didn't do the corners and you missed two panes." Her tone was accusing.

I intended to be ingratiating because I wanted to finish this job. I started to answer her meekly and offer to go back over the work. I started to explain that the windows were difficult because the corners were caked with paint. I started to tell her that I hadn't missed a single pane. Of this I was certain. I had checked them off as I did them, with great precision — one, two, three —

Then I remembered a discussion I'd heard that very morning among members of the "paper bag brigade." I learned that it is a common device of Slave Market employers to criticize work as a build-up for not paying the worker the full amount of money agreed on. . . .

Suddenly I was angry — angry at this slave boss — angry for all workers everywhere who are treated like a commodity. I slipped under the window and faced the old woman. The moment my feet hit the floor and I dropped the rag into the pail of water, I was no longer a slave.

My voice shaking with anger, I exclaimed: "I washed every single pane and you know it."

Her face showed surprise. Such defiance was something new in her experience. Before she could answer, I had left the pail of dirty water on the living room floor, marched into the kitchen and put on my clothes. My ex-slave boss watched me while I dressed.

"I'll pay you for the time you put in," she offered. I had only worked 40 minutes. I could afford to be magnanimous.

"Never mind. Keep it as a Christmas present from me."

With that, I marched out of the house. It was early. With luck, I could pick up another job.

Again I took my stand in front of Woolworth's. . . . I found five members of the "paper bag brigade" still waiting to be "bought" by housewives looking for cheap household labor.

One of the waiting "slaves" glanced at me. I hoped she would be friendly enough to talk.

"Tough out here on the street," I remarked. She nodded.

"I had one job this morning, but I quit," I went on. She seemed interested.

"I washed windows for a lady, but I fired myself when she told me that my work was no good."

It was as though she hadn't heard a thing I said. She was looking me over appraisingly.

"I ain't seen you here before," she said. "You're new, ain't you?"

I was discovering that you just can't turn up cold on the market. The "paper bag brigade" is like a fraternity. You must be tried and found true before you are accepted. Until then, you are on the outside, looking in.

Many of the "new" women are fresh from the South, one worker told me, and they don't know how to bargain.

"They'll work for next to nothing," she said, "and that makes it hard for all of us." . . .

There seemed little likelihood of another job that morning. I decided to call it a day. As I turned to leave, I saw a woman coming down the street with the inevitable bag under her arm. She looked as if she knew her way around.

"Beg your pardon," I said as I came abreast of her. "Are you looking for work, too?"

"What's it to you?" Her voice was brash and her eyes were hard as steel. She obviously knew her way around and how to protect herself. No foolishness about her.

"Nothing," I answered. I felt crushed.

"I'm new up here. Thought you might give me some pointers," I went on.

"I'm sorry, honey," she said. "Don't mind me. I ain't had no work for so long, I just get cross. What you want to know?"

When I told her about my morning's experience, she said that "they [the employers] are all bitches." She said it without emotion. It was spoken as a fact, as if she had remarked, "The sun is shining."

"They all get as much as they can out of your hide and try not to pay you if they can get away with it." . . .

I asked if she had ever tried the State Employment Service.

"I can't," she answered candidly. "I'm on relief and if the relief folks ever find out I'm working another job, they'll take it off my check. Lord knows, it's little enough now, and its going to be next to nothing when they start cutting in January."

She went on down the street. I watched her for a moment before I turned toward the subway. I was half conscious that I was being followed. At the corner of 170th St. and Walton Ave., I stopped a moment to look at the Christmas finery in Jack Fine's window. A man passed me, walked around the corner a few yards on Walton Ave., retraced his steps and stopped by my side.

I crossed Walton Avenue. The man was so close at my heels that when I stopped suddenly on the far corner, he couldn't break his stride. I went back to Jack Fine's corner. When the man passed me again, he made a lewd, suggestive gesture, winked and motioned me to follow him up Walton Ave.

I was sick to my stomach. I had had enough for one day.

Woolworth's on 170th Street was beginning to feel like home to me. It seemed natural to be standing there with my sister slaves, all of us with paper bags, containing our work clothes, under our arms.

I recognized many of the people who passed. I no longer felt "new."

But I was not at peace. Hundreds of years of history weighed upon me.

I was the slave traded for two truck horses on a Memphis street corner in 1849.

I was the slave trading my brawn for a pittance on a Bronx street corner in 1949.

As I stood there waiting to be bought, I lived through a century of indignity.

It was that rainy, muggy day after the two-day Christmas holiday, but there was no holiday cheer in the air. The "paper bag brigade" assembled unwillingly—slowly. These women knew, even better than I, that there would be little trading on the market that day.

I waited with six others one hour—two. Four gave up and left. Then a young couple approached, looked us over, and bargained with the woman next to me. I didn't blame them for not choosing me. She was younger, obviously more fit. She went off trailing behind them.

I was alone. I was drenched and my feet were wet. I was about to give up when a little old woman with a bird-like face asked if I wanted a few hours' work.

I let my fellow workers down, for I went off with my new "madam" with a bad verbal contract—75 cents an hour for an undetermined amount of work, knowing only vaguely that there was general cleaning and ironing to do. What that meant in detail, I didn't know.

By the end of the day I knew very well. Every muscle in my body ached.

On the way back to her home on Morris Ave., the little old woman informed me that she had been hiring girls off the street for 20 years and that she'd never been disappointed.

"I've always picked nice girls," she said. "I knew you were nice the minute I laid eyes on you."

That pat on the back was worse in a way than a kick in the teeth.

"I was almost afraid to ask you to work," she went on. "You look like you belong in an office."

I glanced down at her. Was it in her mind that the old clothing I was wearing was too good for a Negro? I couldn't interpret her expression. She had none.

"What's your name?" she asked.

"Margo," I answered, quickly selecting a name near enough my own not to be confusing. However, five minutes later, she was calling me Margie. By the end of the day I was Mary, a name that to her mind, I suppose, was more befitting my station.

Her apartment had two rooms and a bath, with the kitchen unit in one end of the large living room.

She watched while I changed into my work clothes. She seemed to be taking stock of my strength. Without turning, I could almost see her licking her lips. She had bought a strapping, big animal.

"First, rinse those clothes and hang them on the drier in the bathroom," she said, pointing to the tub. "And then you can dust the walls down all over the house." She handed me a makeshift wall mop.

There were endless chores. I ironed a man's shirt, four full-length ruffled curtains and a tablecloth. I took the stove apart and gave it a thorough cleaning. I cleaned and scrubbed the refrigerator, a cabinet, the sink and tub and shelves above the sink. I rubbed all of the furniture in the apartment with furniture oil.

Through it all, my employer sat unperturbed, watching my every move. Once or twice she arose from her chair to flick imaginary dust from an area I had already been over. Then she'd sit down again to watch me.

She was gentle, and persistent, and cruel. She had bought her pound of flesh and she was going to get every ounce of work out of it.

The pay-off came when she asked me to get down on my hands and knees to scrub all the floors, which were covered with linoleum. I just couldn't do it. I realized with some surprise that the ache in my chest I had been feeling all day was old-fashioned anger. Suddenly it flared. I stood up and faced her.

"I can't do it."

"Can't do what, Mary?"

"I can't scrub all of these floors on my hands and knees. This method of scrubbing went out with the Civil War. There are all sorts of modern methods to make floor washing easier. And if they must be scrubbed that way, why don't you provide a knee pad?"

My words tumbled over each other. But she caught their meaning all right.

"All of my girls clean the floors this way, Mary," she said gently. "This is the way I like them done. Well, finish this one and I'll call it a day."

I gathered strength as I scrubbed the floor. I cleaned with the strength of all slaves everywhere who feel the whip.

I finished the job. After I had changed into my street clothes, this gentle Mrs. Legree counted $3.40 into my hands—exactly what she owed me (by the hands of the clock, at least) minus my car fare.

I was too exhausted to argue about 20 cents.

A 1951 LOCAL REPORTING AND BEATS CLASSIC

⌐ RED SMITH ⌐

One measure of great athletes is how well they perform in the big games. The same could be said of great journalists. The most memorable work stands at the conjunction of creative talent and amazing circumstance. How well does the reporter write on deadline when challenged by a monumental event?

Such an event was the "Miracle of Coogan's Bluff," the playoff baseball game in 1951 when the New York Giants defeated the Brooklyn Dodgers for the National League pennant. Bobby Thomson's home run in the ninth inning became the legendary "shot heard round the world." Thomson entered the pantheon of sports legends, while pitcher Ralph Branca became a symbol of bad luck and futility.

Sitting in the press box at the Polo Grounds that day was Red Smith. He had already been covering great sporting events since the 1920s and once pleaded guilty to editor Stanley Woodward's indictment that he was "Godding up those ballplayers." To be sure, there is a bit of hero worship in this classic column, but who could blame Smith for his enthusiasm. Here was a game with two New York teams, a pennant on the line, in the bottom of the ninth, with the world tuned in.

Smith wonders himself whether he's up to the challenge: "Now it is done. Now the story ends. And there is no way to tell it. The art of fiction is dead." Those short sentences, filled with overstatement, set a tone for the story of a mythic sporting event.

Notice how Smith begins his story at the end, focusing his attention on a drunken fan breaking through police lines and tearing across the field. There is a slight shift in voice when we get to the details of the game itself, a playful recounting of the key miscues that led to the dramatic climax.

It would be hard to find, in any sports column, a better "kicker." That word refers to the end of the column, usually something special and memorable for the reader. In this case it's a single word, a number, that turns out to be a prophecy about the destiny of a good pitcher who makes one fatal pitch.

"In my later years," said Smith, "I have sought to become simpler, straighter and purer in my handling of the language. . . . When I was very young as a sportswriter I knowingly and unashamedly imitated others. . . . But slowly, by what process I have no idea, your own writing tends to crystallize, to take shape. Yet you have learned some moves from all these guys and they are somehow incorporated into your own style. Pretty soon you're not imitating any longer."

Red Smith began his writing career in 1927 at the *Milwaukee Sentinel*, moved to the *St. Louis Star*, the *Philadelphia Record*, and the *New York Herald Tribune* before becoming a mainstay at *The New York Times* until his death in 1982 at the age of 76.

Miracle of Coogan's Bluff

NEW YORK HERALD TRIBUNE • OCTOBER 4, 1951

Now it is done. Now the story ends. And there is no way to tell it. The art of fiction is dead. Reality has strangled invention. Only the utterly impossible, the inexpressibly fantastic, can ever be plausible again.

Down on the green and white and earth-brown geometry of the playing field, a drunk tries to break through the ranks of ushers marshaled along the foul lines to keep profane feet off the diamond. The ushers thrust him back and he lunges at them, struggling in the clutch of two or three men. He breaks free, and four or five tackle him. He shakes them off, bursts through the line, runs head-on into a special park cop, who brings him down with a flying tackle.

Here comes a whole platoon of ushers. They lift the man and haul him, twisting and kicking, back across the first-base line. Again he shakes loose and crashes the line. He is through. He is away, weaving out toward center field, where cheering thousands are jammed beneath the windows of the Giants' clubhouse.

At heart, our man is a Giant, too. He never gave up.

From center field comes burst upon burst of cheering. Pennants are waving, uplifted fists are brandished, hats are flying. Again and again the dark clubhouse windows blaze with the light of photographers' flash bulbs. Here comes that same drunk out of the mob, back across the green turf to the infield. Coattails flying, he runs the bases, slides into third. Nobody bothers him now.

And the story remains to be told, the story of how the Giants won the 1951 pennant in the National League. The tale of their barreling run through August and September and into October. . . . Of the final day of the season, when they won the championship and started home with it from Boston, to hear on the train how the dead, defeated Dodgers had risen from the ashes in the Philadelphia twilight. . . . Of the three-game playoff in which they won, and lost, and were losing again with one out in the ninth inning yesterday when — Oh, why bother?

Maybe this is the way to tell it: Bobby Thomson, a young Scot from Staten Island, delivered a timely hit yesterday in the ninth inning of an enjoyable game of baseball before 34,320 witnesses in the Polo Grounds. . . . Or perhaps this is better:

"Well!" said Whitey Lockman, standing on second base in the second inning of yesterday's playoff game between the Giants and Dodgers.

"Ah, there," said Bobby Thomson, pulling into the same station after hitting a ball to left field. "How've you been?"

"Fancy," Lockman said, "meeting you here!"

"Ooops!" Thomson said. "Sorry."

And the Giants' first chance for a big inning against Don Newcombe disappeared as they tagged Thomson out. Up in the press section, the voice of Willie Goodrich came over the amplifiers announcing a macabre statistic: "Thomson has now hit safely in fifteen consecutive games." Just then the floodlights were turned on, enabling the Giants to see and count their runners on each base.

It wasn't funny, though, because it seemed for so long that the Giants weren't going to get another chance like the one Thomson squandered by trying to take second base with a playmate already there. They couldn't hit Newcombe, and the Dodgers couldn't do anything wrong. Sal Maglie's most splendrous pitching would avail nothing unless New York could match the run Brooklyn had scored in the first inning.

The story was winding up, and it wasn't the happy ending that such a tale demands. Poetic justice was a phrase without meaning.

Now it was the seventh inning and Thomson was up, with runners on first and third base, none out. Pitching a shutout in Philadelphia last Saturday night, pitching again in Philadelphia on Sunday, holding the Giants scoreless this far, Newcombe had now gone twenty-one innings without allowing a run.

He threw four strikes to Thomson. Two were fouled off out of play. Then he threw a fifth. Thomson's fly scored Monte Irvin. The score was tied. It was a new ball game.

Wait a moment, though. Here's Pee Wee Reese hitting safely in the eighth. Here's Duke Snider singling Reese to third. Here's Maglie wild-pitching a run home. Here's Andy Pafko slashing a hit through Thomson for another score. Here's Billy Cox batting still another home. Where does his hit go? Where else? Through Thomson at third.

So it was the Dodgers' ball game, 4 to 1, and the Dodgers' pennant. So all right. Better get started and beat the crowd home. That stuff in the ninth inning? That didn't mean anything.

A single by Al Dark. A single by Don Mueller. Irvin's pop-up, Lockman's one-run double. Now the corniest possible sort of Hollywood

schmaltz—stretcher-bearers plodding away with an injured Mueller between them, symbolic of the Giants themselves.

There went Newcombe and here came Ralph Branca. Who's at
bat? Thomson again? He beat Branca with a home run the other day.
Would Charley Dressen order him walked, putting the winning run
on base, to pitch to the dead-end kids at the bottom of the batting order? No, Branca's first pitch was a called strike.

The second pitch—well, when Thomson reached first base he
turned and looked toward the left-field stands. Then he started jumping straight up in the air, again and again. Then he trotted around the
bases, taking his time.

Ralph Branca turned and started for the clubhouse. The number
on his uniform looked huge. Thirteen.

A 1959 PROFILE AND FEATURE STORY CLASSIC

～ MEYER BERGER ～

If *The New York Times* deserves its reputation for greatness, a case
could be made that Meyer Berger, known to his friends as "Mike,"
was the best writer ever for the world's best newspaper. Berger worked
for the *Times* for 30 years, until his death from ulcers in 1959. He
covered the trial of Al Capone in 1932 and was nominated for a
Pulitzer Prize. He served as a war correspondent in Europe and North
Africa. His story "The Dead Return," an account of the first war dead
brought home from Europe, continues to be circulated among news
writers who treasure great narratives. He won a Pulitzer for his deadline re-creation in 1949 of a shooting spree in which 13 people were
injured in Camden, N.J.

Berger invented the "About New York" column in 1939-40 and
brought it back to life in 1953. He created a pattern of work carried
on by *Times* writers such as Francis X. Clines and Anna Quindlen: If
he could get out of the office and onto the streets of the city, he'd
come back with an interesting story.

Reprinted here is a splendid example of Berger's journalistic art,
the story of a poor, old blind man with a secret past: He was once a
great musician. Published only days before Berger's death, the story is
filled with light and sound, building to a poignant crescendo when
tender care restores an old violinist's art.

Included here are moments of great beauty, language that is both lyrical and evocative. "His head fell to his chest and his white lion's mane—he looks like Franz Liszt—caught feeble light that came through the hospital window." Or, "An audience assembled in the tiled corridor as the strains quivered and hung in the quiet, as they fled in thin echo." But such flights of image and metaphor remain grounded in reality, anchored by a reporter's quest for specific detail: the date of birth, the number of the hospital room, the address of the grocer's shop.

Notice how interested the reporter is in names and lists of names. We learn the names of the blind man's siblings, the names of places where he played, the name of his wife, the name of his Bowery buddy, the names of the nuns, the names of the songs he played, even the name of the violin. Berger brings a poet's ear to these lists, but also a reporter's curiosity. It would be hard to find a better example of the good that happens when great reporting and powerful writing combine on behalf of the reader.

Berger's best columns, as selected by the author, were reprinted in *Meyer Berger's New York*, published by Random House in 1960.

About New York

THE NEW YORK TIMES • JANUARY 23, 1959

Last Friday a welfare worker led a slender, pale old man into the old Straus mansion at 9 East Seventy-first Street. Franciscan nuns run the Eye, Ear, Nose and Throat Division of St. Clare's Hospital there.

The old man was blind. His clothes were shabby. His sunken cheeks were stubble-covered. He tried to sit on the elevator floor as it lifted to the second floor. In dimly lighted Room 203, to which he was assigned, he tried to sit on the floor again.

The welfare woman said: "He has lived a long time in Bowery flophouses. When there are no seats in flophouses, the men sit on the floor."

The old man was shaved, bathed and put into pajamas. He gave his history as though through a veil. His memory failed now and then. He said he was Laurence Stroetz, born in Fifth Street between Avenues A and B on Aug. 10, 1877, when the lower East Side was mainly German.

His father was Frank Stroetz, who played cornet for Squadron A of the old National Guard in the Seventies. The family had a grocer's shop at 165 Second Street. He could remember some of his brothers and sisters—Frank, Hannah, Barbara, Madeline, Annie, Mary.

"All gone, now?" he was asked, and he nodded. The listeners were conscious of mental groping behind the sightless, cataract-covered eyes that might once have been blue. He said, "My wife was Maud Baker." He repeated, "Maud Baker."

"She gone?" He nodded.

"No children?" He said, "No children."

By last Monday the old man had mellowed under the kindly treatment of the dark-clad Franciscan sisters and the white-clad nuns who are nurses. He told of life on the East Side in his boyhood, of how he had taken violin lessons there and of playing in his twenties with professional orchestras.

He said he had been two years with Victor Herbert in the Pittsburgh Symphony Orchestra; with the orchestra in the old Academy of Music in Fourteenth Street next to Tony Pastor's. He told of playing in the Savoy and in the Lyceum when Billie Burke was in "Mrs. Dot," long, long ago. He snatched each memory from the past with difficulty.

He kept talking about Charlie, who had been his guide and companion in one Bowery flophouse or another the last thirty years. He said: "When my eyes began to go, Charlie was my boss in a restaurant in Radio City. I had a broom and a pan. I picked up cigarette butts and napkins. Charlie had his own office."

It took a long time before the old man could better identify Charlie: "He slept in the Majestic, same as me, and in the Alabama." Those are Bowery lodging houses. "He brought my coffee. Charlie was good to me." Then he remembered Charlie's last name:

"Charlie was a Frenchman. He pawned my old violin for me. I used to play in the Hotel Oriental in Coney Island. I played in Beethoven Hall and in the Liederkranz. Charlie Messier—he was a good pianist. He led the boys' choir in the old Mariners' Temple when Dr. Hubbell was there. I played in the Church of The Land and Sea. Mrs. Morris was organist."

The mental scraps had to be snatched before they fled. At 82 they don't stay put, the old man said. A few times he fell asleep. His head fell to his chest and his white lion's mane—he looks like Franz Liszt—caught feeble light that came through the hospital window.

Nurse Josephine Wynne spoke with Sister Pauline Marie. They remembered that Sister Francis Marie had in her room the old Biotte violin that had belonged to her sister, the nun Sister Anthony Marie. Sister

Anthony Marie died in St. Clare's three years ago. Cardinal Spellman had found the instrument for her in Rome more than thirty years ago.

The staff talked with Sister Mary Fintan, who has charge of the hospital. With her consent they brought the old violin to Room 203. It had not been played for years, but Laurence Stroetz groped for it. His long white fingers stroked it. He tuned it, with some effort, and tightened the old bow. He lifted it to his chin and the lion's mane came down.

It was 8 o'clock. Dinner was over. Room 203 was all but dark. Only diffused light filtered in from the silent corridor through the partly open door. The old man had told the nuns he had not played since Charlie had pawned his violin, but the pale fingers rippled up and down the strings as he sought touch.

He played "Sidewalks of New York," true, but quavery. The fingering was stronger in Handel's "Largo," "Humoresque" and "The Blue Danube." Before each number the old man mumbled the composer's name and hummed opening bars to recapture lost melody. The nuns, the patients and the nurses were silent.

An audience assembled in the tiled corridor as the strains quivered and hung in the quiet, as they fled in thin echo. Laurence Stroetz murmured another tune, barely heard by the nuns and the nurses. Then he played it, clear and steady. It was Gounod's "Ave Maria."

Black-clad and white-clad nuns moved lips in silent prayer. They choked up. The long years on the Bowery had not stolen Laurence Stroetz's touch. Blindness made his fingers stumble down to the violin bridge, but they recovered. The music died and the audience pattered applause. The old violinist bowed and his sunken cheeks creased in a smile.

Next week eye surgeons at St. Clare's will try to remove the cataracts. If they do, the Welfare Department will try to place the old violinist in a nursing home to get him off the Bowery. If someone would offer a violin that he could call his own again, he would know ecstasy.

"It would make me feel good," he told the sisters. "It would be wonderful."

JANUARY 26, 1959

Eight violins were offered the other day to Laurence Stroetz, the 82-year-old, cataract-blinded violinist who was taken to St. Clare's Hospital in East Seventy-first Street from a Bowery flophouse. The offers came from men and women who had read that though he had once played with the Pittsburgh Symphony Orchestra, he had been without a violin for more than thirty years.

The first instrument to reach the hospital was a gift from the Lighthouse, the institution for the sightless. It was delivered by a blind man. A nun took it to the octogenarian.

He played it a while, tenderly and softly, then gave it back. He said: "This is a fine old violin. Tell the owner to take good care of it." The white-clad nun said: "It is your violin, Mr. Stroetz. It is a gift." The old man bent his head over it. He wept.

A 1963 OPINION AND PERSUASION CLASSIC

∼ GENE PATTERSON ∼

Gene Patterson held one of the most important newspaper positions of the 20th century: He was the editor of *The Atlanta Constitution* during the civil rights era. From 1960 through 1968, there was a daily column in the paper with Patterson's name on it. None of these, including the ones for which he would win a Pulitzer Prize, was as powerful as "A Flower for the Graves."

Under the tutelage of former editor Ralph McGill, Patterson used the platform of his column to persuade other white Southerners to reject their racist and segregationist past. It was a daunting and dangerous calling.

Public outrage in America reached new heights when dynamite exploded in a Baptist Church in Birmingham, Ala., killing four black children. In his lead, Patterson evokes the image of the mother of one child, holding a tiny shoe in her hand. "Every one of us in the white South holds that small shoe in his hand," wrote Patterson. . . . "Only we can trace the truth, Southerner—you and I. We broke those children's bodies."

By sounding a clarion for reform, Patterson joined a distinguished list of Southern white editorialists whose writing helped change the face of American culture and politics. So powerful was his message that Patterson was invited by Walter Cronkite to read his column on the *CBS Evening News*, an almost unthinkable honor by contemporary standards.

Patterson went on to become managing editor at *The Washington Post*, then editor of the *St. Petersburg* (Fla.) *Times*. In 1977, he became president of the American Society of Newspaper Editors. Under his leadership, the ASNE Distinguished Writing Awards were created.

A Flower for the Graves

THE ATLANTA CONSTITUTION • SEPTEMBER 16, 1963

A Negro mother wept in the street Sunday morning in front of a Baptist church in Birmingham. In her hand she held a shoe, one shoe — from the foot of her dead child. We hold that shoe with her.

Every one of us in the white South holds that small shoe in his hand.

It is too late to blame the sick criminals who handled the dynamite. The FBI and the police can deal with that kind. The charge against them is simple. They killed four children.

Only we can trace the truth, Southerner — you and I. We broke those children's bodies.

We watched the stage set without staying it. We listened to the prologue unbestirred. We saw the curtain opening with disinterest. We have heard the play.

*   *   *

We — who go on electing politicians who heat the kettles of hate.

We — who raise no hand to silence the mean and little men who have their nigger jokes.

We — who stand aside in imagined rectitude and let the mad dogs that run in every society slide their leashes from our hand, and spring.

We — the heirs of a proud South, who protest its worth and demand its recognition — we are the ones who have ducked the difficult, skirted the uncomfortable, caviled at the challenge, resented the necessary, rationalized the unacceptable and created the day surely when these children would die.

This is no time to load our anguish onto the murderous scapegoat who set the cap in dynamite of our own manufacture.

He didn't know any better.

Somewhere in the dim and fevered recess of an evil mind, he feels right now that he has been a hero. He is only guilty of murder. He thinks he has pleased us.

*   *   *

We of the white South who know better are the ones who must take a harsher judgment.

We, who know better, created a climate for child-killing by those who don't.

We hold that shoe in our hand, Southerner. Let us see it straight, and look at the blood on it. Let us compare it with the unworthy speeches of Southern public men who have traduced the Negro; match it with the spectacle of shrilling children whose parents and teachers turned them free to spit epithets at small huddles of Negro school-children for a week before this Sunday in Birmingham; hold up the shoe and look beyond it to the state house in Montgomery where the official attitudes of Alabama have been spoken in heat and anger.

Let us not lay the blame on some brutal fool who didn't know any better.

We know better. We created the day. We bear the judgment. May God have mercy on the poor South that has been so led. May what has happened hasten the day when the good South, which does live and have great being, will rise to this challenge of racial understanding and common humanity, and in the full power of its unasserted courage, assert itself.

The Sunday school play at Birmingham is ended. With a weeping Negro mother, we stand in the bitter smoke and hold a shoe. If our South is ever to be what we wish it to be, we will plant a flower of nobler resolve for the South, now upon these four small graves that we dug.

Chapter 10

THE CRAFT OF WRITING GREAT STORIES

THE BUILDING BLOCKS OF THE STORY

When people tell stories in everyday life, they often report the news first. "My plane was delayed for four hours," they might begin. They might also give more interesting details as part of the story: Perhaps the plane could not be flown into a tropical storm, a passenger got rowdy and had to be restrained, an attempted hijacking was foiled, or the pilot had a heart attack.

Sometimes a long dramatic story can begin with a summary of the news. For example, Shakespeare does this in the first eight lines of *Romeo and Juliet*:

> Two households, both alike in dignity,
> In fair Verona where we lay our scene,
> From ancient grudge break to new mutiny,
> Where civil blood makes civil hands unclean.
> From forth the fatal loins of these two foes
> A pair of star-crossed lovers take their life;
> Whose misadventured piteous overthrows
> Doth with their death bury their parents' strife.

Perhaps if Shakespeare had been a reporter for the *London Globe*, he might have written it this way, using a convention called a *lead*: "A pair of teenage lovers died Thursday, the result of a failed plot to bring their warring families together. Romeo Montague and Juliet Capulet, both of Verona, were pronounced dead, he from poisoning, and she from what appeared to be a self-inflicted dagger wound. 'This is the most woeful story I've ever heard,' said Escalus, prince of Verona and chief law enforcement officer. 'I hope the families learn from this terrible tragedy.' "

In his play, Shakespeare includes the basic elements of news-telling, usually referred to as the Five W's and H. We know Who: a pair of unlucky lovers; What: took their lives; Where: in fair Verona; When: right now; Why: an ancient feud. The full narrative of the drama, what the playwright calls "the two hours' traffic of our stage," provides the How. Who, What, Where, When, Why and How.

Why would Shakespeare bother to write the play if he tells what is to happen in the first eight lines? The answer says everything about the power of story, of a writer's ability to render experience in a way that seems real, so that the death of the lovers, when it comes, hits us with a shocking surprise, even if we've seen the play dozens of times.

Jon Franklin, one of the greatest American newspaper writers, offers this definition of a story: "A story consists of a sequence of actions that occur when a sympathetic character encounters a complicating situation that he confronts and solves."

Romeo and Juliet fall in love but cannot act openly because of the deadly feud between their families. They marry secretly, but their plans go wrong, resulting in their deaths, a tragedy that eventually ends the families' hatred. What a story. What we get in newspapers, argues Franklin, is often something quite different: a sequence of resolutions without complications, or endless complications without resolutions.

The Inverted Pyramid

The search for an explanation must begin at the base of the *inverted pyramid*. For more than a century, this single story form has been the workhorse of American newspaper writing. Born with the telegraph and the Civil War, adopted and perfected by the wire services, the pyramid has served the needs of readers in a hurry, reporters on deadline and editors who love to hack from the bottom.

In the pyramid, reporters organize information in descending levels of importance. The readers absorb the most important news first and continue down the page until their interest flags:

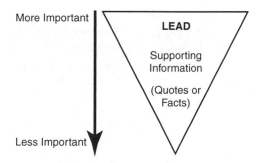

A 43-year-old Seffner man was killed Thursday evening when his car collided head-on with a semitrailer truck, according to a Florida Highway Patrol spokesman.

James Johnson of 143 Oak St. was headed west on State Road 574 when his 1986 Buick inexplicably crossed the median line and hit the truck, the spokesman said.

The driver of the truck, Stan Simmons, 26, of 435 High St., was not hurt, the spokesman said.

The value of such writing is clear: Readers get the most important information early, the reporter can follow a formula on deadline, and busy editors with a space crunch can cut from the bottom without consultation. Such writing is as straightforward and undecorated as a fullback running over left tackle. Some journalists learn no other style.

Some experts feel the pyramid will retain its pre-eminence as a story form, especially in a new media environment, where online communication is often delivered in short, digestible bites of information. Thus, every student must master it.

So why are none of the stories in this anthology written in the inverted pyramid? It has to do with a crucial weakness in the pyramid as a form of communication. "The inverted pyramid is at war with the narrative tradition," says columnist Charles McDowell of the *Richmond* (Va.) *Times-Dispatch*. "We write upside-down and tell stories backwards."

Journalism teacher Melvin Mencher also dislikes the image: "The term is somewhat misleading. An inverted pyramid story is an unbalanced monolith, a huge top teetering on a pinpoint base. It is a monstrous image for journalists, for the top of a story should be deft and pointed."

When badly written, the inverted pyramid peters out into insignificance. One reporter said, "No reader reads more then three paragraphs into a story." For him the inverted pyramid is a self-fulfilling prophecy. Some reporters let the pyramid control the content so that news comes out homogenized. Traffic fatalities, three-alarm fires and new city ordinances begin to look alike, numbing readers with their blandness. In extreme cases, reporters have been known to keep files of story forms in their computers: Fill in the blanks. Stick it in the paper.

Reporters have always tested the conventions of news writing. This anthology is filled with their work. To write like they do, learn a process and practice using a variety of story forms.

The Process of Writing and Reporting

Good writing may seem magical, but it's not magic. Instead, it is the result of a number of rational steps, practiced and perfected over time, of constant writing, rewriting, reading, being edited and talking about writing. Many of the writers in this anthology, when they talk about how they do their best work, describe steps in a process that the rest of us can emulate.

Although the steps need not follow a straight line, one thing is clear: The writing can begin long before the writer commits the first word to paper or screen. Conceiving a story is as much a part of the writing process as revising sentences. The writing is not just accomplished with a pencil or at a keyboard. It is done in the head, with the eyes and ears, and with the legs. It is done in the office, in the field and lying awake at night.

Generating story ideas.   Reporters fall into two categories: those who get assignments and those who generate ideas. And of those who get assignments, there are also two categories: those who do what they're told and those who expand the assignment and make the story their own.

The best writers see the world as a storehouse of story ideas, see through the walls of faceless institutions to find the human characters within them. These writers lack the ability to turn off their curiosity. This passion for knowing carries over into these reporters' lives and influences where they live, where they steer their cars, where they eat, what movies they see and what books they read.

As you read the stories in this collection, consider the tools that these curious reporters use, including tools for generating ideas. Perhaps they clip small items from newspapers and magazines that can be expanded into full stories. Perhaps they "save string," bits of information on specific topics that will be woven into a strong thread that ties a story together. These writers don't wait for stories to come to them. They get off the phone, away from the computer and out of the office.

Collecting information.   No writer is good enough at using stylish language to cover basic deficiencies in reporting. The good reporter's notebook is the repository of wonderful things that will enrich a story for readers: nuggets of information, explanations of complex processes, telling details, revealing statistics, vivid descriptions and the glories of human speech. The notebook will contain at least twice as much as the reporter can use in the story.

Over time, reporters develop more sophisticated ways of hunting and gathering, from a mastery of public records, to computer-assisted reporting methods, to immersion in scenes and events. To maintain credibility with sources and the public, reporters also need to develop many tools for checking and double-checking the facts, ensuring the accuracy of the story and building credibility with audiences and sources.

Finding a focus with the lead.   Writers often use visual metaphors to describe their work, and "focus" is one of them. During the idea and collection stages, the top of the funnel can be very wide, but the neck narrows to form the story.

No tool for finding focus is more important than the lead, the first few lines of the story that establish voice, tone and news judgment. Writers collect lots of tools for writing leads:

1. Keep leads short, knowing that even a very long story can flow from one carefully crafted sentence.

2. Never forget the news. If it is not in the first paragraph, it will appear in a "nut" paragraph near the top of the story. The *nut graph* explains to readers why they should bother reading the story.

3. Indirect leads must have impact. If a lead is indirect—that is, does not get directly to the point—it will still include elements that dramatize the news, foreshadow events or create a sense of foreboding, anticipation or surprise.

4. Never hype a lead. Never begin with the most startling or sensational anecdote if it is not organically related to the news.

5. Place a good quote high in the story to create a variety of voices and a human focus.

6. Put key words in powerful positions. Place subject and verb near the beginning and words with strong impact at the end of the first paragraph.

7. Try not to set standards too high. Not every story merits a memorable lead, but make sure, at the very least, that the lead does not block the reader's path into the story.

8. Use direct leads for important stories. In general, the more important the news, the more direct the lead.

9. Read the lead aloud. Don't be surprised if you see a good writer reading a lead with his or her lips moving. The writer tries to hear the tone or voice of the story.

10. Break the rules. The best writer will often find a great lead that violates all these rules.

Selecting the best material. Reporters may interview 50 sources and quote only five in the story, or go through pages of statistics and use only one. The process of selection works best when the focus of your story is clear.

The process of selection begins early, in the field, when reporters choose some people to interview rather than others, or when they write down a detailed description of one person but not another. Finding a focus during the collection process helps the writer gather needed information in a timely way and write better and faster.

Because writers "fall in love" with their material, the process of selection can seem painful. The British author and scholar Sir Arthur Quiller-Couch talked of the need to "murder your darlings" during the writing process, to cut without conscience those parts of the story that make the writer look clever, especially when those details fail to advance the narrative.

Donald Murray advises writers that "brevity comes from selection and not compression." Whereas the inexperienced writer may be tempted to boil everything down in a story to save space, the veteran learns to use the best three quotations rather than five, and the best anecdote rather than three.

Creating a plan for the story. Stories have shapes. They have parts that fit together to make a coherent whole. They have beginnings, middles and ends. Like a brilliant piece of architecture, a well-made story makes the reader's journey both practical and pleasurable.

Few writers work from a detailed outline, but many make a tentative list of the major parts of a story and the order in which they will appear:

Lead: the scattering of ashes

Flashback three years: Man reveals to his wife that he has AIDS

Flashback 20 years: How they met, fell in love and married

Move chronologically through his illness and death, and her survival

That four-line plan describes the structure of "Three Little Words," a 29-part series that appeared in the *St. Petersburg* (Fla.) *Times* in 1996. Even a long narrative can flow from a simple plan.

Some writing coaches argue that the less time you have, the more you need a moment to plan. Over time, writers learn to do this work in their heads, driving back to the office to work on deadline or just grabbing a bite to eat or a cup of coffee. This part of the process can turn "procrastination" into "rehearsal," moving the writer along more creatively and productively.

Creating a draft. Some writers move slowly and methodically through the drafting of difficult material. Others work quickly to build momentum in the story. The best writers use both strategies.

To overcome writer's block, some reporters lower their standards early in the process, knowing that they can raise them dramatically during the next stage. If a reporter starts criticizing a story too early in the process, not enough progress will be made in the story, leaving insufficient time for rewriting and revision.

Over time, writers collect many drafting tools. They rewrite their notes to master the content of the story and build a basic draft. They write several leads and let the best one carry them forward. They write the ending first so they can see the destination and follow the map of the story to it.

Revising and clarifying. The word *revision* means "to see again," and no great writing is produced without great revising. When revising, writers make changes both large and small. Changes may range from those that affect order and structure, to language preferences, to an altered sense of audience, to a sharper focus, to a better news judgment.

On the level of sentences and paragraphs, writers eliminate clutter, making sure each word does useful work; strengthen verbs and cut adverbs; place strong subjects and verbs at the beginning of sentences; and position emphatic words of key paragraphs and sections at the end.

On the level of language, writers make sure no key word is repeated without intention; translate jargon; seek alternatives to clichés; and dig for the concrete and specific.

To create certain effects, writers adjust the pace of information to suit the reader's learning needs; vary sentence length to create a rhythm; show and tell; reveal character; and strive for voice.

To strengthen structure, writers take advantage of chronology and other narrative opportunities; reward the reader with bright points throughout the story; and make sure the reader arrives at a natural ending rather than a contrived one.

This process—from conception to collection to focus to selection to order to drafting to revision—is not a narrow path, with all the force headed in a single direction. Think instead of the working of the tides. If you stand in the surf, the waves might knock you down, but the undertow might drag you out into strong counter-currents.

In just such a manner, the undertow of the writing process often drags writers a step or two back. A confused focus requires writers to do more reporting. A disorganized structure carries writers back to the focus stage. Problems with word choice may mean writers have not been selective. A working knowledge of the writing process can create a common vocabulary for writer and editor, aiding both to achieve a more meaningful diagnosis of the strengths and weaknesses of the story.

THE LANGUAGE OF JOURNALISM

Some critics make fun of the language of journalists, deriding it as "journalese." Too often, we earn the criticism. We fill our stories with clichés, with the "chopping blocks" and "skyrockets" that lend false color to writing about money. Or we dip our pens in steroids, heightening the drama of fires that always seem to "rage" and of "crime sprees" that always send "shock waves" through communities. Go ahead, critics, have your fun.

But consider this: We don't describe the language of ballet, photography or the violin according to its worst exemplars. When considering their art, the ballerina learns about position, the photographer about composition and the violinist about transposition. So why not think about the language of journalism as an ideal, a set of values and practices that inspire the young writer?

The writers in this anthology invite that kind of lofty thinking. It is true, their accomplishments seem out of the ordinary, a far cry from the routine practices of journalism. They have zigged when others have zagged. But that is not because they have abandoned the language of journalism. Quite the contrary, they have perfected it, drained every drop of energy from it, banged it against the wall to test its mettle, bent it to prove its flexibility and then shaped it into something beautiful and useful.

These prizewinning stories and the best routine stories likely share certain characteristics, which, when added together, constitute the language of journalism:

- The language of journalism is concrete and specific.
- The language of journalism is active.
- The language of journalism makes meaning early.
- The language of journalism is democratic.
- The language of journalism has a voice.
- The language of journalism strives for clarity.

The Language of Journalism Is Concrete and Specific

Writers are not perfect, thank goodness. For example, Cynthia Gorney violates one of the gritty rules of newspaper writing by failing to give us the name of Dr. Seuss' dog. She makes up for it with the detail that the famous author's Yorkshire terrier has a "front end . . . indistinguishable from the back at first glance." She quotes Seuss as admitting, "I've been accused of having drawn him" (p. 169). Good writers can break the rules to create wonderful effects, but you can be sure they are aware of the rules they are breaking.

Gorney's story and others should remind us that the language of journalism is concrete and specific. A saying at the *St. Petersburg Times* requires reporters to "get the name of the dog, the brand of the beer, the color and make of the sports car."

Here's an example of a police story that exemplifies this point. It was a hot, oppressively humid Florida day, and things started to go badly inside a house on 63rd Avenue South. First the air conditioner broke down, making it unbearably sticky for husband, wife and mother-in-law. Mother-in-law's irritation increased when the television set also went on the blink. (Was she watching *Wheel of Fortune, The Dating Game* or *One Life to Live?*) The woman complained to her son-in-law that the television was not working. So he took an ax to the television set. What followed was a standoff with police and his eventual surrender.

The reporter, Doreen Carvajal, writes: "An unemployed welder, enraged by his mother-in-law, axed a television set and held police at bay for seven hours Tuesday while he twirled a pistol cylinder and threatened to shoot himself." Carvajal goes on to reveal that the man's foul mood and subsequent violence were influenced by his imbibing 24 cans of Black Label beer that day. Not Heineken or Budweiser or Coors. Black Label. The reporter wrote down, and put in the story, the brand of the beer.

Good writers, like the ones included in this collection, use telling details to help us see, hear and understand. We learn that Dr. Seuss keeps his father's rifle target on the wall as a spur toward perfection; that engineers fire live chickens at airplane windows to test their safety; that teenage girls wear rhinestone necklaces that form the word *bitch*; that the body of a man lies rotting in a Rwandan schoolroom beneath a chalkboard map of Africa. As you read the stories in this book, notice these telling details, gather similar ones in your notebook and learn how to use them in your own writing.

The Language of Journalism Is Active

Reporters write in the active voice—a term of grammar and syntax. In a larger sense, the best-written journalism comes from direct observation or eyewitness accounts of people in action. Consider Bill Blundell's lead about cowboys:

> The lariat whirls as the man on horseback separates a calf from the herd. Suddenly, the loop snakes around the calf's rear legs and tightens. Wrapping a turn of rope around the saddle horn, the rider drags the hapless animal to his crew. (p. 115)

Such a lead is not a trick of language but the result of dogged reporting, being on the scene when the action takes place. That is where words such as *lariat, whirls, loop* and *snakes* can be found. But even if the reporter is not an eyewitness—which is most of the time—the writing can be active and lively.

Consider Anne Hull's account for the *St. Petersburg Times* of a woman police officer who is assaulted by an armed teenager:

> But there was no way Lisa could have seen it coming.
>
> In an instant, someone forced her down over the hood of the car. A hard object was pressed to the back of her skull, just below her right ear, next to her hair ribbon. Metal to bone: She knew it was a gun. She froze.
>
> "Don't move," the voice behind her ordered.
>
> Maybe it was some other sort of weapon at her head, a lead pipe or something. But a voice in the distance confirmed what she feared.
>
> "He's got a gun." (p. 102)

If the language of journalism is so active, concrete and specific, why are so many pieces of journalism written in language that is passive, technical and bureaucratic? George Orwell condemned such tendencies in his monumental 1946 essay "Politics and the English Language."

"The inflated style," writes Orwell, "is itself a kind of euphemism. A mass of Latin words falls upon the facts like soft snow, blurring the outlines and covering up all the details. The great enemy of clear language is insincerity. When there is a gap between one's real and one's declared aims, one turns, as it were instinctively, to long words and exhausted idioms, like a cuttlefish squirting out ink."

The corruption of language—that is, bad or insincere writing—is a tool of tyranny. "In our time," writes Orwell, "political speech and writing are largely the defense of the indefensible. Things like the continuance of British rule in India, the Russian purges and deportations, the dropping of the atom bombs on Japan, can indeed be defended, but only by arguments which are too brutal for most people to face, and which do not square with the professed aims of political parties. Thus political language has to consist largely of euphemism, question-begging, and sheer cloudy vagueness."

Following Orwell's line of thinking, the job of the political reporter can be said to be, in large measure, a linguistic one: translating the evasive passive ("Mistakes were made") into the accountable active ("The mayor knew of the plan and agreed to it").

The Language of Journalism Makes Meaning Early

The language of journalism is front-loaded. On the level of stories, this is made emblematic by the narrative structure known as the inverted pyramid. But it operates on the sentence and paragraph levels, too, even when the writer chooses, as many of the writers here have, an alternative narrative form to the wobbly pyramid.

> WASHINGTON — President Clinton will announce today he is lifting the 50-year ban on gays in the military, but the change will not occur immediately.

This standard news lead is direct, clear and comprehensible. It achieves the effect described by Don Fry, the influential writing coach, as "steady advance." The writer creates meaning by beginning a sentence with a subject and verb.

In the deep structure of every sentence is a subject and verb. That simple rule generates an infinite number of potential sentences of such astonishing variety that it is rare that an author unintentionally repeats a sentence in a lifetime. If meaning is created by a subject and verb, then a sentence that begins with a subject and verb *makes meaning early.*

Imagine each sentence you write printed on an infinitely wide piece of paper. Each sentence stretches from left to right. A reporter writes a sentence with a subject and verb at the beginning, followed by other subordinate elements, creating what textual linguists and scholars of writing call a "right-branching sentence." We just created one. The subject and verb of the main clause are on the left ("A reporter writes") and all other elements branch off to the right. Many writers, such as John McPhee and John Steinbeck, create page after page of right-branching sentences, but with such variety in length and subordination that the effect is almost invisible.

Look for this kind of sentence from writers in this collection, such as Rick Bragg, describing a poor woman of great generosity: "She spent almost nothing, living in her old family home, cutting the toes out of shoes if they did not fit right and binding her ragged Bible with Scotch tape to keep Corinthians from falling out" (p. 31). This complicated sentence works, for the reader, because Bragg makes the meaning in the first four words.

The right-branching sentence is the staple of effective journalism in the modern era. It was not always the case. Traditional English prose favored a different style, with long introductory passages and the main clause discovered somewhere in the middle or even near the period.

This is the secret of the right-branching sentence: It helps the writer create sentences of infinite length that are equally clear. The AP's legendary feature writer Saul Pett would confound and delight the word-counting editors who preached that no lead should run longer than 21 words. What would they make of his prizewinning profile of New York Mayor Ed Koch: "He is the freshest thing to blossom in New York since chopped liver, a mixed metaphor of a politician, the antithesis of the packaged leader, irrepressible, candid, impolitic, spontaneous, funny, feisty, independent, uncowed by voter blocs, unsexy, unhandsome, unfashionable and altogether charismatic, a man oddly at peace with himself in an unpeaceful place, a mayor who presides over the country's largest Babel with unseemly joy" (p. 175). Sixty-five words, the phrases locked together like boxcars, pulled along nicely by the locomotive and the coal car—the subject and verb.

The Language of Journalism Is Democratic

The language of journalism, described by Hugh Kenner as the "plain style," is, in various senses, democratic. When used powerfully, it flows from democratic impulses and creates a model for public discourse.

"Plain style is a populist style," Kenner writes, "and one that suited writers like Swift, Mencken, and Orwell. Homely diction is its hallmark, also one-two-three syntax, the show of candor and the artifice of seeming to be grounded outside language in what is called fact—the domain where a condemned man can be observed as he silently avoids a puddle and your prose will report the observation and no one will doubt it. Such prose simulates the words anyone who was there and awake might later have spoken spontaneously. On a written page . . . the spontaneous can only be a contrivance."

An American aesthetic of plainness is articulated early and often in the creation of a canon of literature we used to call American. "I am glad you think my style plain," wrote Nathaniel Hawthorne to an editor in 1851. (One wonders whether the editor was praising or condemning the author.) "I never, in any one page or paragraph, aimed at making it anything else, or giving it any other merit—and I wish people would leave off talking about its beauty. . . . The greatest possible merit of style is, of course, to make the words absolutely disappear into the thought."

Orwell puts this sentiment more plainly, despite the help of a simile: "Good prose is like a window pane." The reader notices not the writing, but the world. This value, he believes, grows out of his political motivation: "Looking back through my work, I see that it is invariably where I lacked a political purpose that I wrote lifeless books and was betrayed into purple passages, sentences without meaning, decorative adjectives and humbug generally."

The language of journalism is so plain, in fact, that metaphors or other decorations of prose—because they are infrequent—have a special power: "The deaths," writes Francis X. Clines, "were handled by Gerry Adams, the eerily placid, black-bearded leader of Sinn Fein, the rebellion's political arm, as if he were the Osiris of his people, the king rallying souls to the underworld, to the plain slant of Belfast hillside called Milltown Cemetery" (p. 25).

In his popular book *On Writing Well*, William Zinsser preaches the virtue of simplicity. "Clutter is the disease of American writing," he argues. "We are a society strangling in unnecessary words, circular constructions, pompous frills and meaningless jargon." His search for useless words in his own writing is relentless, as he demonstrates in his revision of his own manuscript. His passion for simplicity is reminiscent of E.B. White's description of William Strunk's classroom lesson on brevity: "When he delivered his oration on brevity to the class, he leaned forward over his desk, grasped his coat lapels in his hands, and in a husky, conspiratorial voice said, 'Rule Thirteen. Omit needless words! Omit needless words! Omit needless words!' "

The Language of Journalism Has a Voice

The language of journalism is concrete and specific; it is active and filled with people in action; the important things come first so that meaning is clear; it is democratic and, as a result, tough and plain.

Does that mean that the language of journalism is nothing like human speech at all?

Speech rambles and turns back on itself; it stumbles and repeats; it stops and leaves gaps; it connects the disconnected; it uses strange pauses and odd sounds. How then can we explain Alexis de Tocqueville's metaphor of speech when describing early America's journalists: "They speak the language of their country, and make themselves heard"?

He was not listening to broadcast journalists such as Edward R. Murrow or Charles Kuralt. He was reading authors and "hearing" them. In that sense, he understood that illusion of speech in prose that writing scholars and teachers call "voice."

The voice of most news stories is neutral and authoritative. Editorials are often written in institutional voices. Columnists, critics and sportswriters often develop distinctive voices that readers seek out over their breakfast cereal and interact with in an imagined form of conversation.

The language of journalism is not like speech, but it is closer to speech than most other forms of writing. This is what Kenner means by describing it as "populist." It also explains the journalistic obsession with quoting, the attempts to represent speech in prose. Too often, especially in government stories, this means experts speaking in code or in meaningless sound bites.

But when eyewitnesses, especially everyday people, are given their voices in print, the effect can be powerful, moving, puzzling, funny or outrageous. These effects are often best accomplished on public radio, where voices can be heard with the full flavor of dialect and nuance of expression. But "a good quote high in the story" can also enhance the drama or sharpen a point.

The Language of Journalism Strives for Clarity

The most valued quality of the language of journalism is clarity, and its most desired effect is comprehensibility. Many lawyers and diplomats value clarity within their discourse communities, but unlike the journalist, they also exalt ambiguity, ambivalence, subtext and even paradox. These have their uses. The U.S. Supreme Court ordered that American public schools must be desegregated "with all deliberate speed," and with that intentional ambiguity tried to effect dramatic social change without inviting chaos.

All journalism exists on a spectrum that curves from the civic to the literary, that is, from information and announcements about hurricane preparedness to long, dramatic narratives about people facing the most dangerous hurricane in the nation's history.

The qualities most valued in "literary" stories are narrative momentum, revealing scenes, sympathetic characters, compelling dialogue, telling details and sharp points of view. These qualities are usually associated with "good writing" or "prizewinning" journalism.

There grows a problem, and it buds out of the image of the spectrum. For in journalism, the civic *is* literary. Just as plainness is achieved through craft and artifice, so is clarity of explanation. When the civic becomes literary, as it often does in this anthology, the language of journalism is used for its highest purpose: to reveal how the world works to readers who are imagined not as consumers or market shares, but as citizens and members of communities.

The craft of the writer must result, beyond all else, in comprehensibility. Journalists must not merely make information available to audiences but truly inform. They must take responsibility for what audiences know and understand about the world. To achieve this, journalists must think not of "the reader" but of "readers," and must seek to bridge their intentions with the differing expectations and experiences of those who turn to the news.

This often involves a set of language skills more often associated with encyclopedia authors than journalists. If it's your job to write something about Einstein's theories that a 13-year-old can use in a term paper, you'd best take a radical view of clarity and comprehensibility. For journalists, such radical clarity means controlling the pace of information, translating technical language, knowing when to show and when to tell, creating analogies to help readers understand numbers and, most difficult of all, knowing when to leave things out. Only skilled writers, such as those in this collection, master these techniques. This anthology offers models to show you how.

WRITING TO INFORM, WRITING TO ENGAGE

In the 1930s, a woman named Louise Rosenblatt began teaching literature to high school students and eventually taught at New York University. As a scholar, she not only studied great works of literature but also was curious about the different ways her students read works such as Shakespeare's *Hamlet* or *Romeo and Juliet*.

She realized early what is now a commonplace: Reading is a transaction in which each reader brings his or her own biography, experiences, prejudices, knowledge and ignorance to the text. The writer may create the text, but the reader makes it a story.

Rosenblatt defines two kinds of reading, which she describes as "the efferent" and "the aesthetic." Excuse the technical language for a moment; we'll be getting to journalism soon. The word *efferent* means "carrying away from." The reader carries away information, things that have some potential utility. Rosenblatt believes, rightly, that most of journalism falls into this category.

- A new restaurant opens in town.
- The city passes a new property tax.
- Four new movies open this week.
- A new drug for AIDS is being tested.

In each case, the reader has something to learn, or carry away from the story, to use in his or her personal life, perhaps to pass on to another. It should be obvious that whatever the reader brings to the text, the writer can help the reader carry something away. The writing must be clear and comprehensible, and not call attention to itself.

But much of the reading we do is also "aesthetic," which is to say that the language is rendered artfully. When we read *Hamlet*, the purpose is not to find our way to Elsinore, or to learn how to dig a grave or poison the tip of a sword. We read *Hamlet* because it is an experience, a virtual reality. It seeks not to inform us, but to form us.

In the United States, and in other cultures, there is a long tradition of storytelling in newspapers:

- Three men, thought lost, are rescued at sea.
- A woman is murdered in her house, and although many neighbors hear the screams, no one calls the police.
- A dolphin rescues a dog.
- A woman's hearing is restored in an experimental operation.

This kind of news cries out for stories, not articles. Stories are told through scenes. They have characters who speak with dialogue. Details excite the senses, making the experience come alive. Stories also have settings, places characters inhabit. We can see things from another's point of view.

Richard Zahler of *The Seattle Times* makes a helpful distinction: "When we write for information, we depend on the traditional Five W's: Who, What, Where, When and Why. But when we write for story, when we thaw out those articles, Who becomes Character; What becomes Plot; Where becomes Setting; When becomes Chronology; Why becomes Motivation."

WRITING WITH "GOLD COINS"

Journalists often write informational articles that have story elements and vice versa. Moreover, they have some tricks of the trade that help them do this. The first is the anecdote, a word often confused with "antidote"—unless we say that the anecdote is an antidote to the poison of dull writing.

The anecdote is a tiny story within a story, "a short account of some interesting or humorous incident." The word comes from the

Greek, meaning "previously unpublished," suggesting some little secret piece of history or biography.

Don Fry suggests a story structure in which anecdotes can be
used as gold coins. "Imagine yourself walking along a path through
the forest when you come upon a gold coin. You pick it up and put it
in your pocket. You walk another mile, and find another coin. Another mile, another coin. Even though you're tired, you keep walking
until the coins run out." In the same way, a reader will more likely
move through an informational story if he or she is rewarded with a
gold coin, a tiny bit of story that intensifies the experience of reading.

So an article can be mostly informational and be brightened by
embedded stories. Or it can work the other way around. The story
can begin with an experience, a narrative, rendered so artfully that
we can see it, hear it, smell it. Remember William Blundell's lead in
his *Wall Street Journal* story about the disappearing cowboy?

> The lariat whirls as the man on horseback separates a calf from the
> herd. Suddenly, the loop snakes around the calf's rear legs and
> tightens. Wrapping a turn of rope around the saddle horn, the rider
> drags the hapless animal to his crew.
>   The flanker whips the calf onto its back, and the medicine man
> inoculates the animal. Amid blood, dust and bawling, the calf is
> dehorned with a coring tool, branded in an acrid cloud of smoke
> from burning hair and flesh, earmarked with a penknife in the
> ranch's unique pattern . . . and castrated. It is all over in one minute.

Fascinating story. But why are we reading this scene? What's the
point? What is the context? It turns out there are few real cowboys
left in an era of cowboy hype. And the author communicates this in
the nut graph:

> Finally, there is a little band of men like Jim Miller. Their boots are
> old and cracked. They still know as second nature the ways of
> horse and cow, the look of sunrise over empty land — and the
> hazards, sheer drudgery and rock-bottom pay that go with perhaps
> the most overromanticized of American jobs. There are very few of
> these men left. "Most of the real cowboys I know," says Mr. Miller,
> "have been dead for a while."

The narrative can slow down, or even stop, for a bit of background or explanation. Think of this structure as the moving train, a
reader's journey created by the writer's narrative line. Every so often,
the train slows down or even makes a whistle-stop, during which the

reporter may speak directly to the reader to explain, offer history or provide context or background.

Stories can brighten information, and that information can enrich stories. Studying this anthology will help you learn the grammar and structure of such stories, especially how to use language that points you there and that puts you there.

MAKING HARD FACTS EASY READING

When some professional journalists read stories like the ones in this anthology, they let loose their frustrations: "Sure, I could write a great story about the Armenian earthquake or the civil wars in Africa. But I don't get chances like that on my beat. I write local stories! I write about sewers! I write about taxes! I write about budgets! I write about utilities! I write about bond issues! I write about water! You tell me how I'm supposed to make that readable and interesting."

Such reporters have a right to their rage because they draw the daily task of writing the toughest stories in the newspaper. No circuses or beauty pageants or oyster-eating contests for these scribes. Only bankruptcies, municipal finance proposals and rate hikes.

But the stance of editors the world over is right, too. Good writing should be in every corner of the paper. Reporters and editors must work together to find new ways to write the newspaper's bread-and-butter stories. Reporters may not be able to write a school board story with the same narrative power that a killer hurricane inspires, but journalists can fulfill their civic responsibilities by using the tools of clarity to make their stories engaging and comprehensible. Too often, under pressure of time and space, reporters say subconsciously, "If I understand it, if I get it into the paper without any inaccuracies, then readers can muddle through it and make whatever sense they can out of the story."

To take responsibility for what readers understand, reporters must write in a way that explains important and complex issues to readers. Then informed citizens can make the daily decisions that affect their lives. Will I vote for the council member who supported that tax? Will I shop there anymore? Will I send my child to public school? Will I sell my house? Should I save my money?

Reporters can apply these tests to their prose. Is it clear enough so that a reader could pass a quiz on the important information in the story? Is it relevant enough that a reader could pass along accurate information from the story to another person? If you asked the reader, "What's important in this story?" would the reader agree with the reporter and editor?

Journalists who can answer yes to these questions are already using the tools of clarity in their work. These techniques help make hard facts easy reading. Writers and supportive editors can apply them on behalf of the reader.

Thinking Tools

Envision a general audience.   A writer's sense of audience controls his or her voice. If I imagine an audience of specialists, my language may become technical and convoluted, like this sentence from an editorial titled "Curb State Mandates":

> To avert the all too common enactment of requirements without regard for their local cost and tax impact, however, the commission recommends that statewide interest should be clearly identified on any proposed mandates, and that states should partially reimburse local governments for some state-imposed mandates and fully for those involving employee compensation, working conditions and pensions.

This sentence assumes an audience of experts. Editor and reporter must play the role of the reader's friend. These prompts might help: "Tell me in your own words what this issue is about." "Can we find a way to simplify this?" "Let's start from the beginning. What exactly is a 'state mandate'?" Help the reader with something that sounds more like this: "The state often tells local governments what to do. But guess who winds up paying for it?"

Tell it to a friend.   Many readers come to the same story looking for different things. It sometimes helps the writer to imagine he is writing for a single human being, and a familiar one at that. When you tell your story to a single person, your voice changes and your language becomes more simple and direct.

The editor can often play the role of this friend. One editor asks his writers to write him memos before they try to execute difficult stories. "When they put my name, Dear Fred, at the top of the page, it makes them write in real English rather than that governmental gobbledygook."

Think graphics. Informational graphics are reaching new levels of excellence in American newspapers. A writer's ability to explain complex issues in words and then illustrate them in pictures provides valuable reinforcement for the reader.

The clever editor invites the writer into the process. The writer should be on the lookout for important information that might be communicated effectively in a chart, graph or picture.

Look for the human side. Writers who write regularly about fiscal policy often fail to escape the clichés of economic writing. Budgets are not human documents, but graphs that look like pizzas. Stories are filled with bottom lines, tightened belts, economic spirals and chopping blocks. These stories seem not to be about people at all. No wonder readers look the other way.

Good writers understand that readers are attracted to the presence of human beings in stories. These humans can be politicians or bureaucrats, or people who are the victims or beneficiaries of public policy.

John Gouch of the *Anderson* (S.C.) *Independent-Mail* explains the plight of black farmers in South Carolina by focusing on the life and words of a single farmer: "Furman Porter was 4 years old when he first walked behind a mule plowing up Anderson County's red clay." The story is about the business of farming. A writer that focuses on a human being—and follows that character throughout the story—helps readers understand an issue's true significance.

Find the microcosm. It's hard to get a handle on a subject as complex as "the American bureaucracy" or "the effects of rising interest rates on the American people" or "the economic impact of high technology on the Sun Belt." The key to writing such a story clearly and well is to find a specific, concrete example that represents the larger reality.

"I know there's a problem with vandalism in the county schools," says the editor to the reporter. "But isn't there one school we can focus on to tell the story?" Or "It looks like more top students are starting their college careers at junior colleges. Let's look at all the statistical evidence for that. But let's make sure we identify a student and a family to build the story around."

Develop a chronology. When writers write in chronological order, they invite readers to enter a story and stick with it. Readers understand the demands of chronology and know that when the timeline ends, they will have reached a heightened level of understanding.

"I always try to find a chronology," says Chris Welles, who has written some of the most complex business stories in American journalism. Welles may be writing about a marketing war between Bic and Gillette, the collapse of a major government securities firm or the criminal indictment of a famous entrepreneur, but in each case he finds a chronological rope that his readers can hang on to.

These opportunities for chronology are not always transparent. But a good editor can help the reporter unfreeze time in the story, often turning flat explanation into action. Good prompts for the reporter include: "When did that happen?" "Tell me the story of how that came to be." "Do you know the history of this problem?"

Consider the impact.   Mike Foley, former city editor of the *St. Petersburg Times*, taught his reporters to avoid writing leads that read "They held a meeting Tuesday. . . ." The meeting itself is not important, argued Foley. What they did or failed to do is important. Did they increase the millage rate for property taxes at the meeting? If so, the writer must communicate the impact to the reader. If necessary, the writer might teach readers how to compute their property taxes based on the new rate.

A city may get a grant to build a plant that will recycle sewage water. The good writer tries to make it meaningful to the reader: "Next year you may be able to water your lawn and firefighters may put out fires with treated sewage water."

Too many stories fail to answer the reader's most challenging question: "So what?" The writer and helpful editor can ask it first.

Cool off.   Killer stories about complex issues often involve intense periods of reporting and learning for the writer. A cooling-off period helps the writer understand what is known and how to tell it to the reader. It also gives the writer, with the help of the editor, time to understand what he does not know or what she has failed to communicate.

Those who try to publish "in the heat" run serious risks. Some reporters, attempting to explain complicated information, get defensive about long, complicated sentences. "Of course it's complicated," they tell their editors. "The idea is complicated." That is a mask for "I don't really understand it, so I'll fog over my ignorance with cloudy prose."

The best reporters know how to step away from a project, if only for a few minutes. They sit back, reflect on the story, and plan a solution on behalf of the reader. When they return to the story, they can see a better way that they missed before.

Read it aloud.   If some writers would only listen to their own stories by reading them aloud, they would come to understand how dense and confusing their prose is. Reading out loud forces the writer and editor to experience the linear nature of the reader's path to understanding. One word follows another; one thought follows another. Writer and editor can hear trouble areas even when they can't see them. Many of the best writers testify that they read their work out loud, or at least read it "in loud," listening to the sounds of their prose in their "inner ear."

Eliminate unnecessary information.   The best way to deal with some difficult information is to leave it out of the story. Too many stories contain too much information for the reader to digest.

Our readers may understand more if we give them less. The key to doing this responsibly is to make tough value judgments on the information we have collected. The result of such selectivity is a more precise, more readable story. If it turns out to be boring and difficult, at least it will be brief, boring and difficult. The readers will be thankful the writer did not waste their time.

Drafting Tools

Slow the pace of information.   A good teacher does not assume students know everything about a subject. Nor does the teacher expect them to learn everything at once. Yet too much writing on difficult subjects is of the "dense-pack" variety: information stuffed into tight, dense paragraphs and conveyed at a rate that takes our breath away.

> The billing structure and data-gathering procedures are geared toward providing cost-based reimbursement to satisfy federal regulations under Medicare, he said, which insures about 40 percent of Arizona's hospital patients.

Who would want to try to pass a comprehension test after reading a story so dense with information? The writer can come to the reader's rescue by slowing the flow.

Consider the beneficial effects to the reader of a story that proceeds at a slower pace:

> When the price of sugar was plummeting last year, the federal government tried to help.
>   Things didn't work out as hoped.
>   What emerged is a complex struggle involving an interplay of governments, sugar producers, Third World economies, corn farmers and two grain milling giants based in Decatur.
>   At stake are the price of sugar, the marketability of corn and the future of high fructose corn syrup.

Jim Ludwick of the *Herald & Review* in Decatur, Ill., shows concern for his readers here by easing them into what is going to be a complicated subject.

Introduce new or difficult elements one at a time.   A tough story to read, and to edit, is the one that introduces 20 characters to readers in a dozen paragraphs. The frustrated reader turns back again and again to keep things straight, or just gives up.

Good editors help reporters introduce one character or one concept at a time. When Chris Welles explained to the readers of the *Los Angeles Times* "how accountants helped Orion Pictures launch its financial comeback," he had to explain "generally accepted accounting principles." That done, Welles was able to deal with each of the accounting techniques used at Orion. He introduced them slowly, one at a time: "Certainly the most unusual accounting strategy used by Orion was what is known as 'quasi-reorganization.' " In this long, difficult story, Welles gives the reader a chance to relax, to think, to understand.

Recognize the value of repetition.   Teachers know the value of repetition. They adhere to the old strategy: "Tell them what you're going to say, say it, tell them what you've said."

Editors tend to be suspicious of repetition. It takes up space. But why not repeat the key information to demonstrate its importance to the reader? An editor can recognize the heart of the story and reinforce it in a headline, a drop quote and a caption.

"I try to teach reporters that if they have an important point they want to make, make it repetitiously but in different ways," says Bill Blundell. "Make it with a figure, make it with an anecdote and then maybe wrap it up with a quote." Variation saves the repetition from being boring and distracting.

"You cannot be explicit enough in communication," preaches scholar John Robinson. "Leaving something between the lines and thinking the reader is going to get it is a very dangerous practice."

Don't clutter leads. The writer and editor must pay special attention to the lead when the story is difficult or complex. If the lead is crammed with information or demonstrates to readers that the subject is beyond their interest and understanding, the reader will turn elsewhere:

> Efforts to improve housing for Buffalo neighborhoods will receive $5.6 million of the city's 1980-81 federal community development block grant money, according to the application to be submitted to the Common Council tomorrow.

The combination of numbers, jargon and needless attribution dooms this lead. The writer could use some coaching from the editor: "How much money is $5.6 million? What will it accomplish?" "There are no people in this lead. Who are the key players? Who will benefit most?" "Explain this application process to me. Is this going to happen or not?" "What do readers really need to know about this?" Perhaps such questions would lead to something more like this:

> Some people in Buffalo think the city needs more and better housing for its citizens. They are trying to do something about it and want the federal government to help. More than $5 million worth of help.

Use simple sentences. Difficult ideas can be expressed in simple sentences. Simple sentences are usually short, clear and easy to read. They contain one clause and one idea. A series of simple sentences also slows the pace for the reader. Each period is a stop sign. The reader has time to digest and assimilate information.

Donald Murray has pointed out what can happen when brevity and simplicity give way to complexity. The result can be a lead like this:

> A 3.6 billion-dollar compromise budget was agreed to by House and Senate Ways and Means Subcommittees yesterday that pares one billion dollars from the previous compromise budget of 4.6 billion dollars, of which 993 million dollars may be restored when it returns to the floor of the Senate next week.

"The more complicated the subject," says Murray, "the more important it is to break the subject down into digestible bites, writing in short paragraphs, short sentences and short words at the points of the greatest complexity when the meaning is too often lost."

Remember that numbers can be numbing.   Numbers turn off most readers, especially when they are packed into paragraphs or when they bump and collide:

> A proposed elimination of the 2 percent property tax rollback will immediately add $25 to each $1,000 in property taxes paid by middle- and upper-income taxpayers. In addition, the state is freezing its contribution to the 10 percent property tax rollback, which has been used as a tool to allow homeowners to keep pace with inflated property values.

This paragraph is not particularly offensive. But a series of such paragraphs can damage the reader's level of comprehension.

Numbers should be handled carefully in a story. Only the most important numbers should be used, and they should be explained in context. Editors can help: "Which number will really tell our readers what's happening?" "That big area of land is just an abstract number. Can we compare it to an area our readers will recognize?" "Those big numbers make my head swim. What else costs that much?" "Can we take those numbers out of the story and put them in a graphic?"

Translate jargon.   It may take a new city hall writer a month to learn the acronymic alphabet soup of municipal government. Suddenly the writer feels comfortable sneaking into stories technical words without explanation.

A problem arises when the journalist's language is contaminated by his contact with specialists. Unless the journalist translates "capitalization" or "amortization" or "depreciation," most readers will be left in the dark.

According to former Page One editor Glynn Mapes, *The Wall Street Journal* defines the gross national product each time it is introduced into a story as "the total market value of the output of goods and services in the nation." *The Journal's* zeal for translating jargon once extended to defining batting average in a story about Ted Williams.

Announce difficult concepts.   Some medicines go down hard, and some concepts, issues or procedures are so difficult that even careful and thoughtful writers cannot make them easily palatable for readers.

That is as it should be. It would be dishonest to give readers a false sense of simplicity. So writers inform readers that certain information will be rough going.

Chris Welles lets his readers know what they are in for if they are to understand the complexities of "risk arbitrage": "Until recently, however, risk arbitrage has been largely unknown beyond Wall Street and only vaguely appreciated even on Wall Street. One reason was arbitrage's image as a highly intricate, arcane, even mysterious art well beyond the ken of ordinary investors." Such announcements change the concentration level of readers and give them greater tolerance for harder information.

Compile lists.   Journalists use the "laundry list" to spell out the most important information in meaningful order. Investigative journalists list their major findings high in the story. A city hall reporter lists the alternatives for financing a new construction project. Lists create order, or at least the sense of order. They demand that the writer convey information tightly. Lists also create white space and typographical structures that invite the reader's eye to move down the page.

Chapter 11

ETHICAL JOURNALISM AND THE CRAFT OF HONEST WRITING

"A writer is a reader moved to emulation," Saul Bellow, the Nobel Prize-winning novelist, once observed. Some readers of this anthology may be inspired to match the quality of the stories they read. But this should be done with great care. Using another person's writing as a model for one's own can reap rewards for the writer and reader only if the journalist avoids the dual traps of plagiarism and fabrication.

These are not new journalistic sins. Making up an 8-year-old drug user for a 1980 feature story, "Jimmy's World," cost *Washington Post* reporter Janet Cooke her career—and a Pulitzer Prize—and tarnished her newspaper's reputation. A 1983 ASNE winner, sportswriter Tom Archdeacon, had to apologize for lifting passages from another writer's book, although he kept the writing award and his job. The list of newsroom transgressors continues to grow, most notably with the 2003 discovery that a *New York Times* reporter named Jayson Blair had plagiarized and fabricated numerous stories, leading to his dismissal and the ouster of the paper's top two editors.

As we revised this collection for publication in mid-2005, journalism's continuing struggle against word theft and serving up fiction as fact struck close to home. Charges of unethical behavior had been lodged against three prizewinning writers featured in the first edition of *America's Best Newspaper Writing*: Rick Bragg, Mitch Albom and Diana Griego Erwin. Bragg resigned from *The New York Times* after he was accused of relying too heavily on a stringer's reporting to

314

write a story. Albom, sports columnist for the *Detroit Free Press* and a best-selling author of fiction and nonfiction, got in hot water when he wrote about two pro basketball players attending an NCAA Final Four game. It turns out Albom wrote the story before the event occurred. When the players didn't go to the game after all, the newspaper suspended him and conducted an internal investigation. Griego Erwin resigned from *The Sacramento Bee* after her editors were unable to determine the existence of people mentioned in several of her columns. Subsequently, the *Bee* could not verify the existence of more than 40 sources and characters in her stories, which is why we decided to eliminate her work from this edition. We decided to keep the prizewinning Bragg and Albom stories in this anthology because there is no evidence that any such problems exist with them.

Writing in *The Yale Review* in 1980, reporter and novelist John Hersey drew an important distinction between journalism and fiction: "There is one sacred rule of journalism. The writer must not invent."

DO NOT ADD; DO NOT DECEIVE

Hersey draws an important distinction, a crucial one for journalists. He admits that subjectivity and selectivity are necessary and inevitable in journalism. If you gather 10 facts but wind up using nine, subjectivity sets in. This process of subtraction can lead to distortion. Context can drop out, or history, or nuance, or qualification, or alternative perspectives.

Although subtraction may distort the reality the journalist is trying to represent, the result is still nonfiction, still journalism. The addition of invented material, however, changes the nature of the beast. When journalists add scenes that did not occur or quotes that were never said, they cross the line into fiction. And they deceive the reader.

This distinction leads to two cornerstone principles: Do not add. Do not deceive. Let's elaborate on each.

1. **Do not add.** This means that journalists should not add to a report things that did not happen. To make news clear and comprehensible, it is often necessary to subtract or condense. Done without care or responsibility, even such subtraction can distort. Journalists cross a more definite line into fiction, however, when they invent or add facts, images or sounds that were not there.

2. **Do not deceive.** This means that journalists should never mislead the public in reproducing events. The implied contract of all

nonfiction is binding: The way it is represented here is, to the best of the writer's knowledge, the way it happened. Anything that intentionally or unintentionally fools the audience violates that contract and the core purpose of journalism—to get at the truth. Thus, any exception to the implied contract—even a work of humor or satire—should be transparent or disclosed.

FOUR SUPPORTING STRATEGIES

Because these two principles are stated negatively, we do not want to nag journalists with an endless list of "thou shalt nots." Here we express four supporting strategies in a positive manner.

Be unobtrusive.   This guideline invites reporters to work hard to gain access to people and events—to spend time, to hang around, to become such a part of the scenery that they can observe conditions in an unaltered state. This helps avoid the "Heisenberg effect," a principle drawn from science in which observing an event changes it. Even watchdogs can be alert without being obtrusive.

Some circumstances require journalists to call attention to themselves and their processes. We have nothing against broadcast journalist Sam Donaldson for yelling questions at a president who turns a deaf ear to reporters. Go ahead and confront the greedy, the corrupt, the secret mongers. But the more reporters obtrude and intrude, especially when they are also obnoxious, the more they risk changing the behavior of those they are investigating.

Make sure that stories ring true.   Reporters know by experience that truth can be stranger than fiction, that a man can walk into a convenience store in St. Petersburg, Fla., and shoot the clerk in the head, and that the bullet can bounce off his noggin, ricochet off a ceiling beam and puncture a box of cookies.

If we ruled the world of journalism, we would ban the use of anonymous sources, except in cases where the source is especially vulnerable and the news is of great import. Some whistle-blowers who expose great wrongdoing fall into this category. A person who has migrated illegally into the United States may want to share his or her experience without fear of deportation. But the journalist must make every effort to make this character real. An AIDS patient may want and deserve anonymity, but making public the name of his doctor and his clinic can help dispel any cloud of fiction.

Fired *Boston Globe* columnist Mike Barnicle writes, "I used my memory to tell true tales of the city, things that happened to real people who shared their own lives with me. They represented the music and flavor of the time. They were stories that sat on the shelf of my institutional memory and spoke to a larger point. The use of parables was not a technique I invented. It was established ages ago by other newspaper columnists, many more gifted than I, some long since dead."

A parable is defined as a "simple story with a moral lesson." The problem is that we know them from religious literature or ancient fables. They are fictional forms, filled with hyperbole. Mike Barnicle passed them off as truth, without doing the reporting that would back them up.

Make sure that stories check out.   Stated with more muscle: Never put something in print or on the air that hasn't checked out. The new media climate makes this exceedingly difficult. News cycles that once changed by the day, or maybe by the hour, now change by the minute or second. Cable news programs run 24 hours, greedy for content. And more and more stories are broken on the Internet, in the middle of the night, when newspaper reporters and editors are tucked in their beds. The imperative to go live and to look live is stronger and stronger, creating the appearance that news is "up to the minute" or "up to the second."

Time frenzy, however, is the enemy of clear judgment. Taking time allows for checking, for coverage that is proportional, for consultation and for sound decision making that, in the long run, will avoid embarrassing mistakes and clumsy retractions.

Report and write with humility.   This virtue teaches us that Truth — with a capital *T* — is unattainable. But even though you can never get it, with hard work you can get at it, you can gain on it. Humility leads to respect for differing points of view, attention to which enriches reporting. It requires journalists to recognize the unhealthy influences of careerism and profiteering, forces that may tempt them to tweak a quote, bend a rule, snatch a phrase or even invent a source.

PLAGIARISM: THE UNORIGINAL SIN

We would amend Hersey's dictate as follows: There is one sacred rule of journalism. The writer must not invent *and must not lift from another writer or publication without giving proper credit.*

What causes plagiarism, the theft of words that Roy Peter Clark dubbed "the unoriginal sin"? Twenty years ago in the *Los Angeles Times*, media writer David Shaw provided a litany that covered most, if not all, of the root causes:

> Laziness. Sloppy work habits. Deadline pressure. Writer's block. Temporary—or chronic—emotional problems. A conscious or unconscious desire to be punished. In the case of several columnists who have plagiarized, the problem is simply that in the day-after-day-after-day grind, they come up empty one day and panic. Perhaps the most common cause of plagiarism is a fear of failure—or a fear of not meeting one's own (or one's editors' or peers') high standards.

To Shaw's list, we would add (in some cases) confusion over what constitutes plagiarism, a dearth of industry commitment to educating newsroom staffs about what constitutes plagiarism and, most important, a shortage of practical strategies to avoid its trap. There are ways to write well and write honestly, however. Here are some techniques to avoid charges of plagiarism, as adapted from Christopher Scanlan's *Reporting and Writing: Basics for the 21st Century*:

- Give credit where it's due. "If you think you should attribute it, then attribute it," advises Thomas Mallon, author of *Stolen Words*, a history of plagiarism. If you use a quote from another newspaper, attribute it, such as "*The New York Times* reported yesterday. . . ." The need for such attribution will probably demonstrate that you need to do your own reporting.

- Copying notes from other stories increases the risk of what plagiarism scholar Marilyn Randall calls "notebook syndrome." Avoid it by putting your notes aside when you write your first draft. Put "Quote TK" ("TK" is shorthand for "to come"), then go to your notes later to verify the exact wording.

- Inform readers about your sources, the way some newspapers and magazines do, with a sidebar or a list of online links.

- When you copy information from a printed source, always record the source, along with the page and paragraph numbers or the

Web address if the source is online. If you're using a computer to copy research material, use a different font or color than the one you use to write the story.

- Quotation marks are your friends. Use them when you copy material verbatim.

- Be a better time manager. Plagiarists are often desperate writers, late with assignments and often scrambling to meet their deadlines. Give yourself enough time to do the job right, and if the pressure threatens to overwhelm you, ask your editor for help.

- Journalism rests on a foundation of honesty. Be upfront about where your information comes from.

The push for storytelling in journalism has also raised the stakes for writers. Reporters are being encouraged to use literary techniques and devices—Tom Wolfe enumerated them as developing characters, setting scenes, using dialogue and reporting details—that have traditionally been the province of the fiction writer. These elements depend on reporting that goes beyond the superficial stenography of quoting what official sources tell reporters and requires multiple interviews, a search for independent verification and, above all, a consuming, sometimes obsessive, passion for accuracy.

But narrative reconstructions require rigorous reporting standards. Here's a checklist of questions suggested by Scanlan and Poynter Institute ethicist Robert Steele, also adapted from Scanlan's *Reporting and Writing*:

- How do I know it happened?

- Who and what are my sources?

- How reliable are they?

- Is my reconstruction based on more than one source? How do I reconcile differences between sources or signal to readers that there may be other versions? Have I tested my sources' recollections against those from other witnesses?

- What degree of confidence do I have in my sources? Have I considered whether their memory is faulty or if they have an ulterior motive for providing an inaccurate version?

- Have I used documentary sources, such as public records, newspaper articles or other source materials, to test people's memories? (Don't just rely on a source to tell you the weather; confirm it with the National Weather Service.)

- What is my purpose? Am I reconstructing an event to communicate the reality of an experience, or am I simply trying to show off my writing skills?

- Are there ways, such as an editor's note or source box, that could inform readers about the reporting behind my story? (Lack of attribution is a hallmark of reconstruction, but it also weakens a story's credibility.)

- Am I comfortable enough with my methods to fully disclose them to my editor and readers? (To buttress the authenticity of narrative writing, the *Los Angeles Times*, *The Wall Street Journal* and *The Providence Journal* have included footnotes with stories to provide sources.)

Under the pressures of daily journalism, facts can be misinterpreted, names can be misspelled and deadlines can be missed. Writers can make many different kinds of mistakes and still maintain their credentials as professional journalists. But cheating is often a fatal mistake, one that adversely affects not only the writer's career but also the health of the profession. Willard G. Bleyer, a pioneering journalism professor, pointed this out nearly a century ago.

"Every fake, whether it deceives few or many, lowers both the newspaper that publishes it and newspapers generally in the estimation of all who know that it is false," Bleyer wrote in his book *Newspaper Writing and Editing*, published in 1913. "It hurts the guilty writer; it hurts the victims of the fake; it hurts the newspaper that publishes it; it hurts journalism generally."

Acknowledgments

Mitch Albom. "Mackenzie Football Star Another Gunplay Victim." Published in the *Detroit Free Press*, December 22, 1995. Copyright © 1995 Detroit Free Press, Inc. Reprinted by permission.

Richard Aregood. "Tugs at the Curtain, but Wizard's Lips Remain Frozen." From *The Philadelphia Daily News*, March 15, 1990. Copyright © 1990 Philadelphia Newspapers, Inc. Reprinted by permission. All rights reserved.

Meyer Berger. "About New York." Published in *The New York Times*, January 23, 1959. Copyright © 1959 by The New York Times Company. Reprinted with permission. Also reprinted in *Meyer Berger's New York* by Meyer Berger. Copyright © 1960 by Meyer Berger. Published by Random House, Inc.

William E. Blundell. "The Life of a Cowboy: Drudgery and Danger." From *The Wall Street Journal*, June 10, 1981. Copyright © 1981 Dow Jones & Company, Inc. Reprinted with permission of Dow Jones, Inc., via Copyright Clearance Center, Inc. All rights reserved worldwide.

Jonathan Bor. "It Fluttered and Became Bruce Murray's Heart." From *The Post-Standard*, May 12, 1984. The Herald Company, Copyright © 1984 by The Post-Standard. Reprinted with permission. All rights reserved.

Thomas Boswell. "Losing It: Careers Fall Like Autumn Leaves." Published in *The Washington Post*, September 30, 1980. Copyright © 1980 The Washington Post Company. Reprinted with permission.

Rick Bragg. "All She Has, $150,000, Is Going to a University." Published in *The New York Times*, August 13, 1995. Copyright © 1995 by The New York Times Company. Reprinted with permission.

Donna Britt. "A One-Word Assault on Women." Published in *The Washington Post*, November 30, 1993. Copyright © 1993 The Washington Post Company. Reprinted with permission.

Francis X. Clines. "In Belfast, Death, Too, Is Diminished by Death." Published in *The New York Times*, March 20, 1988. Copyright © 1988 by The New York Times Company. Reprinted with permission.

Marvel Cooke. "From 'The Bronx Slave Market.' " From *The Daily Compass*, 1950. Copyright © 1950. Reprinted by permission.

Richard Ben Cramer. "Report from the Mideast: Shiva for a Child Slain in a Palestinian Raid." From *The Philadelphia Inquirer*, March 15, 1978. Copyright © 1978. Philadelphia Newspapers, Inc. Reprinted with permission. All rights reserved.

Jim Dwyer. "Fighting for Life 50 Floors Up, With One Tool and Ingenuity." Published in *The New York Times*, October 9, 2001. Copyright © 2001 by The New York Times Company. Reprinted with permission.

Russell Eshleman Jr. "Even for Trees, Age Could Have Its Privileges." "Domino's Bites Back at Tax." *The Philadelphia Inquirer*, March 12, 1991, and June 13, 1991. Copyright © 1991 The Philadelphia Inquirer. Reprinted by permission.

David Finkel. "For Lerro, Skyway Nightmare Never Ends." Published in the *St. Petersburg Times*, May 5, 1985. Copyright © 1985 St. Petersburg Times Publishing Company. Reprinted by permission.